# Socially Collaborative Schools

## Also by the Author

*From School Delusion to Design: Mixed-Age Groups and Values-Led Transformation*

*The Systems Thinking School: Redesigning Schools from the Inside-Out*

*Vertical Tutoring: Notes on School Management, Learning Relationships, and School Improvement*

# Socially Collaborative Schools

## The Heretic's Guide to Mixed-Age Tutor Groups, System Design, and the Goal of Goodness

Peter A. Barnard

ROWMAN & LITTLEFIELD
*Lanham • Boulder • New York • London*

Published by Rowman & Littlefield
An imprint of The Rowman & Littlefield Publishing Group, Inc.
4501 Forbes Boulevard, Suite 200, Lanham, Maryland 20706
www.rowman.com

Unit A, Whitacre Mews, 26-34 Stannary Street, London SE11 4AB, United Kingdom

**British Library Cataloguing in Publication Information Available**

**Library of Congress Cataloging-in-Publication Data**

Names: Barnard, Peter A., author.
Title: Socially collaborative schools : the heretic's guide to mixed-age tutor groups, system design, and the goal of goodness / Peter A. Barnard.
Description: Lanham : Rowman & Littlefield, [2018] | Includes bibliographical references and index.
Identifiers: LCCN 2018016749 (print) | LCCN 2018034150 (ebook) | ISBN 9781475844337 (Electronic) | ISBN 9781475844313 (cloth : alk. paper) | ISBN 9781475844320 (pbk. : alk. paper)
Subjects: LCSH: School management and organization—Social aspects. | Tutors and tutoring. | Mixed ability grouping in education.
Classification: LCC LB2805 (ebook) | LCC LB2805 .B2745 2018 (print) | DDC 371.2—dc23
LC record available at https://lccn.loc.gov/2018016749

♾️™ The paper used in this publication meets the minimum requirements of American National Standard for Information Sciences—Permanence of Paper for Printed Library Materials, ANSI/NISO Z39.48–1992.

Printed in the United States of America

We may not be able to take the school out of the factory but we can take the factory out of the school!

# Contents

# Foreword

We do not describe the world we see. We see the world we can describe.

—René Descartes

Stories are a good way into thinking about organizations as systems. Human systems are about relationships, and so we need to use the language of relationships to describe them. Fritjof Capra knew this when he said that "what is important in a story—what is true in it—is not the plot, the things, or the characters, but the relationships between them."

A few years ago, following an unfortunate chain of events, I found myself in need of some major surgery. A day or two after the operation, my consultant visited to check on my recovery. I proceeded to list one worry after another, describing my various aches and pains and pointing to a scar that wasn't healing as planned. "Okay," he responded. "That's all good then. You seem to be doing very well." I was surprised. I felt far from well and reiterated my anxiety. His response was formative. He said, "In making my assessment, I look at the *whole you*, rather than the parts. If the surgery had failed, we would see systemic symptoms. As a system, you are well and recovering, and I am pleased. I will leave the parts to my colleagues."

I was a system! And, while recovering, I had little better to do than think about that!

As a living system, I was more than just the sum of my parts. As the old Sufi story has it: "You think that because you understand *one*, you must therefore also understand *two*, because one and one make two. But you forget that you must also understand *and*."

As a system, I wasn't just any old collection of disparate parts either; I was, as Donella Meadows describes, an "interconnected set of elements that is coherently organized in a way that achieves something." So I was *parts*, *interconnections*, and *purpose*. And while the parts were quite visible, and the purpose—I hope—was assumed, the interconnections were less so.

The same, of course, is true for the organizations and groups in which we spend the vast majority of our lives. As it turned out, I had plenty of time to consider this after the wise doctor's visit, and I have spent a lot longer since thinking about such matters in my work with schools. And like Capra, it is the relationships between the parts of a school that hold the most interest for me. This is where the real stuff of organizational life happens, and it is also therefore the place where real and lasting change can be made. Conversely, if left unattended, it is also where so much can go wrong.

For schools—like other organizations—are highly complex psychodynamic systems of systems, each with a collective identity that is separate from and different to the elements which make it up. Furthermore, as open systems, schools only exist—and can only exist—in relation to their exchange of information and resources with their environment, including a community of parents, students, and staff. It is only by viewing schools as organizational systems that we can truly appreciate them, understand the nature of their organizational behavior, and ascertain how they might be better managed and led.

Unfortunately, we live in a time when questioning fundamental assumptions like this—particularly in public services—is considered heretical. And this is where Peter's new book comes in.

For example, what could possibly be wrong with the same-age organization of children for pastoral tutor groups? We have, after all, been doing it like this for 150 years! Well, according to Barnard, pretty much everything is wrong with it. In fact, in his analysis, the same-age organizational model at the heart of most schools is the direct cause of a whole litany of school problems and is the very reason why so many attempts at change fail. This heretical proposition, this questioning of the fundamentals, and this *systems thinking* are the springboard to a host of other searching questions that Barnard has the temerity to ask.

Why do schools find *distributed learning* so difficult? Why don't we see a broad adoption of the sort of *innovation* and *collaboration* we so badly need? Why do highly attractive and well-resourced *pro-social programs* fail to successfully address behavioral issues like bullying? Why do we accept such a narrow view of teacher accountability? Why do we have annual appraisals when there is no evidence that they work? Why are staff walking away, and why are students getting ill?

Peter's answer is to mix tutor groups by age. He believes this relatively straightforward, low-cost change fundamentally reshapes the way relationships form, better enables people to connect, and creates a much better environment for learning. Of at least equal importance for me is the impact of such a systemic change on organizational life. Once one becomes aware that everything *can* change, *everything* changes.

When Peter first told me about this book and sent me his emerging draft, I was excited and delighted in equal measure. It was his earlier book *The Systems Thinking School* which clarified much that had previously frustrated me about my consulting practice. What's now clear is that he was just getting warmed up! It is only now, here in *The Heretic's Guide*, that he's firing from both barrels.

I am reminded of another story attributed to ancient Persian folk wisdom:

Nasreddin, an itinerant preacher, is on his hands and knees under a street lamp outside his house, searching for his missing house key. His friend, Mansour, passes by, and asks, "Nasreddin, what are you looking for? Did you lose something?"

"Yes, Mansour. I lost the key to my house. I've been searching here for hours, and I can't find it. Can you help, old friend." Mansour, of course, joins Nasreddin in the sand and grass under the lamp and begins to scratch around for the key. After a time, frustrated at having got his clothes dusty yet not having found the key, Mansour turns to his friend and asks, "But Mullah, where did you last have it?"

"Well, I lost the key in my house," Nasreddin responds. "But there's more light out here."

For Peter in this important book, schools are looking for solutions to their problems in the wrong places. Like the preacher, they look only at what they can see, where the light is better. The trouble is that the causes of most of their issues lie far from the physical or temporal location of the observable problems. The causes are not "proximate" to the symptoms.

Thus, we see the undignified and profoundly unfair focus on teachers as the cause of many schools' current ills. We hear from government and its advisers that a school system can only ever be as good as its teachers, although the reality, as Peter points out on several occasions, is the opposite: They can only be as good—collectively and individually—as the system allows. And what we are now seeing is a system that is not just failing to achieve its most basic purposes, but it has also replaced its basic purposes with instrumental targets and accountability measures.

Peter makes a noble point of not criticizing his *heroes* who, day in, day out, sally forth to teach and lead our schools, and I agree. However, given the availability of this book, and the reams of academic evidence and practice-based research it references, there can be no further excuse for inaction on the part of those paid vast sums of money to be system leaders. For them, and for others, this book should be required reading, primarily for its promotion of systems thinking in school leadership, management, and policy. Sadly, it may not be for a while. Too many are unwilling or insufficiently robust to cope with the higher level of scrutiny Peter promotes. And sadly, as the anecdote about consultancy has it, there's still good money to be made in prolonging the problem!

But for those enlightened souls (and I see plenty of them in my work) who do choose to follow the systems wisdom of Ackoff, Argyris, Deming, Schein, Meadows, and Wheatley (among others), and approach schools as complex adaptive systems, changeable through careful design, there is hope. For them, it is clear how the organization of schools, as currently conceived, inhibits—perhaps even prohibits—the achievement of their critical purposes. It is also clear how, in a system ravaged by the malignant paradigm of New Public Management, leaders can't lead, so they boss; teachers can't teach, so they leave; and worst of all, children can't be children, so they disengage.

Having exhausted all reasonable means in his attempts to encourage system change, Barnard turns here to heresy, which he knows may irritate, disturb, and provoke. He may be on to something, but it is the breadth and quality of his analysis that is his most potent weapon, complemented by an intimate understanding of how schools work. This book could only be written by a teacher, and a head teacher at that.

Above all, the Heretic's Systems Guide to Better Schools clarifies that education is "all" about relationships, and the planned organization thereof. Arguably, there's never been a more critical time for this to be drummed home. Our only hope for arresting schools' current malaise is humane, relational, and maverick leadership, informed by the behavioral sciences and a willingness to question long-held assumptions. This is a guidebook for such heretics.

Vive la Révolution!

Ben Gibbs
Restart-Ed & the Relational Schools Foundation
Cambridge, UK
January 2018

# Acknowledgments

As ever, I must thank those whose ideas underpin much of my ramblings. In the USA, Professor Frank Duffy's expertise in systems approaches to school transformation and kind remarks inspired all three of my recent books, beginning with *The Systems Thinking School* through to *From School Delusion to Design*, and finally this, the last in a mini-series extolling the virtues of mixed-age organization as the key to systemic change.

Behind this book is a binding philosophy that views the school as a living system, an idea expressed in the work of Margaret J. Wheatley, Myron Kellner-Rogers, and others. It is by far the better alternative to the machine metaphor. For me, John Seddon's Vanguard Method is preeminent among practical applications of systems thinking to the public sector; terms like *failure demand* and *value demand* should be an indispensable part of any school's management vocabulary. John explains systems better than most.

There are many other players who have inspired my journey. Among them are Niels Pflaeging and his book *Organize for Complexity*; John Atkinson, Emma Loftus, and John Jarvis and their curated work, *The Art of Change Making*; and, of course, the inspirational *Thinking in Systems* by the late Donella Meadows. Mention should also be made of the excellent NHS white paper by Helen Bevan and Steve Fairman, *The New Era of Thinking and Practice in Change and Transformation*, and the excellent report *Creative Public Leadership* from Joe Hallgarten et al. at the RSA. All provide further scaffolding for this book. Mention should also be made of Frederic Laloux, whose book *Reinventing Organization* builds on the foundations of Peter Senge's great work, *The Fifth Discipline*, and is an indispensable read.

Thanks too to Debbie Sorkin, national director of Systems Leadership, who provided me with a boatload of extra reading material and listened patiently to my ramblings about how schools might be the spur for systemic change.

While writing, many other publications and research documents came along. Among these was Lucy Crehan's *Clever Lands*, which for me was the first systems approach to school culture of its kind. Another came from Charlotte Pell, Rob Wilson, and Toby Lowe in the form of *Kittens Are Evil—Little Heresies in Public Policy*. A third was *Collaborative Professionalism*, the report for WISE by Andy Hargreaves and Michael O'Connor.

The big surprise was Google and its company research on team construction and soft skills; Google couldn't have been more helpful. There are many others. It is a joy to know that so many people are thinking in systems and follow in the footsteps of organizational gurus no longer with us, including the great W. Edwards Deming, Donella Meadows, and Russell Ackoff.

Over a long time span, it has been my privilege to work with many hundreds of schools mainly in the UK but also as far afield as Qatar, Australia, Japan, China, and South Africa. The people who work in schools remain my heroes, and all have generously shared their experiences and taught me far more about systems than I was able to teach them. Their kind words and feedback about the difference vertical tutoring (mixed-age organization) has made to their schools have helped more than I can say. These schools have blazed a trail, and we should learn from their pioneering spirit. This book is about them.

Thanks too to Dylan Wiliam and Jonathan Haidt whose tweets, observations, and writing have kept me on the right side of sanity over the years.

Finally, I'd like to thank Patricia George who takes my scribblings and somehow makes them into something readable despite both the language and large pond that separates us. Any other errors, typos, and unintended mistakes are down to me. Having succeeded in reaching my three score and ten, my enthusiasm to check is not what it used to be, so I apologize in advance. Call it an age thing!

I must mention my family: how Patricia, my partner of so many years, has put up with someone who foolishly thinks he can write books is beyond me. Hopefully, this will be the last—a promise made and broken five times!

When I started writing, my son was at schools and playing rock guitar for school bands. He graduated to hard-core punk rock (as he should) traveling the world with his band Gallows. His current band, Gold Key, is a return to Pink Floyd, Muse, and Queens of the Stone Age. It seems at last, we are all on the same page. Their first album, *Hello Phantom*, has been critically acclaimed—if you don't buy the book, at least buy the album!

# Introduction

The first part of this book is about the school as a system, so it's important to describe what a system is, and to do this I'll adapt the description offered by Donella Meadows. In this case, it's a collection of students, parents, and school staff (our players) who are connected in a way that results in a distinct pattern of behavior over time. By including parents, the system has the potential to reach beyond its own borders. What makes this system effective or otherwise is its connectedness. The more connected, the more 'systemsy' it is and the better it is at absorbing complex demands. Like all systems, schools are subject to the vagaries of external forces and reforms. These act upon them in various ways and, despite the range and intensity of these disturbances, the school as a system always responds in a way that is characteristic of itself.

But this book is about two systems. The first is the universal management model used by schools to organize teaching and learning, the familiar mode of self-construction based on the simple idea that students of the same age should be grouped together in tutor time and for classes. Everyone is familiar with such a school, and most of us have attended one, so we should all know how the typical same-age school works. This first system is now close to celebrating its 150th anniversary and continues to act in a way that is both contrary and dysfunctional but one that is characteristic of itself. Not only has it hardly changed at all, but all attempts at school reform have proved ineffective. It is why I like these wonderfully quirky and difficult places so much. Lots of peripheral change go on, but the school's system remains the same.

However, rather than blowing out the candles and celebrating, the suggestion is that we quietly bury this old model and start a new system, a second system. This book sets out very precisely the building blocks for what that second system looks like and the first steps on the journey needed. Such a transition costs nothing other than a change of mind—a price many are unwilling to pay given that it is extraordinarily high! While such first steps are relatively easy to implement, it will be for pioneering schools to complete the management journey as best they can. As things stand, the same-age model universally applied, based on same-age groups, is unable to take us to a better world and is unable to evolve. It is anti-learning.

## A SECOND SYSTEM

The second system is one that schools call vertical tutoring (VT). This term describes a model that many schools in Australia, New Zealand, and the UK have adopted, and involves mixing the age groups in tutor time (homeroom time) in a very careful way. This small change is all that schools adopting the second system require but the transition has to be conducted in a way that follows guidelines on child development and psychology, not assumptions. These guidelines have been hard won by schools that have made the transition and recorded here for others. Any assumptions and any transfer of same-age management thinking into VT will make matters far worse; the school will become a parody of itself. In fact, nothing must be assumed. These prototype mixed-age organizations are now in a position to innovate further organizational change in a landscape devoid of signposts and high in apprehension.

VT schools with their unique mixed-age tutor groups have started a process of connectivity, a system *under construction*. While the philosophy and social psychology of mixed-age schools is very much in place, these schools are not yet in a position to take the next steps in their transformation and that next step will require considerable courage and community support. The destination of these schools sometimes goes under the name of the *learning organization* and to get to this place requires *self-organization*, the ability to adapt, diversify, learn, and create new structure. Whether the destination is achievable or not, the journey is important and must be undertaken. Escape from the same-age prison of the past will not be easy, but the mixed-age approach is the key to this particular cell door.

This is not to say schools don't learn. Every day the staff are involved in solving all kinds of problems, dealing with some and referring others to superiors. People follow all the practices and protocols to the letter minimizing their use of initiative, innovation, and creativity. Each passing moment strengthens the school's sense of self, its identity and most precious asset, and this makes the school very resistant when it comes to change.

Vertical tutoring relies on the creation of mixed-age groups as the school's organizational base. It uses houses (schools within schools) rather than year groups and age-grades as the school's basic structure, something psychologists call a nested system. There are social and psychological guidelines to be followed regarding how such groups are formed, meet, and work, all important matters that will be outlined as we go. In VT schools, tutor groups meet for a short time each day, and these tutor groups are populated to ensure each is balanced from students of all age groups, genders, and abilities.

This is the easy bit, but it isn't change, just the seedbed. Change occurs when the dialogue between our players starts to change and flow and the power of decision-making and agency in the organization moves to the edge to better absorb system demand. Without this change, the door is open to entrepreneurs, consultants, leadership impresarios, teaching experts, program writers, and more, all bent on earning a living from system demise and all solving problems that don't exist while bent on keeping the school's same-age narrative the same. At a time when questions are being asked about system viability, costs, and purposes, schools need to seize the initiative, but to do this they will need to develop as learning communities more than ever.

## HERESIES AND INCONVENIENT TRUTHS

It will not have escaped attention that the word "heretic" forms part of the book's title! Heresies question long-held assumptions, and this poses a problem. Because of the wonderfully obstinate nature of schools, the characteristic response to any external disturbance—such as that posed by a heretical statement—is unlikely to be well received. Placing that risk to one side, here is the heresy at the heart of this book: In every respect, the same-age system is just about the worse way possible to organize a secondary school. It doesn't work, has never worked, and schools cannot make it work. Typically, teachers don't give up trying.

There the heresy is written. Few will accept such an assertion but it is a statement that is not only easy to defend but also has the weight of social psychology and learning on its side. The statement is an inconvenient truth, an inherited design assumption, and one likely to be rejected out of hand and regarded as a threat to any school's identity; it is not something that schools want to hear having spent so many decades trying to make same-age organizations work. A school will accept such a proposition only if it understands that the change from one system to another is in its interests, a construct that can enhance its identity and aids its long-term survival. To paraphrase W. Edwards Deming, schools don't have to change; their survival is optional.

Sometimes, it's not possible to fully appreciate the nature of a problem until the problem is solved. The many hundreds of schools that have successfully changed their organization from one based on same-age tutor groups to one based on mixed-age tutor groups have the potential to remove significant obstacles to learning and build (as many have) new connective structures that more actively support learning. They are happier places than they were. From where VT schools now stand, the problems experienced when they were organized by same-age become glaringly obvious. From inside the same-age system, everything seems normal; difficulties are accepted and the daily grind continues. Everyone performs as best they can, and the staff who walk the corridors of our schools, regardless of how they are organized, strive every day to make a difference.

It isn't possible to make such a heretical statement, one critical of same-age structure, and to expect to walk away unscathed. Many will cry foul and disagree. Schools do not like such comments and the research community prefers for the moment to ignore such a proposition. A major challenge, therefore, is to keep readers interested despite this and other heresies arriving thick and fast; fortunately, readers will agree with many of them. The fact is we demand an awful lot of our schools and their ability to deliver depends entirely on the degree to which they are connected as systems. Collaboration and connectedness in a school is everything. There's just one problem; even at their best, same-age schools are only partially connected.

## THE BOOK

So, this book is about schools as organizations. It tells a systems story of their abuse, why schools are misunderstood, and how schools can get themselves back on track. Essentially, this book is about how schools can wrest back their sense of purpose and values, and how they can revitalize community and regain what many call the goal of goodness.

Such a topic involves questioning many of the fundamental beliefs and received assumptions that underpin school management and leadership, and it is this heretical approach that gives the book its title. Through no fault of their own, schools are not in a good place and the collateral damage to the well-being of staff, students, and family life is increasingly evident. We have reached a point where our schools (even those doing well by the success measures of the day) need systemic change, and the intention here is to provoke and offer an alternative but safer view.

The first step is to increase our understanding of the nature of the school as an organization, and this means exposing any assumptions likely to lead schools off course. The second is to unite the component parts of the school to get the school back together as an interconnected learning operation. It seems that old school values have been spirited away and substituted with cheap imitations; we need schools and communities to claim these back and not assume they still hold good.

But for schools to wrest back control, they will need to abandon same-age organization for a short time each day and transition to a mixed-age base. Grasping such a seemingly insignificant, heretical, and outlandish concept is not only the key to their future success but also is in all our interests. Schools make their own decisions, and it is not in their nature to accept such a proposition lightly—if at all! But it is a fact that a significant number of schools have successfully switched from one system to another and are unlikely to ever return.

This book encourages schools that have yet to take the plunge to do so and for those that already have to make more progress. The way relationships form in a school determines far more than imagined. A same-age system is separational, learning-restricted, and (we'll learn) high-risk. A mixed-age system, even for short time each day, is collaborative, learning-enabled, family-oriented, and low-risk.

Paola Gallo (2016), chief people and culture officer and member of the Executive Committee of the World Economic Forum, wrote this:

> The point is that we all know what is important but—ironically—we tend to do the opposite. We are prisoners of cheerfully miserable cognitive dissonance. Relationships matter, not only in our personal life but also in our professional life. The way we define success is broken . . . by taking part in the rat race, we became so self-absorbed and busy trying to win this race that we forget that even by winning it, we will still remain rats.

When we start messing with schools using crude evaluations and take professionals for granted, we embark on a road to perdition likely to end in a very nasty place. For those of us who suffer vertigo, peering into such an educational abyss is not something that is easy to stomach and many parents and teachers are choosing to walk away. When governments and businesses undermine and ignore core beliefs and values, schools cease any aspiration to become learning organizations and start to become teaching systems devoid of the need for the human connectivity on which so much learning and so much of our shared future depend.

We know what is important but do the opposite. To be a teacher is to have a genuine sense of commitment. Teachers are connectors, purpose seekers, and learners who wish to contribute to a better, more ecologically minded and safer world by sharing their knowledge. Their karma is to make a difference, not make things worse.

When we discount such matters and narrowly redefine what counts as success, the well-being of those trying to make the system work, including our children, takes the inevitable hit. There are schools that offer pockets of resistance but identifying such mavericks, heretics, and disruptors is insufficient to halt the universal trend to convergence and sameness.

## THE READER'S BRIEF

Attached (appendix 1) is a list of heretical statements that challenge the assumptions we make about schools and schools make about themselves. You'll also find these and others scattered throughout. They are there to disturb the way we think about schools and the way schools think about themselves, and you may choose to read these first. Be warned, you may consider them on first reading to be outrageous and unacceptable but they are what they are, and what many mixed-age schools see from their newly acquired systems perspective. There is no intention to undermine schools and the talented individuals who work in them, quite the opposite.

One overriding aim of this book is to place schools in design rehab and show how capable they are of change and how they can become better at self-management and self-organization. If there is to be a change of direction, schools and their communities must lead it and show how they can restore deeper values and create a more secure future for us all.

To understand this book, a very simple brief is needed. A same-age system is one where tutor groups are peer-based. A mixed-age system is one where tutor groups are carefully mixed by small groups of different ages. The broad assumption is that these groups usually meet for a very short time (twenty minutes) each day without any pro-social programs. Both systems are powerful change levers and deserve our fullest attention.

Otherwise, this book is a travel guide for those who want to make schools healthier and more relevant places of learning and want to explore the complexity of transformation, connectedness, and redesign.

Writing about systems is not easy, and every chapter is connected to every other chapter. It is the nature of systems thinking to appreciate the whole picture, how things connect and relate, all at once. This doesn't lend itself to the linearity of separate chapters; those who prefer to read books from back to front will have no problem here!

Otherwise, the book is loosely based on Kurt Lewin's three transformational elements: unfreezing, cognitive change, and refreezing. Readers are invited to see the school as a living system with certain characteristics that define its behavior, including the way it reacts to those who dare disturb its slumber and call it to arms.

In later sections, we'll explore the history of management as applied to schools. What we learn is that very little has changed, and that history keeps repeating itself. It appears that schools are trapped in a reinforcing feedback loop from which there is no obvious means of escape; it seems that confirmation bias has become endemic. In particular, we explore business management practices that turn out to be short-term, destructive, and counterproductive management practices (the neoliberal folly that is New Public Management).

Finally, an attempt is made to set the whole in historical perspective using the work of Frederic Laloux and in particular his ideas on culture and consciousness. This enables us to explore alternative management approaches curated from other organizations.

As far as this book is concerned, springing the many system traps starts with understanding how the school goes about the process of building learning relationships, and this means understanding the difference between same-age and mixed-age organization.

So, the heretic's guide to school management: twenty minutes to make the world a better place!

# THE SCHOOL AS A LIVING SYSTEM

In this section, the main actors appear. These are school workers, students, and families. These complex learning relationships are put under the system microscope. The idea behind the socially collaborative school, its connectedness, is what makes it a system. All players contribute and engage. Collaborative professionalism is not enough. The socially collaborative school requires all to participate in the learning journey. Everyone and everything has to be connected.

The first chapters involve looking at schools and the issues they face from different perspectives using two very different metaphors: the machine and the living system. This is because the way we look at schools tends to define them and their behavior. An attempt is made to show that schools are much more complex than we imagine, and this gives rise to inconsistencies and assumptions. We are convinced that teacher quality is all that matters forgetting that teacher quality depends on the system used by the school to support players (students, staff, and parents). Teachers cannot be disconnected from the rest of the school.

Systems concepts are introduced including leverage points, places in a system where a small change has a domino effect, one that determines the system's behavior. Donella Meadows described these as small changes that can lead to big changes. She discovered that organizations were often aware of change leverage points but constantly pushed them in the wrong direction. These are interpreted as we go along. Same-age organization is one such lever. In this first section, it will be shown how this small design specification has become an obstacle to the learning and to a safer future; it stalls evolutionary change. Its original purpose aided a process of separation and limitation and still does. It remains the direct cause of the system's behavior and mind-set and the root cause of the many problems schools face today.

Changing this seemingly benign lever to a mixed-age approach sets in play a completely different pattern of behavior, one that allows both professional and social collaboration. It is not possible to change schools for the better using the design thinking that stems from the same-age industrial system, hence the challenge of this book. In short, there is a big difference between a system in which people sometimes collaborate and a socially collaborative system where collaboration is a designed-in requirement. One keeps things the same while the other evolves at a rate commensurate with its calling. Teaching is not a leverage point, neither is curriculum, leadership, or new technology; none change system fundamentals.

Health issues, bullying, and parent partnership are viewed from a different perspective as part of the fallout from the past (the use of same-age systems). The school is explored as a living system and its biological nature exposed. The theme of system transformation using a mixed-age approach is introduced, one that redesigns both system and thought and one that neither separates nor limits.

# Chapter 1

# Systems, Purposes, and Problems—A First Look

In this section, some of the major themes are introduced that enable us to look again at schools and how they operate. Set out next is table 1.1 that urges caution whenever we consider the school as a system. In the table are two sets of descriptors pinned under two very different *system drivers*. These drivers set in motion two very different kinds of organization, two very different ways of seeing, and two different approaches to solving problems. One creates problems and works on their solution, while the other predicts and designs out problems before they start.

The same-age system where tutor groups are peer-based requires constant reform and the road traveled is littered with failed attempts at schools change. They never operate as intended and require constant tinkering. Unfortunately, this approach to change and improvement invariably fails in complex societies (like the UK and the USA for starters) where social mobility is low and inequity high.

The failure of reform, PISA league tables, and the influence of effect lists (among others) have led to a widespread belief that there is an inherent problem with teacher quality. There is a problem with professional and pedagogical development and innovation caused by the system in which they operate, and this does not allow us to assign blanket quality judgments on teachers. They do what they can within the system circumstances in which they work. There isn't a teacher quality issue but there is a systems issue, and we'll explore this convenient fallacy throughout! (By the way, heretical statements work both ways!)

The real problem rests with the system itself, the way the school operates as an organization and the management constructs it uses. Today's schools have inherited a deeply embedded industrial way of working, and this has made them unable to adapt quickly enough to their context and environment.

It does no favors for teachers and learners and no fault should be attached to schools; they have simply been unable to evolve, and this means that something concerning the system in use needs attention.

A school is designed as a closed system, so much so that the school is the inadvertent creator of its own challenges and issues. They are design faults and so can be designed out; they cannot be taught out! Bullying is in this category.

The real problem with school improvement is the way we see the problem. Any mistake at this point means that wrong assumptions are drawn. We either start to solve a problem that is marginal to the whole (e.g., acting directly on teachers), or we confuse cause and effect and choose to treat symptoms because that is what we see. For example, we see poor behavior or notice a lack of student perseverance and try to address the issue by introducing a plethora of pro-social programs. The school tries to teach its way through the social dilemmas and challenges it faces. Schools do this because they cannot fathom the same-age cause right under the school's nose.

Schools are often led to believe that they are dealing with students who have a character deficit, poor attitude, and inherent laziness. For a few, this may seem to be the case but the first recourse should be to look again at the system and not rush for a hoped-for fix. The problem is knowing what to look for in a system but in every case we need attention should focus on same-age groups, the basic building block of the social and learning fabric that is the school. Understanding why this is so is the key!

Throwing money at system defects without addressing system causes only makes matters worse. To do so increases complications, bureaucracy, and costs in the forlorn hope that the perceived problems will be somehow resolved and go away. When this reformational strategy inevitably fails, the teachers are blamed and the school is accused of not trying—an apparent leadership problem!

## ORGANIZATION BY AGE

This section illustrates two very different approaches to school organization. The one in universal use based on peer groups and the one in which hundreds of schools (a handful in comparison) have spotted the system's same-age design flaw and opted for a mixed-age strategy.

In table 1.1, some of the initial features are set out to describe features of the two approaches. More will be added as we go and the ones below explained.

System 1 thinking is fast, intuitive, prone to error, and to the bias of past experience. System 2 is effortful and is who we think we are. We think of

**Table 1.1.   Organization by Age as System Drivers**

| Same-Age Grouping | Mixed-Age Grouping | Key Sources |
|---|---|---|
| System 1 Thinking (assumed) | Systems 1 and 2 Thinking | Daniel Kahneman |
| Theory in Use | Espoused Theory Practiced | Chris Argyris and Donald Schön |
| Complicated | Complex | Niels Pflaeging |
| Lower-Order Consciousness | Higher-Order Consciousness | Frederic Laloux and Peter Senge |
| Machine Metaphor | Living System Metaphor | Margaret J. Wheatley |
| Reductionism | Holism | Russell Ackoff |
| Self-Construction—Closed | Self-Organizing—Open | Alvarez De Lorenzana |

ourselves as rational experts, System 2 thinkers, and that the organizations we design (like schools) make perfect sense and are in-line-up with research and social psychology. It wouldn't cross our minds that designing a school where tutor groups are organized by same age is a massive assumption and a grave error, one that has too long gone unquestioned by our indolent System 2.

The fact is the fast System 1, which Kahneman advises us actually runs the show, has limited experience of a mixed-age alternative, so discounts such a proposition despite the evidence (below), a position that our lazy and presumptuous System 2 is all too willing to accept. The challenge here is to get System 2 to wake up and ask some serious questions of intuitive System 1 and the design assumptions that underpin same-age grouping.

Sometimes schools reach a point when they figure out they are missing a trick. They sense something is incongruent within their working milieu and have the courage and humility to seek a second opinion, an outside systems thinking view. They recognize that their teachers are actually quite good, that staff are all working hard and are well intentioned, and that something else must be wrong. They then go in search of solutions and try to envision schooling differently but often remain prisoners of the past rather than the admirable escapees and disruptors we need them to be. Meanwhile, they adapt to the existing circumstances as best they can, maintaining their strong sense of identity.

Today, when so many issues like mental health and well-being are going awry, that sense of things not being right is now a full-blown reality. Morale is low, teachers are walking away, and despite everyone working harder the health of students and teachers is becoming a major issue. Costs are increasing and this in systems terms is a sure sign of a quality issue in the service provided; but if it is not teachers, what is it? What is happening?

## DEMAND

Let's introduce a systems concept at this point. In school, let's imagine that everyone is a customer of everyone else and everyone is a service provider—staff, students, and parents. All have learning and leadership tasks to perform and this requires an ability to draw down from the system all that our players need to make progress and do their work. We might call these learning and teaching needs, part of the *value demand* on the system. By dealing with these needs first time round, the demand is absorbed and costs go down. If the school as a system is unable to meet these needs (value demand) first time, the school is left to deal with *failure demand*. This requires significant extra work downstream and drives up costs over a lifetime. Everybody pays.

Over time, failure demand in a same-age school builds and the system requires more social programs, fixes, and add-ons. Things start to get complicated but from within the school it is difficult to appreciate the nature of attendant problems and their cause. The old remedial ways continue unabated using means that have failed in the past. After all, everyone is working hard and no one intends for things to go wrong. When things do go awry and reforms fail as they must, it is a sure sign of an internal systems problem, not a people problem. Failure demand requires everyone to work twice as hard to correct errors not dealt with first time round. The reaction inside the school is to solve the problem, something Chris Argyris and Donald Schön (1978) called single-loop learning, a practice that involves the use of more support staff and social programs; in turn, this increases bureaucracy, management, complications, and costs.

The incongruence schools experience and the *miserable cognitive dissonance* described earlier by Paola Gallo are caused by the differences that arise between *the theory in use* and *the theory espoused* (Chris Argyris). What schools think and claim to be happening (espoused) is not reflected in reality (in use), and many examples will come to light as we proceed. For many students and teachers, schools are being separated from their core values yet schools still offer a convincing and values-led rationale for all they do. But what happens under close systems examination bares scant regard to the values and aims that schools claim. School principals and head teachers think they run the show but invariably it turns out that the show runs them.

## WORKING WITH SCHOOLS

The feedback from hundreds of schools considering transition from the same-age model reveals minor variations on an old industrial management theme; put bluntly, there has been no substantive change to the school's basic means of organization and management, its self-construction, in over a century. All such schools appear to operate very similar management systems. Although the world has evolved, schools continue with their old operational structures and this is leading to a whole range of dysfunctional behaviors and unresolvable management issues. The role of systems thinking is to expose any disconnectivity and find a means of reconciling what is *espoused* or assumed to be happening as opposed to what is practiced (*theory in use*).

There is a clear systems link between same-age organization and endemic school bullying, disengaged parental partnership, inadequate learning support, and communications. Later chapters are devoted to these areas. These are areas where schools claim expertise but for all the efforts schools make, the same-age system prevents any successful impact. Same-age organization determines how the school constructs itself, so there should be no surprise at the expectation that things can go very wrong very fast at any time in such a system. These observations come from schools that have abandoned the same-age system for a mixed-age system. Only when schools have changed system do they see with any clarity the design faults of the same-age system they have abandoned.

Over time, the industrial architecture used by the school has become less flexible, more complicated, and less able to adapt to the many new challenges that have arisen. It is now the single causal source of most (not many) of the challenges facing schools. The *typical school* has remained closed as a system and finds it difficult to evolve in line with its environment—an inability to become self-managing and *self-organizing*. In essence, it is the same-age school's karma to languish behind the evolutionary learning curve. The more that the industrial hand-me-down rules of the system become operationalized and institutionalized, the less they are questioned as working assumptions.

## PLUS ÇA CHANGE

The proposal here is simple; at the causal base of the school's operation is the same-age assumption that controls how the school operates. Few see it as an issue; it operates in the background and is considered benign by researchers and policy-makers but is in effect the original design *leverage point* that determines how the school operates as a system, one that commands how a secondary school is organized, managed, operated, and led. Just like the students, the school staff, administrators, and school leaders have to adapt to the one-size, same-age system.

So, why make such a heretical assertion? The answer is simple. Schools that have knowingly changed from a same-age system (knowingly!) are able to demonstrate improved learning relationships at all levels and have managed to realign values and purpose. In these schools, bullying has declined dramatically, staff and student morale has improved, and parent partnership has become integral to learning and support. Their *system in use* is their *espoused system* and has the potential to move further in a self-organizing direction toward a fully functioning socially collaborative school.

In other words, schools only appreciate the obstacles to learning and teaching posed by same-age organization after the same-age system is dissolved and a new design (mixed-age) is incorporated in its place. From inside the same-age school, the industrial mind-set rules the roost and substantive change and innovation are not on the school's bucket list.

We rarely question system fundamentals like same-age grouping, choosing instead the reductive simplicity of single-loop approaches to learning, effectively solving problems as they emerge in easy, low-risk, repeatable ways as opposed to dealing with the complexity of underlying cause (double-loop learning). Such a strategy leads to an accumulation of ever more complicated problems over time. Reductionist thinking learned over time renders us incapacitated; it becomes difficult to think in systems, to see the big picture, and appreciate how elements should connect. Reform seeks out repairs and replacement parts and is unable to handle fundamental cause and redesign.

When a school starts to question system fundamentals, it engages in *double-loop learning* and this (and only this) leads to any systemic resolution of organizational problems. All school reforms are invariably single-loop in nature, and this means we persist in trying to solve problems separated in time and space from their cause. The exponential call for pro-social programs is entirely single-loop serendipity in essence.

Schools looking at table 1.1 may not like the list of descriptors applied (the list gets longer the more we look). Surely, they will claim, we belong in the second column. Not so. Until a school is reflective enough to question the same-age assumption, to change the way it thinks, and starts to raise fundamental organizational issues from the perspective of community, parents, students, and staff, it remains firmly in column 1 in table 1.1.

Nearly all the ills effecting schools result, one way or another, from same-age organization, the central heresy of this book.

## WHAT THE RESEARCH TELLS US

Set out below is the research that reveals why same-age grouping in tutor time should be abandoned and changed to mixed-age. At the heart of same-age schools is a contradiction. While same-age schools claim to cherish the child's safety and psycho-social development above all else, their practice is way out of kilter with the evidence base and reliant solely on hand-me-down assumptions.

It should be stated from the outset that much of the relevant research explores the challenge of mixed-age *teaching groups*. The focus of this book is on tutor or homeroom time. Fortunately, the past twenty years have seen a high number of schools making the transition from a same-age to a mixed-age tutorial system. This means that a sufficient cohort of schools has engaged in field trials, modification, correction, and retrialing. Failed mixed-age systems have been largely abandoned, while successful working models have flourished (Barnard, 2010, 2013, 2015). These not only provide a template for socially collaborative schools but are also designed with child development and social psychology in mind. Otherwise, research into secondary schools regarding the use of mixed-age tutor time is sparse to say the least.

There is significant unambiguous research into mixed-age teaching groups and in particular their social and cognitive advantages. Here is a brief overview from Song et al. (2009)

> The benefits (perceived and real) of the idealized model of the multiage program are many, including: helping to develop students' social, emotional, and verbal skills and self-esteem; enabling students to learn at their own pace; building a caring child-centered and project-based learning environment; and improving student attitudes toward school and school work, which results in increased attendance, etc.

It seems that schools that have transitioned to mixed-age tutor time (VT) have avoided the perceived complications of mixed-age classroom teaching—now decimated by age-related testing—but have nevertheless reaped the advantages of social gains and improved learning relationships between actors offered through dedicated mixed-age tutor time. The advantages of multiage approaches from social learning theory (Song, 2009) include learning from children who are both novices and experts, developing intellectual and communication skills, encouraging cooperation, and leadership development and (presumably) a concurrent increase in self-esteem.

Some schools (untrained in systems approaches) decide to omit Y7 (eleven- to twelve-year-olds) from vertical tutoring arguing (and assuming) that they need a degree of protection. Most schools, however, include Y7 and claim these students to be significant beneficiaries of mixed-age grouping; even so, schools should note that care has to be taken with numbers to avoid "social insecurity" (Cornish, 2015). It is argued that the concentration of same-age peer groups is a major factor in aggressive, antisocial, and destructive acts in the USA (Bronfenbrenner, 1970). Similarly, Salmivalli's (2009) meta-review of peer-group bullying indicates that the classroom populated by same-age peers is not as safe as schools assume.

> The group (i.e., classroom) in which bullying takes place differs from many social groups in an important respect: the membership is involuntary, which means that the victim cannot easily escape his or her situation. The other group members cannot just leave, either. Although students cannot choose their classmates, social selection processes (Kandel, 1978) take place within classrooms, resulting in cliques and friendship dyads that consist of similar others. (p. 116)

Even in mixed-age organization, group membership is involuntary and has to be decided with considerable care, expertise, and knowledge of individuals. There is mounting evidence that bullying is very much a group process (O'Connell et al., 1999; Salmivalli et al., 1997; Sutton and Smith, 1999). Given that most schools as organizations are based entirely on peer group structures, it can be argued that any totally same-age system provides the perfect seedbed for bullying to occur. The question then arises as to why schools should choose to ignore research, social psychology, and child development, and continue to use the same-age system as the basis for school organization. Any answer can only appeal to a combination of tradition, misinterpretation, and assumption. The research strongly infers that same-age groups may be harmful to a child's development and certainly restrictive and puts at risk the social and psychological development of young people for the convenience of testing by age.

Because mixed-age groups maintain their core relationships throughout schooling, it is suggested (Marler, 1976; Sherman, 1980) that this sense of belonging acts to promote pro-social behavior and reduces aggression. Today, schools are under severe pressure to incorporate technical pro-social programs covering well-being, resilience, grit, and character development within a curriculum already under pressure. The argument here is that these attributes and dispositions may be better accrued from mixed-age design. For example, schools in the UK are being trained to deal with mental health issues (effects) rather than addressing the same-age organizational cause, further complicating schools and leading to increased costs.

Part of this issue suggests that students are not being given the developmental opportunities they need from same-age schools. For example, children given leadership responsibilities for others assist the teacher and provide role models for others (Lougee and Graziano, 1985), indicating that ideas and dispositions involving character are better designed in than added on as programs for perceived character deficits. William Miller (1995) of the Washtenaw Intermediate School District of Ann Arbor, Michigan, notes that "educators have merely accepted the age-graded organizational structure as a way of doing things within the system of public education. As our society has changed, so must our schools."

The excellent overview of McClellan and Kinsey (1999) and a key reference in this paper notes that the interest in social behavior is of importance because of its role in cognitive development (Rogoff, 1990; Tizard, 1986; Vygotsky, 1978). While the dominant universal school model is the factory in form (Cuban, 1989), McClellan and Kinsey note in their overview of same-age and mixed-age classrooms that same-age structures are out of kilter with neural research:

> There is increasing evidence that this model is inconsistent with a wealth of recent research on the developing human brain (Caine and Caine, 1991; Huttenlocher, 1990; Kandel & Hawkins, 1992; Squire, 1992) and the kinds of educational strategies that bring about optimal learning and development. Ample research (Ames, 1992; Johnson et al., 1984; Johnson and Johnson, 1991; McClellan, 1994) demonstrates that children think more, learn more, remember more, take greater pleasure in learning, spend more time on task, and are more productive than in individualistic or competitive structures.

Many schools see mixed-age tutor groups as ideal preparation for the development of student leadership and mentoring. This is consistent with evidence (Fuchs et al., 1996) that such students are more effective in facilitating cognitive growth in others and in helping others to solve problems (social and intellectual). In the research literature, it is difficult to find a dissenting view with regard to the considerable social and cognitive advantages of mixed-age groups. While there is a debate surrounding the suitability and effectiveness of mixed-age classrooms (in a high-stakes system), there was none about social and learning benefits. The social and psychological basis for mixed-age groups is clear and unambiguous.

## Chapter 2

# Reacting to Disturbances

When big trouble hits (the latest damning report recommendations from government!), a school reacts to events in two distinct ways. It can rearrange the deckchairs on the *Titanic* while the orchestra keeps playing, or it can abandon ship and live to fight another day—if rescued or incorporated into a school chain! Both options are high-risk and tragic in their way. An alternative for the school is to create a more joined-up organization, one that is more resilient, flexible, and adaptive to external shock. In systems terms, such an organization should exhibit multiple working pathways and connections between different sources of information (students, staff, and parents).

So what kind of things are going awry that should be of concern? Let's have a bit more detail.

Deborah Spratling, a psychotherapeutic counsellor working with young people, described teaching as "a beautiful profession transformed into a beast that is damaging mental health" (TES, November 2017). We'll come across more evidence of this kind later. Meanwhile, Michael Fullan et al. (2017) speaks of *the unique configuration of challenges* we face that are only resolvable through learning and especially for those who feel disenfranchised and hard to reach.

For Fullan, desirable engagement with learning garners its strength locally and builds out from the base where our players engage. If this is so, getting the base right at ground level where students meet is essential to create the optimal conditions for what Fullan calls *deep learning*. The suggestion here is that group composition by mixed-age is critical to Fullan's proposals. Fullan notes the difficulty many young people have in creating a pathway to jobs yet to exist, and their sense of hopelessness in belonging to an institution that often seems to them as irrelevant and uncaring.

## MORE SYSTEM PROBLEMS

Julian Astle (2017), in a recent RSA report, brings attention to *gaming* in the system, caused in part by the severity of the UK's harsh version of accountability (itself a naïve attempt to make the existing same-age system work well!).

> With governors and trustees fearing for their schools, and Headteachers fearing for their jobs, our punitive accountability system has come to dominate almost everything some schools do, distorting professional priorities and practice and narrowing and hollowing out the education our children receive.

There are few in schools and among parents who would disagree with Astle's view, something he describes as a *betrayal of education's progressive promise* and one likely to deter students from further learning. Astle continues:

> So focused have our schools become on achieving the proxy goals of passing tests, hitting targets and climbing league tables, that they risk losing sight of education's higher purposes, like individual fulfilment and societal progress.

This sets the scene for the arena we are entering, one where cognitive dissonance is the norm and collateral system damage the result. For all the school policies on safeguarding, it seems that the school itself is far from being a safe place to be and that nothing in its aging management architecture makes much sense anymore. When governments throw money at problems, they engage in single-loop learning solutions that treat symptoms rather than the underlying cause; countries that invest heavily in equity and fairness tend to be happier and more productive, and rarely see schools as problematic.

So what of the many schools that try each and every day to make the current system work? How can we understand what is happening from a systems perspective, and how can we help schools rescue the situation before they go under for a third time? In particular, how can we get schools to start looking at management and leadership in a very different way? Schools have far more potential than they themselves think and are packed with talent.

Secondary schools (from junior high upward) recognize that the huge effort applied by staff rarely seems to result in gains made. While schools busy themselves with the task of passing standardized tests, so much of value is lost or assumed. The linear equation on which school management depends (effort = outcomes) is focused on results rather than process and often fails to pan out in terms of value.

Any errant analysis of this problem creates a system whereby teachers are compelled to work ever harder. Meanwhile, each day seems to bring new system repairs, new effect lists, new examination requirements, new curriculum fixes, and new pro-social add-ons; but instead of helping, schooling gets more and more complicated until time evaporates, work-life balance becomes almost impossible, and costs rise inexorably. The school weakens and tires as it exhausts itself.

Julian's is one of two recent reports (we'll come to the other shortly) that point to a handful of schools that seem to have bucked the system by retaining their learning values. In Astle's words, "They are all driven by a sense of mission that goes well beyond the narrow demands of the accountability system." While the report is strong on system faults, the examples and solutions offered are insufficient to effect substantive system change. Most are interesting and welcome projects battling insurmountable odds and should be cherished but ultimately they remain single-loop in essence.

Such models must still work around the basic same-age management structure of the school and so will always lack the power to inspire systemic change. Though helpful, the exemplars show little evidence of double-loop learning, but they are nevertheless exemplars of how teachers can exercise greater control and agency in the learning process. Their strength is to increase the joy of learning.

What becomes clear when working with schools is that teachers aren't the problem that requires resolution. They are as good as the system in use allows them to be. Similarly, there is no shortage of leadership potential in schools. The problem with leadership is its single-loop preoccupation with fixes and add-ons and its inability to distinguish system cause and effect.

What we have, as Astle rightly identifies, is a systems problem. Schools have moved far from their stated purposes and freedoms. They are now heavily controlled to the point of micro-management and are becoming universally convergent. Given that schools have no power to resist this forced march to oblivion, they would be well advised to gather their remaining energy and formulate an improved survival strategy while they still can.

The fact is, the UK system, like so many others, was never designed to develop the potential of all children, and according to Professor Diane Reay (2017), it still isn't. Reay goes further. We have moved away from approaches that work to ones that don't. In an epic single sentence, Reay says,

We have been bombarded with a plethora of educational policies such as standards, testing regimes, league tables, school choice, academies and free schools, the return to traditional models of both primary and secondary curriculum, performance and managerialism, academic and vocational streaming, punitive strategies such as naming and shaming of schools, and a preoccupation with "school improvement" and "school effectiveness" (Smyth and Simmons, 2017), all of which have had little or no impact on educational inequalities, and many of which have increased children's stress and reduced their levels of wellbeing.

The system, Reay says, is profoundly unjust and one that leads to demor-alization, demotivation, and physical and mental distress among children, and particularly working-class children. It is a system shaped by class in the 1870s and the ideas of the time still permeate management practices today, perhaps more so. "English Education is becoming increasingly fragmented and atomized with a diminishing sense of collectivity and collaboration."

If this is so, and many believe Reay is correct in her analysis, schools have a problem. English education, like so many similar systems, has become a business, and, as the good professor says, the inequities generated have become reinforced by the neoliberal drive toward markets, regulation, indi-vidualism, and competition.

Hallgarten and colleagues (2016), in an exceptional report by the RSA to the World Innovation Summit for Education (WISE), drew attention to the defining characteristics that continue to maintain the industrial model of formal schooling. They note the remarkable resilience of these features as influences on management, teaching, and learning:

- Front-loaded to age sixteen, or increasingly nineteen;
- Teacher-directed and driven;
- Largely building and classroom-based;
- Determined by age grouping;
- Based on set, standardized curricula;
- Privileging specific academic subjects;
- Privileging certain modes of knowing; and
- Assessed by standardized tests.

The fundamentals of schooling have not changed. The authors note,

> This is not to suggest that all of the above characteristics should be abandoned; rather it is to draw attention to an important distinction: that "improvement" and "change" are not the same as "innovation" and "transformation." . . . Most improvement efforts take the parameters above as a given, and make incremen-tal changes around them.

We are talking about the assumptions used to determine the way schools operate as learning systems. Readers might note the determination by age-grouping in the fourth bullet point above; this for me is the critical observa-tion. The school in its current form is only able to operate at the level of incremental and temporary change and is denied the fundamental changes or transformation that is common parlance in the research literature. Same-age structure is not just a separational feature of school organization, but a limita-tion that prevents the school from adapting; ultimately, it has a disabling and demoralizing internal effect.

The school does all it can to create organizational calm; it seeks the order needed for learning, no matter what chaos it faces from reformers banging on the front door with urgent requests for their latest questionnaire. The Senior Management Team (now renamed the Leadership Team or Administration Group) seeks control knowing there is much that can go awry in the daily life of a school. Staff in a wonderful school in Brisbane, Australia, transitioning to a mixed-age system, referred to the Admin Block as *The West Wing*! Graham Leicester (2013) sums up what is happening:

> Educational system leaders are good at producing development programs which are frenetic and burdensome to practitioners, incomprehensible and disruptive to both parents and learners but ultimately leave the essentials of the scene completely unaltered. (p. 13)

On the one hand, we have schools close to palliative care and on the other we have authorities asking ever more of them. The answer involves the school moving from weak *self-construction* (where they are) to strong *self-organization* (where they need to be), a transformational process that starts with acceptance of mixed-age organization. But to achieve this requires a much deeper understanding of the school's organizational form and in particular the consequences of same-age design, a factor so seemingly benign that few seem willing to question its credentials.

## COMMON OBSERVATIONS OF PEER-BASED SCHOOLS

Without exception, in every school that employs same-age groups as their organizational base the following signs are easily detectable:

- High system disconnectivity, separation of teachers, students, and parents;
- Overreliance on job descriptions and line management;
- A plethora of complicated policies, practices, principles, procedures, and protocols;
- Recycled management ideas inherited from the distant past or planet;
- Assumptions about child development estranged from child psychology;
- High failure demand. Repeat work; and
- Reliance on the past to solve problems of the present.

No criticism whatsoever should be leveled at staff and the care they heroically exercised despite the system in use. It is no wonder we are witnessing a spike in mental health issues, loss of well-being, and people unable to perform as they should; it is the system, not the participants, that needs attention.

The result, however, is self-deceit and self-delusion on a grand scale. Even care is not what it seems. It is the living system's way of coping with the cognitive dissonance that threatens its identity. No one in the school is at fault. This means that the leadership and teacher quality problems that reformers and authorities are trying to fix are not the problems that need attention. In the end, the school is part of a bigger system and teachers cannot be expected to compensate for the inadequacies of any wider system failure to tackle inequity and social mobility issues. Teachers and their schools are only part of any solution but they can do so much more and all want to!

Despite the odds, schools still strive to fathom out what they can do better and how they might draw from their vast reservoir of human potential and creativity. In particular, they want to innovate and have more agency and this requires courage given the punitive risks they face. Unfortunately, the industrial toolbox they've inherited was designed for maintenance of a machine, not for a living system like a school.

## SYSTEM LEVERS

In table 1.1, the first column contains the system descriptors that best describe the schools of today, the system in use; the second column describes where schools think they are or what they *espouse*. The purpose is to provide a systems reality check and then show how schools can transform from a teaching organization to a learning and teaching organization.

To switch from one column to another requires a change from same-age organization to mixed-age organization, something that requires considerable care and expertise. It also requires abandoning much of what schools consider to be normal management processes. In other words, we are dealing with two very distinct system change levers. Each sets in motion a very different system.

Same-age leads direct to a teaching system and mixed-age to a learning and teaching system, a mixed economy. Today, schools are prisoners of a same-age system leverage point. Fortunately, we are at a time when neoliberal ideas are almost spent and many schools injured by the experience seek a return to agency, values, and vision. Some, having tried everything in their received repertoire, turn their attention to the use of mixed-age tutor groups. They have heard stories about cultural change from other schools and wonder what might happen if they took a similar path.

Explore the research literature, however, and you'll struggle to find any mention of such a seemingly odd school improvement strategy, but it is there nevertheless, writ large in child development and social psychology. So why is it ignored? The answer can only rest in the power of the received industrial mind-set and the failure of our System 2 to question same-age system assumptions and to innovate to a more viable option. Absence of systems thinking means we have failed to appreciate the power of *system leverage points*, places where a small amount of effort sets in motion a domino effect that determines the way a system behaves.

What came as a surprise was the range of schools that wished to consider changing their system. It included renowned independent schools, grammar schools, schools that struggle in neglected backwaters, high-performing state schools, church schools, single-sex schools, and more. There is no common denominator other than the wonderfully disruptive quality of school leaders who have the temerity to question system fundamentals.

The journey that mixed-age schools have begun is also the first step toward collaborative and social professionalism. It is where schools were heading in their own faltering way before the storm of NPM (New Public Management) threw them onto the rocks. So, like all good journeys, we need to begin by plotting a better destination.

*Chapter 3*

# From Collaborative Professionalism to Social Collaboration

The previous chapter showed that attempts to fix the existing same-age school system rarely have the impact intended. No matter what we do, problems or recruitment and retention, training, funding, and concerns about outcomes continue unabated, while other problems such as staff morale, well-being, and mental health issues arise as if from nowhere. When attempts are made to rectify these without addressing the fundamental cause, the system fails to respond. Systems thinkers know that any kind of piecemeal approach can only lead to complications and the creation of more problems elsewhere.

In the next few chapters, I'll try and illustrate exactly how organization into same-age groups distorts learning relationships and causes many of the problems noted so far, besides preventing system transformation. We'll do this by looking at connections between players and the way same-age organization prevents connectivity and collaboration. In metaphorical terms, there is an incongruity between the school as a living system that seeks an answer to what it feels the world is asking of it, and the machine whose capabilities are restricted to sorting, sifting, and batching.

## THE CHALLENGE OF COLLABORATION

High on John Hattie's (2017) effect list are two important issues. These are the belief teachers have in student achievement and collective teacher efficacy (CTE). This is an important combination, one that is plain common sense and needs no research. We can surmise that this is a good organizational practice as far as teaching and learning is concerned, in which case it is important to understand how a school might encourage such collective efficacy at a systems level. Joining a system to more of itself is always helpful.

Here is the heresy. Collaboration will always be an add-on; if it occurs at all, it can never be the normal way of working in a same-age organization no matter how desirable and efficacious. The hype (espoused) rarely matches the practice of the system in use; in fact, it can't. While schools are always able to point to exemplars in their organization of how well they collaborate, these fall well short of what is needed. Merely being an advocate doesn't make a practitioner. Let's drill down into the area.

Collaboration is at the heart of the learning organization and is defined by Peter Senge (1990) as follows:

> organizations that encourage adaptive and generative learning, encouraging their employees to think outside the box and work in conjunction with other employees to find the best answer to any problem.

Unfortunately, the schools we have created are traveling in a very different direction and few can claim to be working in such learning organizations. Even so, teacher collaboration is generally accepted as a strategy for improving system effectiveness. All we need to do is get people to collaborate. Given that most people like to collaborate, share ideas, and feel supported, this should be relatively easy—shouldn't it? It advances better teaching and learning strategies besides and makes us feel more engaged; it is also an extension of attachment theory so offers significant psychological benefits.

But it isn't so simple. In the previous chapter, it was stated that for collaboration to work the system derived from same-age organization must be abandoned. It is necessary to go further and propose another heresy and defend it. Collaboration in a same-age system is not achievable except at a marginal and superficial level, neither can it lead to a learning organization even if it is a step in the right direction.

Schools may be perplexed by this. In a school, conversations are happening all the time; people are forever exchanging information and working as teams to get the work done. After all, a school has all the appearance of a collaborative organization provided it escapes close systems scrutiny. Collaboration is actually an add-on in form and as such is limited in effect; in a linear system, its adoption can even be seen as problematic given the narrow measures of success (pass rates) in use. Collaboration is actually very difficult to implement because it is not the way schools were designed to work.

So what schools are offered is a sensible strategy which cannot be realized to full effect in a system based on same-age organization. Schools would like to collaborate more but they don't. They run out of time and energy dealing with failure demand. It is not because they are not listening—they are very aware of the research base that underpins the value of collaboration (connectedness in essence). It is because implementation is difficult and largely dependent on energy reserves that schools don't have. We think people won't or can't collaborate but once again, the real problem is the same-age system in use. The reason is complex.

## RETRACING THE PATH TO COLLABORATIVE PROFESSIONALISM

Given the influence of Hattie's analysis and effect list, it should be no surprise that the next big thing touted is *collaborative professionalism*, not professional collaboration! This is fine and on the surface seems to make perfect sense; people generally enjoy collaborating and are often far more effective when they do. It is a great idea and a sensible strategy. But those who promote this idea know that there are implementation issues that require considerable reworking of the existing model. Schools in their same-age structure are not ideally set up for such a way of working.

To help us understand what is happening, let's track the thinking of two eminent thought leaders in education: Michael Fullan and Andy Hargreaves (2012). By following their journey, it is easier to ascertain direction and the precise point where the same-age system blocks the path to collaborative learning and teaching. Hargreaves and Fullan introduce us to a concept called *capital*, in essence an investment in people and their professionalism.

There are two basic kinds of capital investment that Fullan and Hargreaves propose. There is the current short-term business approach whereby teaching is simple, requires minimal training, can be driven by simple logistics and data, and yield a profit. In this increasingly familiar model deeply established in the political psyche, Hargreaves and Fullan describe the purpose of public education as no more than

> a market for technology, for testing products, for charter schools and companies and chains and their look-alikes in Sweden and England and other parts of the world.

But there is an alternative view (professional capital) that sees teaching as hard, challenging, and technically difficult. Hargreaves and Fullan explain this as follows:

> It requires technical knowledge, high levels of education, strong practice within schools, and continuous improvement over time that is undertaken collaboratively, and that calls for the development of wise judgment. Over time, professional capital policies and practices build up the expertise of teachers individually and collectively to make a difference in the learning and achievement of all students. (p. 37)

A worry with this otherwise laudable statement is the implied acceptance that it is all about teachers and seems to accept the existing model of the school as benign. We keep trying to change teachers rather than the system that determines so much of their behavior. Yet the school as a system has the bigger role to play and that role must support ideas like professionalism and agency—if it can.

There is agreement supported by research that when teachers are given time for collaboration, the reward is more effective teaching and learning and better outcomes. Fullan and Hargreaves suggest that professional capital has three components:

- Human capital (the talent of individuals),
- Social capital (the collaborative power of the group), and
- Decisional power (the wisdom and expertise to make sound judgment about learners that are cultivated over many years).

The advice from Fullan and Hargreaves is that *social capital* is the way to go, something they refer to as *using the group to change the group*, and a recurrent and vitally important theme of this book. We are all on the same page. Fast forward to 2017 and Fullan rebadges this phrase into *Using the World to Change the World*. It is a profound analysis, but having identified what is needed by way of teacher improvement the writers are less forthcoming regarding the impact of the current system in use.

Although we are offered exemplars of collaboration in schools, it is not clear in any practical and organizational sense how a school as a system can go about building such capital, the *how*. We only know that they should.

## THE THEORY OF COLLABORATION

Fullan and Hargreaves nevertheless set out the design parameters and the idea that the road to improvement involves joining up a number of moving parts. In particular, they pinpoint an important tenet behind the psychology of systems thinking. When teachers collaborate, they are better placed to deal with the variety of student needs or system demand; such an approach makes the system seem temporarily able to absorb value demand, *using the group to change the group*.

Hargreaves and Fullan reference Carrie Leana (2011). She tells us how the term *social capital* was used by James Coleman (1990) when comparing students in different kinds of schools. He described social capital as the "norms and relationships between adults and children that are of value for a child's growing up." He attributed much of student success to the support networks (parents and community) prevalent in and around schools.

Carrie Leana confirmed the essence of this research in a large-scale program in New York (2005–2007) but took a narrower view.

> Most striking, students showed higher gains in math achievement when their teachers reported frequent conversations with their peers that centered on math, and when there was a feeling of trust or closeness among teachers. In other words, teacher social capital was a significant predictor of student achievement gains above and beyond teacher experience or ability in the classroom. And the effects of teacher social capital on student performance were powerful. (p. 33)

There is a major fork in the road at this point. If we follow Coleman the social scientist, we end up with a broader view of collaboration, a bigger picture of the power of the system pulling together as a community of people. In particular, we are shown the importance of influence and support from adults and mentors (older students), both an endemic feature of mixed-age organization and so of particular importance for those children who lack support at home and in their friendship groups and community.

Social collaboration is a given in a mixed-age situation; it is flexible, joined up, and designed in. Uri Bronfenbrenner's ecological systems theory is of this kind, as is Bowlby's attachment theory. *Social collaboration* can be added to column 2 of table 1.1 as a powerful system feature and there is little doubt that Coleman would be an advocate of vertical (mixed-age) tutor groups. Using the group to change the group!

But we are taken down a cul-de-sac whereby the same-age system is regarded as benign by inference. This is the road of those beguiled by a belief that the *great teacher in every classroom* can somehow be constructed without reference to the system that shapes participant behavior and so much of what happens in school. We are offered professional collaboration, which has an unwanted side effect. It doesn't change the system in use one iota and we end up with a good concept and a system unable to fully exploit its merits.

At its best, collaboration is more than just a dialogue between teaching professionals anxious to develop pedagogical expertise and mastery; it is highly complex and involves not only a diversity of group thinking that extends to students and parents but also a sense of group purpose, belonging, and even emotional support. We'll discover more of this later when we look at Google and the Oxygen and Aristotle Projects (chapter 15). It is why the talk now is of collaborative professionalism, not professional collaboration.

For Coleman, *social capital* is an inclusive concept and one that underpins mixed-age organization, a concept that requires greater systems acumen and attention by schools. For Coleman, the difference in performance (between public and private schools) is more a matter of social capital than teacher capability alone. He echoes the ideas of Pierre Bourdieu (1930–2002) on *cultural capital* and *habitus*, which are likely to confer advantages at school.

So, the idea is that we move beyond professional collaboration to collaborative professionalism, a wider and more inclusive concept and way of working, one that leans toward the idea of social capital. The equity and social mobility so often absent beyond the school gates have to be addressed within the school by reconnecting our players, and this is what the mixed-age system does.

Coleman recognized that collaboration involves a more elaborate social network that extends beyond teachers to parents and students. All have a role to play, and how this multiplicity of roles is played out and how these players are connected are determined by the system in operation. Schools open (mixed-age) to genuine partnership will enjoy more success in social collaboration and support, and this makes the role of the school critical in how it builds the collaborative and social partnerships between players.

The point being labored is this: collaborative professionalism in a same-age setting will always suffer separation and limitation issues no matter how well executed. The mixed-age setting builds collaboration with immediacy from the base. The students in a mixed-age setting are the first to learn how to use the group to change the group in ways that support learning, the start of a domino effect. It is a theme we'll return to.

As far as our two systems are concerned, the following descriptors apply. The same-age system assumes that connections are all in place and functional but this is not so. Parents, students, and staff are separated as groups and are rarely in the same place at any one time. Schools often see their task as protecting teachers from parents and the electoral blast at the door. There are always major issues when it comes to communication and parental engagement. The mixed-age school system is collaboration dependent. It cannot run as a system without the social collaboration of all players, and this makes it a very different system!

Fullan and Hargreaves suggest that when teachers are able to collaborate they become nation builders. The question is, what sort of nation? Far better to design a collaboration-dependent school, one more likely to build a collaborative kind of nation than one separated out and limited. The fact is young people learn a great deal from the system in which they work and from the nature of the working relationships to which they belong.

Today in the UK, we are witness to a system that history will show has all the separational hallmarks likely to lead to a future black swan event. Many think that this is where we already are.

## GROUPS AND INFLUENCE—CANADA

While we may agree that collaboration is an essential ingredient for teacher development, it is difficult to implement and can never be professionally endemic in a linear, same-age system. While good teaching may improve test results, it is questionable whether it can improve civic society without a thorough consideration of how all learning relationships in the school combine to support learning.

For collaborative professionalism to be truly successful, it has to involve the wider community of students and parents besides being securely sited in social psychology and community. In the end, teaching and learning is a social and passionate affair. Peter Block (2007) reminds us that it is unwise to design services and solutions exterior to (in this case) the school as a community and expect them to work. He suggests that change requires different thinking, one group at a time from the base up. He also suggests helpful inversions such as the idea that *the learner creates the teacher* and *the future creates the present*!

For me, the mixed-age school is the seedbed of collaborative professionalism. Otherwise, the concept is just a concept. In system terms, the step from professional collaboration to collaborative professionalism is sensible; the bigger step is social collaboration and the challenge is to create the systemic conditions needed in schools. It doesn't work the other way round!

Among the countries she visited, Lucy Crehan (2016) nominated Canada (Ontario) as the preferred choice for her children. This shouldn't be a surprise. When Canadians rebuilt their education system, they made a number of sensible decisions. Top of the list was the rejection of the top-down UK model based on a *delivery unit*, a model that has led the UK to its own unfortunate plight and dismembered form. Instead, our Canadian cousins chose to consult with teachers and build upward from the base.

On their journey, governments took sage advice and wise counsel from eminent educationists like Fullan and Hargreaves. In the end, they created a system not only able to balance conflicting learning demands but also able to align accountability with support rather than punishment (Crehan, 2016, p. 236). It is a system built by adults for their children and their future, one with considerable group buy-in.

It should be no surprise, therefore, to see the concept of collaborative professionalism set out by the Ministry of Education for Ontario in memorandum No. 159 (2016). It is worth taking a moment to note what is said.

As part of the transformation process, all education professionals will work together to build on Ontario's solid foundation of achievements through the establishment of trusting relationships that value the voices of all, encourage reflection and support professional growth. A culture of collaborative professionalism is grounded in:

- Professional learning that supports and enables the conditions for student achievement and student and staff well-being;
- Recognition of and building on the strengths of all individuals to support professional growth;
- Leadership practices that value the expertise and inclusion of all voices, perspectives and roles;
- Commitment to building professional capacity at all levels;
- Professional practice informed by research, evidence and knowledge arising from the strengths, needs and interests of students and education professionals;
- A trusting environment where school, school board, and union leaders and the ministry create the necessary conditions, including consideration of time and resources, that enable teams to learn with, and from, each other.

This vision is sound and in line with cultural values of those doing the learning and teaching work in schools. It sounds like a group approach. But where the language of the memorandum later gets tricky is in its approach to implementation. Schools in their hierarchical, same-age form aren't well-suited to embrace collaborative professionalism, though Canadian schools seem more proficient than most.

Bringing us up-to-date, Andy Hargreaves and Michael O'Connor (2017), in their recent report to WISE, describe collaborative professionalism as follows:

Collaborative professionalism is about how teachers and other educators transform teaching and learning together to work with all students to develop fulfilling lives of meaning, purpose, and success. It is organized in an evidence-informed, but not data-driven, way through rigorous planning, deep, and sometimes demanding dialogue, candid but constructive feedback, and continuous collaborative inquiry. The joint work of collaborative professionalism is embedded in the culture and life of the school, where educators actively care for and have solidarity with each other as fellow-professionals.

Let me quibble with these defining and well-intentioned characteristics: what is really needed is a system that is collaboration dependent; otherwise, teaching and learning cannot transform to its potential. Neither do we want collaborative professionalism *embedded* in the system we have. *It needs to be the system*! The life and culture of the school have to be collaborative, and this means more joined-up and this means the same-age system cannot be the underpinning culture.

Again, we are offered a compelling picture of what a school that practices collaborative professionalism might look like and offered possible exemplars.

How this embeds itself in the life of the school in its current same-age, organizational form, however, remains hugely problematic. It does seem that the old industrial model remains unscathed in its current form and somehow gets through this redefinition of learning unscathed. Even so, this abridged definition (which goes on for quite some length to include all current thinking) still has to contort its way around the system in use.

## THE DESIGN PROBLEM

Hargreaves and O'Connor take a further step to a better model through their provision of ten guiding system tenets (appendix 1). It is always a joy when systems thinking is called upon to turn theory into practice. In so doing, Hargreaves and O'Connor return us yet again to a simple, distilled concept. Using the group to change the group is a steady state only achievable in a mixed-age system, one designed solely with such group dynamics in mind.

The challenge is to recognize full social capital and the system cohesion required to release the creative power of all groups in a school, in effect to make them operational. Teachers are not separate from the system but integral to it, which is why they cannot easily be singled out for special attention or blame. Teachers cannot change the system through better teaching. Better teaching comes when teachers change the system in a way that enables greater agency and organizational learning,

There is a small problem; teachers do not work in the kind of learning organizations advocated by Peter Senge; they work in teaching organizations, and teaching, as W. Edwards Deming and Russell Ackoff used to say, always gets in the way of learning. The mixed-age model or vertical tutoring (VT) doesn't create a learning organization but is the first critical step toward one. It is the learning gateway through which schools must pass and has the better chance of designing in collaborative and social professionalism, a paradigm that extends leadership and engagement in learning to include parents, students, and community.

The model described by Hargreaves and O'Connor falls into the trap of accepting same-age organization as benign. The only way that the school can adopt more collaborative professionalism is to add it on in temporary form and hope it sticks. Collaborative professionalism cannot be a desirable form on a to-do effect list but needs to be the way schools work and should include students, staff, and parents. Why? Because they are a vital source of energy and information in the system. All groups are important, and the combinations are many.

Put bluntly, the system used by the school has to be collaboration dependent, not separational and limitational, and this requires three things.

- First, we have to understand how the linear, same-age system and an industrial mind-set leads to limitation and separation and how it restricts collaboration and the development of the full range of complex relationships (social capital) on which learning and teaching relies. (Unlearning or unfreezing).
- Second, schools have to adopt a mixed-age system design strategy in the vacuum created by the abandonment of a deeply entrenched industrial mind-set. (Change).
- Third, schools must exercise the agency, autonomy, and trust needed to develop organizations that are collaboration-dependent. This means system change. (New learning and refreezing).

So, what of the tenets nominated by Hargreaves and O'Connor (appendix 1). As we travel through this book, most will arise because the conversation is about living systems and how they work. I'll leave you with the most important one, number 10. "In collaborative professionalism, everyone gets the big picture. They see it, live it and create it together."

While this is exactly what is needed, application is stymied if the school is operating in a way that restricts the input of players and sets the school in a direction where teaching to the test is the chosen modus operandi. Any big picture and practice must be complementary. A same-age system is inflexible by design and is entirely dependent on add-ons and fixes to make it functional. A more *systemsy* and helpful definition is as follows: Within the bigger picture, everyone 'gets collaboration'. They see it, live it and are dependent upon it.

This is the learning organization of Peter Senge and is what systems thinking is all about, seeing the big picture and how it works. It is also a completely different model. The difficult bit involves ridding ourselves of received assumptions, risking system change, and adopting new system management and leadership ideas. Somehow, schools have to cease their addiction to fixes and add-ons and rethink their end-to-end operational practice. It returns us to ideas about how people work best.

David Hargreaves (2006) described school design and organization as the most challenging of the nine gateways to learning available for development. The challenge is elegantly expressed by King and Frick (1999).

> Just understanding the need for redesign, however, does not provide us with the necessary skills to create alternative schools. All too often, reform efforts fail because we lack the abilities required for systemic design; we cannot analyze the existing school model holistically and recreate it from the ground up. Instead, we often remain entrenched in our current notions of education and only tinker at the edge of schools, making minimal changes. With the grandest

of ideals, designers often aim towards creating a new school that looks entirely different from traditional education, only to find that the resulting system is very similar to the traditional classroom.

It seems we are distracted by what we see rather than the underlying connectedness on which a system depends—the bit we assume and don't see. We handle numbers in preferences to collaborative relationships, and it seems we are unaware of our cognitive dissonance. The anthropologist Gregory Bateson (2000) refers us to a concept he calls *an ecology of mind*, the difference between the way nature works and the way we think it does.

*Chapter 4*

# The Pusher, the Puller, and Thinking Differently

In this chapter, we pursue management thinking and the business of *value demand*. In particular, we pursue our investigation of two systems and take a first look at pro-social programs, why we have them, and the form they take.

For this section, the heretical starter takes the form of two questions that go like this. Why do we tolerate a system (same-age) that acts counter to the collaboration it promotes and needs? Given that the same-age system in use is causing so much damage, why do we try and fix the kids and the teachers rather than the system that is causing everyone so many problems?

The sad fact is the world is a messy place, dangerous and unfair. In complex societies where the difference between haves and have-nots is increasing, social mobility is almost static and the path that schools are obliged to travel involves survival in a competitive market, one not conducive to building collaborative networks and good learning relationships.

This has led Dirk Van Damme (2015), head of OECD/CERI, to pose a fundamental question.

> Are our education systems really geared to support learning, to foster social learning and to create learning societies? Or are we merely maintaining credentialism, systems of selecting, screening and signaling people?

The two systems (same-age and mixed-age) that started this journey evoke very different ways of thinking about schools and systems and the responses to challenges. First, we'll cover push-and-pull management styles and systems, and then we'll look in detail about how each responds when the pressure to perform increases.

## WHEN PUSH COMES TO SHOVE

Schools find themselves in a world where schooling and economics have become irrevocably intertwined. Today, researchers often begin by examining schools in terms of their (economic) efficiency, productivity, and return on investment. Push comes from concerns about economic performance in the global market, and schooling has been hauled back into the economic mix.

When the return on school investment is poor and the output data low, questions are raised about teacher capability and the competence of school leaders. The same-age system in use isn't regarded as anyway problematic and seems perfectly suited for the job of selecting out the high flyers needed. Any deeper school rationale and values are set aside.

Such an approach does not seek system change. It infers a tougher, more market-oriented approach to system leadership (Hanushek, 1986), a push system rather than a pull system, one that sides more with the machine metaphor used to separate, sort, and batch for delivery. In time, a causal link is claimed that relates teacher effectiveness directly to a child's economic prospects (Hanushek et al, 2014, 2016), and although the figures for such a proposition are often hotly contested (Komatsu and Rappleye, 2017), the damage is done.

Politicians grasp such research like manna from heaven. It confirms their errant bias that school leadership is weak, teaching standards are low, and that schoolchildren have a deficiency of character when pushed to work harder.

The economic view understands the school as a center of production. It proposes that production can be increased by raising the achievement bar, setting stretch targets, and acting directly on teachers who will be held directly accountable and dismissed or rewarded as appropriate. While there can be little doubt that school quality and economic performance is linked, such a link is far from simple and assessing teachers based on test data far from secure.

In their paper, John List, Jeffrey Livingstone, and Susanne Neckermann (2016) note that forty-three US states require evaluations of teacher performance that include measures of their students' achievement. Their research indicates that test results are not a fair measure of a teacher's performance but are influenced by the importance that students themselves attach to standardized tests and the effort they choose to apply. This calls into question the use of such data and their validity as a tool for teacher evaluation and indicates a sense of student detachment from the school process.

This crude push management is very different from the Canadian approach described earlier. Push managers spot what they perceive to be a problem (teacher quality, strength of leadership, and student dispositions to learning) and then contrive to fix the problem without a full systems understanding of the issues. This can mean narrowing the work to produce better data in desired areas, ensuring everyone is permanently on-task, rewarding work against perceived outcomes, increasing accountability, limiting training and professional development to *what matters*, and, of course, public shaming. Unsurprisingly, teachers respond by teaching to the test, the very opposite of the recommendation made by Hargreaves, Fullan, and O'Connor.

As teachers assume the role as agents of delivery, the effect is to increase dependency on the center (a la Maccia and Maccia 1966, SIGGs hypotheses). The *pusher* offers short-term fixes and long-term dependency and has a dulling effect on the school as an organization. The last thing a system like a school needs is teachers asking what they should do and how they should teach! Push managers ensure work is done and tasks completed. They drive solutions without thinking too much about the problems that need resolving and tend toward command and control structures (table 4.1).

## PULL

Pull systems take a different tack in line with systems thinking and schools should think carefully about which method suits their purpose. Pull is all about teams and collaboration; the manager pulls expertise from the teams, and the teams pull down the resources they need from the system. Pull relies on quality relationships and, as David Langford and Barbara Cleary (1995) say, quality resides *in the very relationship between teacher and learner*. But it should also reside in every other school learning relationship, and a heavy price is paid for its absence.

A pull system requires team participation, one where the enabling servant leader is often dependent on followers for solutions to problems; leaders are in part defined by their followers. In such a system, customers (teachers, parents, and students) are able to access the resources needed to do the job, in effect to absorb complexity itself defined as the variety of value demand on the system. A pull system studies value demand (what participants need to make progress) and then designs the best means to absorb that demand.

In an environment like the school, beset with a huge amount of variety, it makes sense for those doing the work to have control of what is going on. The manager's role is to manage the system in a way that best that enables the people doing the work to perform at their best. Seddon (2008) calls this *a different way of thinking* (table 4.1). Any mistakes in meeting value demand create *failure demand*, errors that have to be rectified downstream; these become very costly both in school and beyond.

Once the school has a handle on demand, it should concentrate on *flow*, the means by which information and mutual support services travel to where they are needed, the system's connectedness. The manager is there to ensure that any obstacles to flow are removed.

It is helpful to introduce John Seddon's take on the two systems. He differentiates between command and control, the type of approach used in schools and on schools, and systems thinking, the kind of approach needed in complex and collaborative service systems. All the evidence suggests that schools aspire to systems approaches but are trapped in the command mode.

In Jelmer Evers and R. Kneyber's book *Flip the System* (2016), Tom Bennett writes:

> The over-emphasis of a top-down hierarchy based on saturation levels of prescriptivism has produced a burden that alienates many from their profession. Their opinion, their entire craft is marginalized to the point of obsolescence. The teacher is no longer a professional, but a delivery system. (p. 253)

Finding a collaborative way back from where we are going will not be easy. We started with a simple systems table (table 1.1). The simplest way of understanding the same-age model and the thinking behind it is to compare it with schools that have adopted a mixed-age approach based on systems thinking principles. It is possible to have a mixed-age system while retaining the command mind-set but this is high-risk. Instead of becoming complex, the school just gets more complicated.

Table 4.2 sets out the main differences between the two approaches to school organization gleaned from schools that have made a successful transition.

The systems thinking approach builds a very different system, and the points set out (above) require careful consideration. It is not only different conceptually but also practically and lines up with child development and

**Table 4.1. Different Thinking (Adapted from Seddon, 2009, p. 70)**

| *Command and Control* | | *Systems Thinking* |
|---|---|---|
| Top-down, hierarchy | PERSPECTIVE | Outside-in system |
| Functional | DESIGN | Demand, value, flow |
| Separated from work | DESIGN-MAKING | Integrated with work |
| Output, targets, standards | MEASUREMENT | Capability, variation: related to purpose |
| Contractual | ATTITUDE to CUSTOMERS | What matters |
| Contractual | ATTITUDE to SUPPLIERS | Cooperative |
| Manage people and budgets | ROLE of MANAGEMENT | Act on system |
| Control | ETHOS | Learning |
| Reactive, projects | CHANGE | Adaptive, integral |
| Extrinsic | MOTIVATION | intrinsic |
| PUSH | Style | PULL |

**Table 4.2.   System Descriptors**

| Same-Age System | Mixed-Age System (Vertical Tutoring) |
| --- | --- |
| Large tutor-group size (25–30) | Uniform group size around 18 (20 max) |
| Tutors selected from available staff | Everyone a tutor regardless of status |
| Requirement to teach SEL | No taught program (SEL designed in) |
| Limited mentoring by older students | Every child a mentor and a leader |
| Empathy and others taught/added on | Empathy designed in as the school culture |
| One tutor per group | Two tutors per group (lead and co-tutor) |
| Tutor time at the start of the day | Tutor time before morning break (ideally) |
| Data sheets as reports | Reports require written improvement strategies |
| Year heads act as super secretaries | Heads of house act as heads of school |
| Parent evening short five-minute slots | Full academic tutorial forty minutes minimum |
| Parents disengaged | Parents fully engaged (summative assessment) |
| Induction process serendipity | Induction involves older students as mentors |
| Precarious friendship groups | Stable in-group loyalty and security |
| Confidence at risk | Secure base to venture out and explore |
| Psychologically errant assumptions | Psychologically secure |
| Child known by data sheet | Whole child known, grown, and developed |
| Deficit in grit, resilience, character | Learning dispositions designed in and grown |
| Focus on teacher/leader | Focus on the enabling system |

learning support. Instead of add-ons and fixes, all the necessary system ingredients are designed in.

The mixed-age approach surrounds the child with a pro-school support structure where every child is known and belongs. The group size is reduced and the number of tutors doubled to include everyone employed by the school. All older students are mentors and all are leaders, empathy designed into the system. How this model builds becomes clearer as we proceed.

As schools, we must learn how dispositions to learning and desired character traits can be designed in, lessening the need for pro-social programs and making them complementary perhaps, rather than *de rigeur*. Only by switching to this model is it really possible to appreciate the nonsense that is the same-age system and the problems it causes. The cost is twenty minutes a day.

The main difference between the two is the potential the mixed-age system has for social and academic collaboration, distributive leadership, and collective teacher efficacy. We can even add Piagetian programs to the list, which require an almost empathetic knowledge of where a child is at and how to move them on. Everything is a learning relationship, and much of this is not as visible as claimed. These are difficult add-ons in a same-age network but become designed into a same-age system, reflecting how the system works. The mixed-age system is all about connectedness, the capability, and power of the teams on which the system depends.

## THE MIXED-AGE RESPONSE AND PRO-SOCIAL PROGRAMS

We have to move from a situation entirely dependent on teachers to one dependent on organizational collaboration, one where every child, parent, and all staff must also be leaders and learners. The kind of same-age thinking that dominates school management is in the command column (table 4.2). It exists in practical terms because the same-age system produces a high degree of failure demand, relational issues that go awry, and disconnected relationships that aren't easy to address. In broad terms, staff and student well-being is in decline because the system in play lacks the capability needed to grow the resilience in players. In fact, it acts to lessen their resilience. The fix is not to reprogram participants by offering them resilience training but to reprogram the system—to stop it behaving like a machine and enable it to develop as a living system.

Resilience in a system depends upon its connectedness. The more network ties learning relationships and social partnerships (alternative support structures and pathways), the more resilient the system. Any failure here means that the isolated participants have to work considerably harder and this is detrimental to health and well-being. The same-age school has few cards to play to address these matters and relies on its extensive referral and support systems to deal with any negative effects that arise from the system. Complications and costs increase, and quality diminishes.

When this reaches overload, the school turns to the teacher (who else) to improve output and the delivery of pro-social programs to address relational matters. Principals are persuaded that kids, who are unable to cope or for whom school isn't working, lack resilience, grit, character, and a can-do mind-set, matters fixable by a daily session of mindfulness or a new pro-social program. This is completely understandable in the short term but clearly wrong as a long-term strategy.

This kind of well-intentioned thinking is on the rise but seems to be another attempt at fixing system fallout with more add-ons. It is up to schools whether or not they wish to have a system that continues to cause significant collateral damage that has to be corrected or make a switch.

There is evidence from Flook et al. (2015) and even the producers of Sesame Street, and the Kindness Curriculum developed at the University of Wisconsin, that there are early-years advantages to pro-social programs. SEL experts will produce endless data to support the effectiveness of such programs, but this doesn't tally with experience. Besides, it may not be the content of the program that is important but the possibility of being listened to and respected in a stress-free environment, one where a learning relationship with a teacher is more likely to form.

The only data offered here come from schools that have made the change to mixed-age organization and the degree to which mixed-age approaches are aligned with child development, motivational psychology, and systems thinking. Otherwise, it seems strange for schools to adopt pro-social programs in part to fix the problems caused by the school.

But this book is heretical. We should not tolerate a system that is causing loss of well-being and problems with resilience and grit. Helping students adapt to a system that does little to recognize their individual potential and to develop their social competencies may seem sensible but fails to deal with underlying cause, the system itself and the behavior it generates. Such an approach is counterproductive and merely serves to maintain sameness. Everyone pays a high price.

Mixed-age systems use social capital to lay the foundations of the collaborative school. We make assumptions when we don't understand things. We see elemental parts rather than their connective tissue. The principal manages by separation while preaching the collaboration the same-age system denies, and this always leads to limitation. At no time is the school leader able to control teacher quality, let alone motivate. We need help to think again about how our school system got broken and how the parts can be better assembled so that learning conversations can once again begin. Student performance is a whole school and community matter, and moving toward such a model has to be beneficial to all.

Here's the challenge: how do we get schools to understand the school as a complete living entity rather than a bunch of disparate parts linked only by policies, protocols, regulations, and directives? How do we enable the group to change the group and reconnect all players relationally? How do we enable the collaboration that frees up the system and enables all learners and teachers to perform optimally and with joy? How do we return the school to its fundamental purpose of making a difference and the goal of goodness?

In a school, the humble form tutor is the catalyst, the information hub around whom the system is organized and on whom the system depends. The tutor is the *school whisperer* and commands the power of the pack, using the group to change the group! If we are truly seeking change and a better learning system, it is necessary to understand how the tutor role can be developed, supported, and sustained. When this happens, teaching and learning improve too. Everything is connected.

## Chapter 5

# The School as a Living System—Disturbances and Fast Fixes

This book must be so frustrating. Schools want books that offer management tips, ways to improve teachers, attract staff, train leaders, and better manage their difficulties—and more money! Please, more money. But it's all here; it's just a question of seeing. Money used to manage specifications, complications, failure demand, fixes, and add-ons is money wasted, while money used to design-in quality, connectivity, and learning relationships saves money, lots of it!

Crudely measuring teacher performance and setting output targets has no immediate interest here because it diverts attention from learning and quality. Providing the organizational conditions for staff, student, and parent collaboration and engagement is by far the more important system challenge—besides schools only have so much energy. Such well-intentioned provocations and heretical statements are sticky; they make us think and react, and tend to linger longer than simply *sharing*, but they can have a temporary, adverse effect. They may prevent change, especially if the provocation is counter to everything recipients believe.

Provocations don't affect machines, and the machine has become the mind-set metaphor used to explain how the same-age system works. It has few human qualities. We grease the wheels, hit the brakes, change gear, and replace broken and nonfunctioning parts. We train people as if they were the machine parts. Even here, much is explained in terms of change levers and systems. But machines are static and repetitive and go wrong, and people have to work around them or be part of the operating process, cogs in the so-called wheel.

But the same-age education system is a machine that requires more and more attention, more toolboxes, more snake oil, more fixes, more training courses and add-ons, and more ancillary support. It is easily exploited by program sellers. It only appears to work well when the variety of demand from learners is fairly homogeneous and their attitude to the process of teaching and learning one of cultural acceptance and compliance. It works less well in social contexts where the variety of demand is more complex and system faults are exposed.

By now, the realization should have dawned that any attempt at system reform that acts to repair, replace, or improve component parts, including teachers, pedagogy, programs, policies, and more, invariably falls exasperatingly short of expectations and can even make matters worse.

Any connection between same-age structure and the failure of reform may seem unlikely, almost an aberration, but that is precisely what is proposed and set out in tables 1.1, 4.1, and 4.2. We need a system that is more self-managing, where self-reform or self-organization is built-in. There is a direct and irrevocable link highlighted by research (chapter 1), and the sooner we shift our System 2 systems thinking into gear (classic machine metaphor!) the better.

If school managers were trained as systems thinkers and able to look critically at managing the system rather than managing those trying to make it work, they would see how same-age organization negatively affects how our players (teachers, students, and parents) operate. Bringing school managers to that level of awareness is one of the many challenges here, and that requires a change in the metaphor used to describe human systems.

Having mentioned the idea of *the school as a living system*, it is time to put some meat on the bones! There are two broad approaches to *living systems*. In this chapter, we start with their biology and how they evolve and then move on to how they behave, in effect to explain how schools operate as organizations. This will lead to a deeper understanding and more spiritual sense of school, one with an ecology of mind as advised by Margaret J. Wheatley and Myron Kellner-Rogers (1996).

## CHANGING THE METAPHOR

Approaching the challenge of change using the heavily contextualized but inaccurate language of education together with its accompanying machine metaphor means going round in circles and becoming hung-up on system fixes and add-ons, the reform agenda, and a debate about *what works*. As Dylan Wiliam says, everything works somewhere! Besides, machines have no intelligence, so treating a school like one makes no sense. Schools are neither pushed nor driven; they either evolve or end. We need to change the metaphor.

The work of Maturana and Varela (1980) on *evolutionary biology* offers a far better insight into what is happening. Instead of machines and factories, organizations like schools are seen as *living systems*, and living systems are biological. As such, they react to environmental change, such as attempted reforms that pose a threat to the way they normally work, in predictable ways. In short, living systems react badly to disturbances: they react biologically but never quite obey, and this is an important feature of schools and a clue as to how best to work with them.

Over time, schools make subtle, imperceptible changes. In the view of Tyack and Cuban (2004), they *tinker to Utopia*, a slow but safe process of adaptation. This is fine in normal circumstances when evolution is equally slow, but not so good when demand on schools becomes more intense and searching questions are posed as to their economic value, teacher quality, and school leadership. As a living system, the school's biological drive is to survive and maintain identity (how it sees itself). Like any living system, it tries to control its environment and is sensitive to any change it perceives as a threat. To be accepted by a living system like a school, any change has to conform to the way the living system works. A school will accommodate many small changes, but nothing likely to overly interfere with what it perceives to be its main functions and drives, the way it has become accustomed to working.

The switch from the machine metaphor to that of a living system is subtle and takes us into the realm of consciousness and insights into how confirmation bias works. This offers a better perspective into the nature of schools and system behavior. Set out below are the main biological features adapted from John Atkinson (2015) and interpreted here for schools.

- The school (a living system) assesses the degree of threat that change brings and will always question its necessity. It will resist change that threatens its survival, the way it normally does things. External change is unwelcome unless the school initiates and controls it in ways that allow the school to maintain the way it typically operates. (This explains much about column 1 in all the preceding tables.)
- The school will change only if it becomes deeply disturbed in some way. It prefers not to be disturbed and will seek to dilute the disturbance or resist as necessary! But it will make small adaptions. This book is a disturbance! Heresies are a big disturbance, but they change nothing. Only the school as a living system can decide to change.
- The school controls change and how any change can occur (*We'll do it our way* is the school's dictum). Because the (same-age) school operates as a closed system, change in any one part has an unavoidable knock-on effect

to others and is often detrimental. It is less resilient to change than it thinks but still resilient (stubborn).

- The school understands the present only in terms of the past. It can change but in ways based on previous experience. It is self-referencing and understands the *now* only by what has happened before. It relies on hand-me-down methods and coping strategies that have helped it get by previously.

- Finally, a biological system has strict routines and relies on repetition and predictability; any breakdown in routines can have dramatic consequences to its well-being until the school is able to revert to its previous stable form. If, for example, it changes from a same-age system to a mixed-age system but is unable to break from old management practices, it could find itself in trouble and double-back fast.

The school as a living system is not conducive to reform in its present unevolved form. While a machine is created for a mechanical purpose, a living system has a nature that is more prone to self-determination. It aspires to be self-organizing. Treat a living system like a machine and it develops severe cognitive dissonance, whereby a belief in values is usurped by (say) a concern for passing tests, a condition resolved only through the ambivalence of self-deceit or identity protection. The living system is concerned with maintaining its identity and its survival above all, and this offers a far better way of understanding a school's organizational characteristics.

Unfortunately, reformers keep asking this amazing entity to act in ways that are contrary to its well-being and ours. We give it arbitrary purposes and measure its performance using standardized tests. In essence, the more we see schools as machine-like, the more they choose to act that way and the less we can ask of them; worse, the living part of the system starts to fail. So while the machine metaphor exists, little of substance will change. The education system becomes more machine-like, churning out sameness and compliance as it goes. The general trend is not diversification and evolution but convergence and sameness.

A school will not readily change from a same-age system to a mixed-age system unless it sees a good reason to do so, one that enhances its identity (how it perceives itself) and survival chances. Those schools whose identity is locked into the same-age system haven't completely lost touch with their values; misplaced optimism tells them that something might yet come along and save the day, an optimism not borne out by history. The school as a living system yearns to be self-organizing and spends more time on its own self-development rather than fighting off the nagging disturbances of reformers.

To change, therefore, the school as a living system requires compelling reasons, and in making such a change it will want to take as much control of that change as possible, even though this (as in the case of a change from same-age to mixed-age organization) can dramatically increase the risk of error. If, for example, it switches to a mixed-age system but maintains any of the descriptors set out in column 1 in table 4.2, it can suffer a near-mortal wound and will need to revert back to its previous form—at considerable cost to its identity.

For any transition from a same-age system to a mixed-age system to be successful, the change must strengthen the school's identity and the way it sees its self-organizing role, in essence what it feels the world is really asking of it. Because identity in a living system is everything, the risk associated with transformation is high. Any mistake (lack of training, uncertain leadership, and use of previous management assumptions) can be catastrophic, causing it to retreat wounded to its previous form. Today, the risk of failure is higher. The head teacher may be quietly removed and the school culled or forced into a chain gang of schools where it will need to conform. It will find itself in a place where the need for creativity and innovation is no longer required and self-organization becomes a dream.

The school as a living system has to achieve a sufficient level of consciousness to recognize that the same-age system it uses is the cause of its pain, its inability to evolve, and its slow demise; otherwise, it can never achieve the self-organizing capability it cherishes.

It tends to react most when the threat is greatest. That time is now, in the hiatus between the paradigm of New Public Management and Public Value Management (discussed later, chapter 13). To retain its values, it must take a calculated risk and seek an alternative path, one that better promotes its chances of survival; to do this, it has to connect to more of itself and become more adaptable and complex, a feature of all human systems.

Most, however, will continue to use add-ons and self-help fixes, while a few pioneering schools will choose to transform and evolve. Many schools will voluntarily opt for the protective custody of privatized groups beguiled by the false promises of greater collaboration and distributed leadership. This temporarily lessens any disturbance but at a considerable cost to the school's identity and the diversification of the future demands.

The work of Maturana and Varela explains much about school management behavior, including the school's legendary penchant for repetition and complicated routines—policies, practices, protocols, principles, and procedures. But eventually the school hits a paradox; the more the school tries to simplify to enable the machine to work better, the more complicated (not complex) it becomes. Simplification causes failure demand and mistakes; failure demand increases workload and complications: complications increase costs. A mixed-age self-organizing school is of itself complex, and this gives it an increased capacity to absorb the variety of demand on its system.

## WHY A KISS REQUIRES CAUTION

Same-age schools are complicated not complex. They seek to control complexity rather than embrace it. While keeping it simple (KISS) seems like a great maxim, it requires considerable caution. For example, the change from detailed written reports to computerized data sheets may seem like a welcome time-saver that protects teachers and reduces workload. Unfortunately, data sheets exclude important information about learning that prohibits parental engagement and support; they can also mislead students. The effect of what seems a time-saving change is itself a kind of system lever but a dangerous one to activate.

Data sheets are separational and limitational. They act to minimize information and flow, and, while this may seem efficient at a superficial level, the effect is to reduce social collaboration in the learning process. When this happens, there is only one result, failure demand. The system has no ability to intervene early, complication occurs, and the system requires more add-ons and fixes.

This leads to a second error. It is possible to put data reports online. This further reduces the need for home/school collaboration. These are all bad decisions destructive of engagement, collaboration, and Piagetian ideas. It seems that the same-age system is minded to maintain its borders by defining what counts as information and partnership because it can see no other way forward. The defining feature of a living system is its complexity not its simplification.

Like throwing a stone in a pond, the ripple effect of simplification (trying to reduce complications rather than embrace complexity) is widespread and ultimately increases workload and complications caused by failure demand. In a same-age system, there is a rule that any attempt at simplification leads to complication, and complication requires more human resources (ancillary support staff), more bureaucracy, and increases costs. Doing things right the first time absorbs demand and reduces costs. The teacher loses every time and so does everyone else. What starts as a time-saving exercise in a same-age school always has unintended consequences.

At the core of a living system is the idea that survival depends upon community, a self-determining network of souls able to collaborate, solve problems, and be adaptive. To achieve such a state, the school has to continually connect to more of itself, a concept used throughout systems thinking. Kellner-Rogers & Wheatley (1998) noted the high rate of reform failure during attempts at organizational change:

> Leaders end up managing the impact of unwanted effects rather than the planned
> results that didn't materialize. Instead of enjoying the fruits of a redesigned

production unit, the leader must manage the hostility and broken relationships created by the redesign. Instead of glorying in the new efficiencies produced by restructuring, the leader must face a burned out and demoralized group of survivors.

The point Kellner-Rogers is making is important. If we go about change in the usual way using measures, targets, and plans, it seems to result in bad outcomes. Schools often want to set up a prototype group to experiment or a mixed-age pilot group not realizing that nothing can be learned from such an isolated exercise. Sometimes you just have to learn, jump in, and hope that you've got the basic understanding and organization right. This is what a living system does because it has the unnerving ability to make sense of chaotic conditions.

## LIVING SYSTEMS

Within a living system like a school, any thinking needs to be nonlinear in form, forever connecting ideas that build the school's identity and sense of moral and ecological purpose. This book may be full of challenging statements, but the school will decide the degree to which it wishes to be disturbed and whether or not it feels it can reinvent itself by adopting an improved persona.

Otherwise, the governing industrial mind-set we impose on school management is psychologically incompatible with the living system's highly independent and collaborative nature. To really understand a living system like a school involves a consideration of all the learning relationships that comprise the whole, the degree to which people are connected to each other, and how they work and collaborate to solve problems and do the learning and teaching work. After all, a living system is composed of other living systems—at the moment!

The challenge to a living system is the degree to which it is able to understand itself and its connectedness; so for a school to make a change from same-age organization to mixed-age, there has to be a system payback, one that enhances its identity and betters its chance of survival. The school has to accept that such a change is necessary for self-preservation.

At first sight, the situation seems very difficult. Such payback rests in the ability of the school to tackle cognitive dissonance and move from separation to collaboration, limitation to fulfilment, linearity to nonlinearity, complicated to complex, and system in use to system espoused (table 1.1)—matters that require a mindful change in management and leadership and an ecological shift. This will be described later as a move from Alpha to Beta management.

First, there has to be an acceptance that the same-age iteration, beset as it is with relational issues and disconnections, is so harmful to its well-being that it can no longer fix itself with the add-ons it applies.

It is the deep organizational system changes that create a more joined-up version of the school, one that enables the school as an organization to learn and adapt (self-organize). The more connected the system, the more it learns, and the more it starts to feel better. Such a metamorphosis offers ecological and evolutionary advantages that are more capable of optimizing performance, releasing creativity, and finding the sense of freedom and agency schools need. The school has to learn to work in ways that are in tune with human nature not against it.

Remember, these are not just metaphysical aspirations but doable actions and achievable. However, they require unlearning the industrial model and learning new ego-free approaches to organization, what Frederic Laloux later calls a shift in consciousness. For the change to be successful, the emphasis must be on participation by all parties. People want to be involved in complex changes and to have a sense that they own the change, even though this often at first appears to be messy, illogical, and irrational.

Deep in the psyche of the school, any kind of separation and limitation is undesirable and by now we should be aware of what is happening in schools and why. Schools tend to suboptimize; they break down into silos of powerful and disconnected subgroups that tend to their own survival and identity needs, which can be detrimental to the well-being of the whole. For the school to learn, survive, and maintain identity, everything—all the multifaceted feedback loops between teachers, students, and parents—must work together. Synergy and flow are vital to the living system's circulation.

## REACTION TO CHANGE

Given our metaphorical understanding of schools and change, this chapter concludes with examples of management change and why they have failed or will fail. We have lost much of our innate inability to think holistically, and this has created a blind spot, described by Daniel Goleman (1998) as follows:

> The mind can protect itself against anxiety by diminishing awareness. This mechanism produces a blind spot: a zone of blocked attention and self-deception. Such blind spots occur at each major level of behavior from the psychological to the social. (p. 22)

Same-age schools are only partially joined up. Look at how responsibilities are distributed and the length of job descriptions and the constant need for border maintenance! One way of coping or justifying such separation and limitation is to pretend this isn't the case and that everything is in perfect working machine order; another is to change the subject to reduce the anxiety; another is to build a false rationale around the perceived benefits of same-age structure and treat any change (something the Jedi master Obi-Wan Kenobi called *a disturbance in the force*) as a threat.

Self-deceit creates an interesting conundrum. To recognize what to avoid, the system at some level has to know what it needs to avoid, and to do this, it relies on instinct and past learning. Telling a school to adopt vertical tutoring (VT) or mixed-age groups doesn't work. The school has to become aware of its limitations and separational self; it has to become reflective if it is to be open to other possibilities. All that is known about vertical systems comes from people in schools able to see a challenge and find a unique solution from a diverse perspective.

## THE SCREAMING OF THE SEAL

In his book *States of Denial*, Stanley Cohen (2001) explains how people, organizations, and governments dismiss or disavow information that is overly challenging or disturbing, their way of maintaining identity when threatened. They turn a blind eye and, in some cases, distort the truth and claim what Donald Trump delights in calling *fake news*. Now that we have a feel for living systems, we can look at an example of what happens when reformers try and change the way a school works.

First, look back at the road traveled. It is littered with failed reforms, abandoned schemes, major reports, lost funding streams, projects that ran out of energy, and more besides. Yet, reformers persist in trying to fix what seems to them to be broken or not working (now the turn of teachers and school leaders), pointing out how and why other cultures and jurisdictions seem to be doing so much better. No matter what is thrown at independent-minded schools, the school will fend off most and adapt others to its cause. What it will not readily do is change its fundamental behavior, its way of doing things. It has no experience of *different*.

A classic example of a failed reform in the UK is the SEAL (social and emotional aspects of learning) program. I've chosen this because it is the reformational way of dealing with complications arising from the system in use. Instead of complexifying the organization to cope, add-ons and fixes are applied. There are more examples, many more.

But let's begin with a small heresy: one of the best ways to ensure minimal change in a school is to set up a working party or, in this case, a pilot scheme. Both give the appearance of change and both create change activity, but little of substance occurs and the chance of error is high in the current circumstances. Both end with disappointment. What is really needed is the school as a complete research unit in its own right and as a complete pilot if organizational learning is to occur.

Otherwise, there is no disturbance. It may seem cynical, but both are likely to peter out when enthusiasm wanes, the funding stream dries up, or the lead player departs the stage and the next big thing (fix) arrives on the scene. SEAL was just such a fix and an add-on—a government strategy designed for whole school change, a kind of off-the-shelf social pro-social program packaged for schools. Based on Daniel Goleman's work on emotional intelligence, it described itself as follows:

> A comprehensive approach to promoting the *social and emotional* skills that underpin effective *learning*, positive behavior, regular attendance, staff effectiveness and the *emotional* health and well-being of all who *learn* and work in schools. (DfES, 2007a, p. 4)

The arrogance of this claim is staggering if well intentioned. As such, it represented one big disturbance and one mega fix or add-on! We have to admire reformers for their zeal. This is a massive claim, and yet schools rarely talk of SEAL, the big pro-social program and game changer, anymore. Had they been asked, Maturana and Varela would have pointed out a small problem; whole school change imposed like this is not on a school's bucket list—not even close. What the reformers had done is completely misread how schools behave and react as living systems.

The reformers made four wrong assumptions. First, they assumed that social or pro-school change occurs through teaching courses. Second, they forgot that schools decide whether or not they wish to be disturbed and to what extent. Third, whole school change requires everyone's participation, not just that of the course deliverers. Fourth, they thought that such a program was a system change lever. These are all big errors of judgment and bad systems thinking.

If anything is wrong, the theory is that it can somehow be solved by the teacher! This is a bad theory but one schools cling to in a disconnected system. The reformers suggested that a pro-social program would have a domino change effect. All that the pilot schools had to do was put in the effort to support the program, and all would be well. When sensible heads see claims like this, their instinct is to run for cover in disbelief. Their experience of past efforts to bring about change urges considerable caution. They quickly calculate the cost benefits and know the sums don't add up.

Expensive pilot schemes were rolled out, and the reform process began. Building on Goleman's ideas of emotional intelligence (1995), the SEAL initiative aimed to support children aged three to sixteen years in areas such as social awareness, managing feelings, motivation, empathy, and social skills. The project was built on the assumption of a perceived problem with young people who failed to respond to schooling in positive ways.

No one recognized that schooling itself might be the problem, so the task was to design a program to *fix* the kids so that they could cope with the system that was causing them problems. We still see similar programs today!

In 2011, the government's evaluation was published (Humphrey et al.) covering the twenty-two schools involved in the pilot. There was hardly a positive word to be said for SEAL except through gritted teeth. The largely negative evaluation is littered with insights congruent with the biology of living systems:

> Finally, in terms of impact, our analysis of pupil-level outcome data indicated that SEAL (as implemented by schools in our sample) failed to impact significantly upon pupils' social and emotional skills, general mental health difficulties, pro-social behaviour or behaviour problems. And analysis of school climate scores indicated significant reductions in pupils' trust and respect for teachers, liking for school and feelings of classroom and school supportiveness during SEAL implementation . . . SEAL had not produced the expected changes across schools.

The researchers found it difficult to understand why their evaluation was out of kilter with meta-studies and previous research into the impact of social and emotional learning (SEL) programs. Meta-research by Durlak et al. (2011) claimed that such programs produce positive academic and life outcomes; for every $1 spent, the return is $ 11. Goleman (2005) noted that very few schools had SEL programs prior to 1995, but since then they have grown in popularity worldwide. Pro-social programs are unusually big in US culture and increasingly popular as change agents elsewhere. Goleman writes:

> In some states and nations, SEL has become the organizing umbrella under which are gathered programs in character education, violence prevention, anti-bullying, drug prevention and school discipline. The goal is not just to reduce these problems among schoolchildren but to enhance the school climate and, ultimately, students' academic performance.

Excuse my use of litotes, but any rational person looking at the USA and the UK might comment that this approach doesn't seem to be working all that well! My argument (another heresy) is that SEL programs are not the universal fix claimed and act to prevent system change. They are an expensive and often futile response to a defective system incongruent with child psychology and dependent on highly specialist teaching. They come into their own only when the damage is done and few other avenues open.

The cynic might say that such programs rely on a system that turns out sufficient quantities of collaterally damaged goods (failure demand) to be fixed through expensive consultancy fees and the sale of programs. The kids aren't the problem; the problem is a system that causes negative behaviors and is unable to recognize and respond to the variety of students' learning and social support needs on a minute-by-minute basis.

There is a place for SEL other than as a job creation exercise, but in its present form it is a system add-on, a fix for the collateral damage inherent to the same-age school model. Far better to create a system that designs-in social collaboration, empathy, and support rather than one that adds these on as an afterthought. Schools intuitively know this.

Let me say immediately that some of the best teachers it has been my pleasure to work with are PSHE or SEL specialists. They make a difference because of who they are but shouldn't be expected to compensate for a same-age system causing problems, itself a kind of suboptimization. Change the system, and empathy and well-being become designed in as interpersonal system behavior allowing PSHE and SEL to resume its important complementary role rather than simply grow unchecked and unevaluated.


## THE SCHOOL FIX FOR MENTAL HEALTH

The more interesting question about SEAL and other programs is where they come from and why. One being written today is a program to teach school practitioners in the UK how to be the lead professional on mental health issues in their school. You may remember the words of Professor Diane Reay and the connection made between the nature of schooling and the decline in well-being.

Once again, a system-related problem of significant concern has arisen. The usual governmental response above all things is to be seen to be active. In this case, it is to provide a quick but hugely expensive but completely unworkable fix by ensuring that in every school there is yet another *named person*, this time responsible for supporting students with mental health issues. Unfortunately, it is simply not feasible to implement a high-quality national training program for such posts, let alone fund the ongoing post and its attendant bureaucracy.

Here is another example of a system add-on that ignores cause and so adds to costs and system complications. It is System 1 riding roughshod over our indolent System 2. Such a solution won't work because it is not a solution. The cause remains untouched, which means there is every chance of the deterioration of mental health getting increasing. In effect, it will divert the school from dealing with its own disjointed way of constructing human relationships by continually trying to fix what it inadvertently keeps breaking.

## CONSEQUENCES OF SPEED

Fortunately, others seem to have spotted this folly. Jamie Peck and Nik Theodore (2015) talk about *fast policy*, ideas that appear attractive and spread like wildfire through sprawling social platforms. Schools seem particularly attracted because they fail to disturb anything in particular. Education is awash with unsorted advice that leads to knee-jerk responses and acts as a kind of educational pill-popping exercise at a swingers' party in which schools feel obligated to participate.

Another classic example is resilience. A few years back, resilience became an issue from out of nowhere. Today, schools have incorporated resilience into their aspirational values as an add-on. *We produce resilient young people*, schools now proclaim! Resilience is not something that can be taught; the better way is to grow resilience by ensuring the school as an organization nurtures individual and group connectivity and support. The mixed-age base provides the security needed for such a task and a secure base to venture out and return.

Such is the speed of social change today that when a problem is spotted, a fix seems to be instantly available. Sometimes, the fix or add-on is available before the school even recognizes it has a problem. For example, *character* suddenly arose as a problem that schools didn't think they had, and don't!

Not only it seems that UK children have suddenly developed character deficiencies, but it also turns out that children in complex societies, low on equity, are besieged by dispositional, social, and learning deficits. It seems they are also low on grit, perseverance, and a can-do mind-set; in fact, it is surprising they can get to school at all, let alone be repaired by the latest program!

## THE SEL INDUSTRY

Schools and governments are subject to vast flows of information and channels of communication whose headline pronouncements tend to stick. In a fascinating paper, Ben Williamson (2017) tracked down the sources of such ideas and how they are captured and forged.

> In the last couple of years, social-emotional learning has emerged as a key policy priority from the work of international policy influencers such as the OECD and World Economic Forum; psychological entrepreneurs such as

Angela Duckworth's "Character Lab" and Carol Dweck's "growth mindset" work; venture capital-backed philanthropic advocates (e.g. Edutopia); powerful lobbying coalitions (CASEL) and institutions (Aspen Institute) and government agencies and partners.

Williamson notes that the US Department of Education has even produced a *grit* report while the UK established an all-party committee to produce a *Character and Resilience Manifesto* (2014) in partnership with the Centre Forum think tank. There is much wrong with the way schools manage their affairs but nothing that warrants such a stream of unnecessary and unwanted input. Williams describes what is happening as follows:

> In sum, social-emotional learning is the product of a fast policy network of "psy" entrepreneurs, global policy advice, media advocacy, philanthropy, think tanks, tech R&D and venture capital investment. Together, this loose alliance of actors has produced shared vocabularies, aspirations, and practical techniques of measurement of the "behavioural indicators" of classroom conduct that correlate to psychologically-defined categories of character, mindset, grit, and other personal qualities of social-emotional learning.

Instead of schools designing a system that grows resilience and a can-do mind-set, it seems they increasingly franchise it out to other providers to do the work. Unfortunately, this approach is a betrayal of the learning relationships schools should be building and an admission that schools are unable or unwilling to admit that they are experiencing system-related design issues. Williams refers to the work of Agnieska Bates (2016b) who writes:

> The last 20 years has witnessed the spread of corporatism in education on a global scale. In England, this trend is characterized by new structural and cultural approaches to education found in the "academies" programme and the adoption of private sector management styles. The corporate re-imagining of schools has also led to the introduction into the curriculum of particular forms of character education aimed at managing the "emotional labour" of children. (pp. 66–81)

It seems that the old selection process, over a century old, continues. When we have reductionist thinking incapable of finding and examining design flaws, the reaction born out of such an approach is to seek solutions that seem to fit the imagined problem. Walk into any school, and the last thing you will notice is a shortage of character and characters. What complicated schools have to learn is how many of the problems PSHE tries to tackle are problems of the school's own making; most can be designed out by paying attention to the way groups are arranged and organized. All that's required is a little systems redesign, a move to mixed-age organization.

From this book's heretical perspective, it seems that there is a strong case in which SEL is fast evolving into an industry involved in producing saleable products, courses, and programs designed to produce the right kind of people with the right competencies for FutureWorld, itself determined by SEL advocates through the OECD. It seems that the Foucaldian theory of government and power offers a plausible explanation of what is happening in the world of schools.

The problems that schools try to tackle are system related, caused by the way the school self-constructs. Senge (2006) put it this way.

> These problems were "actually systems" that lured policymakers into interventions that focused on obvious symptoms not underlying causes, which produced short-term benefits but long-term malaise, and fostered the need for more symptomatic interventions. (p.14)

Surely, what is needed is an emotionally intelligent school that ensures a sense of belonging, one that practices wholeness based on social psychology rather than the separation, division, and limitation of a hand-me-down model reliant on separation and limitation. The only viable means of doing this is through mixed-age organizational design and subsequent changes to school leadership and management.

When this happens, the living system thrives because it finds a better way of realizing its identity. Good design enables organizational learning, and this is the real antidote to ambulance chasers and teachers being persuaded to leap onto the nearest passing bandwagon regardless of the inherent consequences of reckless speed.

## Chapter 6

# More Disturbance—Bullying

So far, this book has been generous in suggesting that the same-age schools we have are *systems*. If they are, they are bad systems. Margaret J. Wheatley (1999) argues that schools generally fail the systems test.

> They are not systems because they do not arise from a core of shared beliefs about the purpose of public education. In the absence of shared beliefs and desires, people are not motivated to seek out one another and develop relationships. Instead, they co-inhabit the same organizational and community space without weaving together mutually sustaining relationships.

It is an important distinction. Same-age structures lead to fragmentation and separation, while mixed-age schools are all about building connections. This brings us yet again to the social consequences of these two very different organizational forms.

Negative behaviors like bullying are rarely out of the news, yet no organization works harder than schools to tackle the problem. Unfortunately, it seems that as soon as schools get on top of one kind of bullying, another manifests itself online or elsewhere. As resources switch to deal with the new problem, perhaps cyber bullying, the original one flares up again and the challenge of relational learning is never properly resolved despite new programs designed to plug the latest hole in the pro-social dam.

Kellner-Rogers tells the story of the head of a junior high school who broke with administrative tradition and adopted only three rules at his school. Instead of adopting endless rules and policies that governed everything likely to go wrong, the school opted for complexity and very broad guidance. The head understood that complexity cannot be controlled but has to be embraced. These are his school rules:

1. Take care of yourself.
2. Take care of each other.
3. Take care of this place.

These broad rules built a thematic consensus, one able to absorb complexity and create a sense of belonging, matters that will help us in this section. Schools are not organizations that give up trying and all have invented endless rules and creative solutions to counter bullying, including the kind of SEL programs discussed in the previous chapter.

Some have introduced ideas like *anti-bullying ambassadors* to step in and support others when things go wrong. This may seem sensible but is high-risk from a systems perspective and counterproductive! In a mixed-age situation, everyone is an anti-bullying ambassador. School anti-bullying strategies have limited success as far as prevention is concerned, and most are designed to deal with fallout after the event. Anti-bullying initiatives accept that bullying is an omnipresent phenomenon, so schools need to prepare for it, know what to do, and have safe places; rather than prevention, schools resort to add-ons and fixes. When these fail, schools pull in an outside agency or revert to the latest pro-social program.

So, let's continue with a second heretical statement and disturb the school organism some more—a strategy we know can sometimes meet with a bad reaction! But here it goes: the same-age system of organization used by schools is the single major cause of school bullying! Let me say immediately that research to back this up (chapter 1) may be tangential but is strong. The feedback of schools that have adopted vertical or mixed-age tutoring (VT) using a systems thinking approach shows a measurable decrease in antisocial behavior and a marked increase in pro-school behavior (Barnard, 2013, 2015). Again, we need to take a slight detour to understand what is happening and this means going back to school.

## SCHOOL RESEARCH

Research into mixed-age organization is sparse, but many have documented their experience online and all welcome visits from other schools. This documentation reveals that schools trained in vertical tutoring describe themselves as happier (changed), safer places. They often note a marked reduction in bullying, a marked rise in empathy, a reduction in exclusions, and an increase in productive learning relationships. In other words, a change of strategy,

**Table 6.1.   Staff Perceptions of Influences on Learning**

| Choice | Rank Order: Who Has the Most Influence on Learning +/- Combined? (Horizontal, Same-Age System) | Estimated Influence on Learning as a Percentage (Should Add Up to 100%!) |
|---|---|---|
| Teacher | 3 | 15% |
| Tutor | 4 | 5% |
| Family | 1 | 35–45% |
| Peers | 2 | 30–40% (increases over time) |

relationships, communications, and the capacity to design-in empathy and support seems to prove more effective than pro-social programs alone.

As part of a training program, members of staff were divided into small groups and asked to complete a small diagram (table 6.1) as part of a five-minute exercise. If they disagreed with the group, they could either change groups or form their own group. The staff comprised teachers, administrators, and ancillary workers, many of whom were parents. The best way of studying the effectiveness of a service system is to examine the places where users and providers interact, the place where value can be added.

Over the course of eight years, this exercise was completed by many same-age schools during VT training and involved an estimated 7,500 staff. They were asked to place in rank order who they thought had the most influence on learning. They were then asked to add a percentage value to back up their conclusions. The results across different kinds of school were remarkably similar and set out below. The sole purpose of the exercise was to start a conversation about systems. A fuller account and system implications are in Barnard (2013, pp. 116–118).

One of the original purposes of this exercise was to ascertain the degree to which tutors operating in a same-age system judge their own effectiveness. There would be good reason for leadership teams to be concerned if tutors felt that the job they were doing was in any way inadequate. None of this had escaped the attention of leadership teams, but then none were able to impact on the situation. Tutors in a same-age school (one that had recognized there was a problem and wanted to change systems) rarely rated themselves and their work in terms of learning influence above 5%.

All schools are aware that at top of the Hattie effect list is the teacher effect, but from a systems point of view there are other equally or more powerful influences. While the school in its same-age organizational form is highly teacher dependent, other relational factors mustn't be dismissed.

Contained in this chart is part of the reason that so many schools change systems. Schools understand that to improve as an organization, a key focus has to be on partnering and supporting the main influencers on learning to ensure a positive effect, something recognized earlier as the socially collaborative school. To downgrade or ignore what is happening within peer loyalty groups and at home makes the teacher's job significantly more difficult.

The chart recognizes that all players have a significant role to play and that such a role has to be pro-learning and collaborative—in effect, joined up as a system. If uncritical schools and training agencies follow concepts like *visible learning* and *effect lists* garnered entirely from the same-age model, they tend to act on teachers alone ignoring the matrix of networks (including collective teacher efficacy) that hold the whole together. This in turn leads to externally imposed distortions and irrational practices such as arbitrary measures, targets, and appraisal and rewards systems.

It seems that the living system has strong views on effects. The concern here is the influence (positive and negative) of peer groups regarded by staff as strong and in line with family. So what has all this to do with bullying? The heretical statement (above) is not a slight on teachers or schools but a criticism of same-age systems and our ongoing inability to understand schools from a systems thinking perspective. Just as learning is a complex organizational issue, so is bullying. Both contain errant assumptions concerning psychology and intervention.

Specifically, the school's way of organizing itself into same-age peer groups, the inherent part of a school's self-construction and the industrial design strategy, is the direct cause of bullying and many other negative behaviors. Schools report that bullying declines as soon as groups are reconstituted and stabilized with care as an empathetic mixed-age milieu. While many factors contribute to bullying beyond the school gates, the actual cause (the one within the school's immediate sphere of influence) is the school's same-age structure, a system built on sketchy assumptions about child development and the use of design principles no longer credible.

Schools may be so affronted by such a suggestion that they stop reading immediately but nothing here is a criticism of schools and teachers; we are talking systems just as our children talk "social." Clair Fox (2016) provides good reasons to engage in more challenging rhetoric in a world of micro-offenses without crying foul over disagreements—no matter how provocative.

Negative behavior is a symptom of something not right, support not given, conversations not had, child psychology misapplied, relationships not built, and assumptions about fixes and add-ons not thought through. The immediate organizational reaction of a living system is to protect identity and reject such seemingly extravagant ideas. Not our school, they will say! We have anti-bullying ambassadors, safe places, school counsellors, and an effective PSHE program. We are on top of the problem! And, no, we are not in denial!

No one knows more than me how stubborn and single-minded schools can be and any talk about group change sparks a fierce debate. Outside, where parents meet and in corridors where children talk, there is a range of opinion on group makeup. Surely, some argue, same-age groups are the very foundation of a good education and an orderly school. Mix the age groups even for a short time each day and there will be chaos! Parents and students will complain. Bullying will surely increase, not diminish. Parents will say they don't want their child mixing with older ones who might be a bad influence. All that this will do, they say, is increase bullying. Students, too, are initially wary about such a disruption and the prospect of losing friends.

In fact, parents don't say such things. My experience is that parents want to be informed, be involved, and most get mixed-age groups straight away. Why? Because they were raised in families and now have families of their own. It was the older ones they turned to and the older ones who provided the shoulder and the wise words.

Neither will such a heresy impinge on those who believe they have cracked the bullying problem and claim that bullying in their school is minimal and under the school's control. For such places, same-age groups aren't a problem, self-deceit is. After all, it is a means of protecting identity, who we think we are. We'd expect self-protecting strategies to kick in and for the school to cry foul, turn a cold shoulder, a blind eye, or perhaps an infamous polite shrug.

Ask any school about the strategies it uses with regard to bullying and the school will wax lyrical about its procedures and practices—its anti-bullying ambassadors, the latest revised policy, its safe places, the anti-bullying show put on by a visiting actors' group (the one the head teacher was forced to attend), the anti-bullying certificate on the wall, and the school's list of protocols, procedures, policies, practices, and fallback mechanisms. What such a biological organism cannot appreciate is that its original design governs its self-managing ways, including the way the school goes about its work and the reconstituted ideas it uses to solve problems.

It doesn't see itself and its same-age organizational base as a problem—a blind spot—because this is an integral part of its identity. The school keeps any change within the bounds of its identity; superficially, it self-constructs a response to bullying in the form of system add-ons and fixes, a response mechanism gleaned from past thinking, how it normally operates, and what it knows. It is a response designed to have minimal impact on the way the school operates. There is no change to the school's fundamental, same-age working arrangements and the cause of most of its woes.

The school's response is to fix things with minimal disruption to its being. It can never fathom that the way it organizes and connects itself, the way the socio/learning relationships work in the school, is the underlying cause of considerable damage. Its priority remains survival. After all, it has survived in its current separational form for over a century. Its elemental parts are designed for set routines and predictable behaviors, and these must continue unabated. Unpredictable behaviors have to be fixed and add-ons applied to ensure compliance.

To change in any fundamental way, the organization has to become aware that there is a better alternative, one likely to aid its survival and enhance its identity. School anti-bullying strategies are memetic, some quite creative, and they spread from school to school and jurisdiction to jurisdiction, comprising all there is in the school's management and leadership repertoire.

This bewildering catalog of reform strategies, best practices, pro-social programs, surveillance methods, and fixes is an indication of the school's creativity, endeavor, and desire to care. They reflect the way the organism thinks, how it deals with threats, and the way it goes about solving problems. It is an irony that the twenty-first-century school is tasked to produce problem solvers yet is ill-equipped to recognize and resolve problems of its own design; a closer look at bullying might help.


## PEER GROUP BULLYING

Bullying covers a range of behaviors whereby individuals or groups repeatedly attack, humiliate, and/or exclude a relatively powerless person. There is considerable evidence that bullying is very much a group process (O'Connell et al., 1999; Salmivalli et al., 1997; Sutton and Smith, 1999). Given that most school organizations are based entirely on peer group structures, there exists a perfect seedbed for bullying to arise. The foreword to Christina Salmivalli's (2009) meta-review of peer group bullying reads as follows:

> The group (i.e., classroom) in which bullying takes place differs from many social groups in an important respect: the membership is involuntary, which means that the victim cannot easily escape his or her situation. The other group members cannot just leave, either. Although students cannot choose their classmates, social selection processes (Kandel, 1978) take place within classrooms, resulting in cliques and friendship dyads that consist of similar others. (p. 116)

Salmivalli accurately identifies an important system design flaw: same-age school organization. Students joining the secondary school are placed involuntarily and arbitrarily (by and large) into same-age groups from which there is no escape. Very little thought has gone into this process at this critical time, and what thought that has taken place is the wrong thought. Schools lay the perfect conditions for bullying to occur.

No matter what the tutor does during secondary school induction, a social selection process is unavoidable during peer-based tutor time. Of course, bullying spills out of classrooms and links with other peer groups and is not so much confined to spaces as to opportunities. The point is this: same-age school organization creates the optimum conditions for bullying to occur. Schools unable to figure out the mixed-age organizational base needed to design bullying out persist with recycled ideas unable to see they are the cause.

Students form groups and seek the shelter and friendship of others, a sense of belonging; others are isolated or rejected, and schools organized by same age can do little to intervene in this process. Once in motion, anti-bullying strategies arrive thick and fast but after the fact, after the damage is done. The same-age root goes unnoticed and unaddressed as an organizational issue. In the case of bullying, the research is thorough, deep, and insightful.

## A Child's First Day at Secondary School

Having worked with hundreds of schools, the same errant strategies spread far and wide. It becomes obvious that the way schools go about organizing the induction process for new students is built entirely on errant assumptions about happiness, attachment, and in-group loyalty. All induction days are variations on a familiar theme. All same-age schools produce bullying behavior within the first hour of the first day.

Each child finds himself or herself in a peer group of (say) twenty-six other students, many unfamiliar to them. The tutor is tasked *to get to know* the children, sort out timetables, and complete any administration needed. Often, the tutor engages the new students in what he or she calls *getting-to-know-you* type activities including team games and circle time.

It all seems so harmless. But what is really happening when peer groups play and interact is socially complex, beyond the tutor's control, and unexpected.

Some children are able to choose others as their friends. Some get reluctantly chosen; some find themselves isolated as the leftovers; others are overtly rejected; some decide they don't like certain others, and all of this happens under the tutor's nose and during getting-to-know-you and circle time! It is all so much *One Flew over the Cuckoo's Nest*. The aim is that children should have a happy first day. For some, it is one of the worst days of their life but they won't tell.

The tutor thinks he has helped the students make friends and settle in, a bit of harmless fun. Everyone seems happy after all. But the children leave the activity with a very clear idea about the behavior of others, who to avoid, who poses a threat, who is kind, and who might be their friend if they get chosen. They behave like the biological living systems they are, protecting their identity and being the best they can be, putting on their best bravest face. The system has separated them and limited them and is teaching them how the world works, their place.

Meanwhile, the potential for things to go very wrong is high and likely to have lasting ramifications. It is far more *Lord of the Flies* than the school realizes, as groups form and group behavior takes over. 'Use the group to change the group,' just as Fullan said (chapter 1) only this time, for the worst. Schools organized by peer tutor groups enable bullying on day one and spend five years trying to fix what they broke! Kids may spend a lifetime recuperating. Some will occasionally deal with their problem-solving issues and return, armed to the teeth, with vengeance in their hearts.

Schools report that they constantly tinker with their induction process, changing timings and methods but the substance and the assumptions remain. It is something they are intuitively never happy with. The system responds in its way, not by changing fundamental practice but tinkering with routines and making minor modifications based on past references. The mantra of the school is, 'we'll do it our way'. When schools say this, there is a cast-iron guarantee that nothing of substance will change—ask anyone foolish enough to call himself or herself a school reformer.

In short, the school as an organization responds to its environment in ways that are the least disruptive to its routines and the core activity of teaching; it self-administers treatment to system symptoms with sticky-back plasters while ignoring any underlying pathology.

Research indicates that bullying is mainly a group phenomenon, and many are drawn into it as bystanders and assistants usually of same age. For same-age schools, the tutor group is far from being the safe haven it claims; it is the catalyst for bullying and is where so much bullying begins.

It may seem an odd thing to say about such a complex issue, but organizationally it boils down in part to a numbers problem, one that leads to relational issues. A single tutor can never get to know so many students quickly enough, and teachers take even longer. Consider the number of students that any individual member of staff is required to get to know!

In a same-age system, there is a dangerous lag in the time taken for learning relationships to form, and a student may never find the kind of support from peers or staff conducive to learning and safe passage through the school. In a mixed-age situation, there is no time lag. The system is designed to build safe learning relationships and support with immediacy.

The same-age school tells the child that if he or she is bullied or worried this is what he or she should do. The school outlines its coping mechanisms, anti-bullying ambassadors, mentors, pastoral care support system, and its counsellors (and, now, mental health coordinators). It backs this up with pro-social programs as prevention strategies.

Despite these reassurances, the school knows that things will inevitably go wrong. Over time, such a process starts to get very expensive, absorbing energy and time while new complications such as Internet bullying and sexting arrive on the scene. The problem that same-age organization has is its singular inability to ensure that group behavior is pro-school and pro-social, that children feel safe, the factor that topped Google's Aristotle list of group requirements (chapter 15).

Anti-bullying policies require ever more fixes and add-ons, but the problem is never solved because the cause is never realized. Recent reports suggest that bullying remains a concern with 90% of UK schools; the remaining 10% are in denial! Such schools are paying dearly for social *failure demand*—the price of not dealing with the problem at source, first time round. Teachers get tired and jaded, kids switch off, and parents complain. Soon, another crisis will occur.

Had the vast range of anti-bullying strategies worked, there would be no bullying. But then, bullying is a strange concept. Like chaos, it's hard to work with; damp it down in one area and it reappears in another. It disrupts learning, and in some cases students (and staff) pay a heavy price through the pain of broken relationships and the onset of mental health issues. These are matters that are becoming worse, not better; the fixes and add-ons are not working as effectively as hoped.

## BETTER DESIGN AND THE MIXED-AGE TUTOR GROUP

Schools think they are dealing with prefabricated social issues that creep in from the turmoil of family life, gangs, social technology, and more, and so they respond accordingly. But a response is not the same thing as an intervention; bullying can be greatly reduced by designing it out rather than in. In previous books (Barnard, 2000, 2010, 2013), the design parameters are set out, and readers will find more later on. At the risk of repetition, the following general considerations guide such a process.

1. Any intervention needs to occur before the students even get to the classroom and that is why mixed-age tutor groups are vital and where they come into their own.
2. This makes the first hour of school induction a critical time. How this is organized is of the highest importance if pro-school behaviors are to overcome any negative ones.
3. Tutor groups have to be mixed by age and ability. In dog whispering terms, the aim is to create a balanced and self-organizing and self-supporting pack!

4. In a mixed-age setting, two tutors meet four students, not twenty-six! This means they form a learning and support relationship fast. The new students feel known and attached.

5. They then engage with four older students from the same group who do all the induction work, showing them the ropes. This enables a second set of learning relationships to form. The group changes the group. No games are played at this time! Every child is a leader and mentor. Empathetic relationships form. The child doesn't have to choose friends because they are there already.

6. Every adult employed by the school is a tutor regardless of his or her status, including the head or CEO. This aligns everyone with school purpose and builds a belonging system.

7. Every room in the school is used, allowing tutor group sizes to reduce to around eighteen students.

8. The younger students are now ready, after a very short induction, to go to the classroom.

9. Later, they will meet the rest of the tutor group, all of whom are experienced and understand the induction process and feel they belong in their mixed-age tutor group and are safe.

10. Tutors meet tutees for twenty minutes each day before morning break: they never teach PSHE but practice it every day with tutees by building secure and supportive learning relationships.

Readers can now see why and how the tutor becomes the information hub of the school, the synaptic link able to pull down from the system what is needed to maximize and support learning. This puts the tutor in an ideal position for summative assessment; the whole management structure of the school has to be reformulated around this central concept of information, flow, intervention, and ongoing support.

In a mixed-age environment, new students find themselves meeting people already empathetic toward them, by design. The child does not have to vie for friendships but joins a network (family) of fellow travelers all on different stages of their learning journey eager to help and empathize. This is not social engineering but simply a means of putting people in touch with who they were best meant to be, induction into a wider, safer, more supportive family-style network. In effect, the school fulfils the intrinsic needs of child development.

The school adheres to Abe Maslow's hierarchy of needs, Uri Bronfenbrenner's ecological systems theory, and Bowlby's attachment theory and for once gets the psychology right.

It is an environment where bullying becomes a surprise rather than an expectation. Mixed-age tutor groups provide a time and place where resilience, grit, and a can-do mind-set can be grown and developed, not added on.

It is a place of belonging, one like *Cheers*, a place where *everybody knows your name*. The power of the group changes the group, just as Michael Fullan suggested it should.

Implementation of mixed-age structure carefully thought through enables the school to connect to more of itself. The tutors assume the critical role of group leaders and information hubs. In such a structure, it is possible for hierarchies to form and reform as needed because the organization is plasticized with the potential to become a viable system. It is around this that school management is built. Instead of *self-construction*, the school moves to a whole new ball game called *self-organization* whereby the school can learn, innovate, and be adaptive.

If schools continue as they are with same-age assumptions, the future will supply kids with some kind of techno wristband to wear in school. This will warn them of rising stress levels, signaling that they should leave the room and head for their nearest *safe place* and engage in deep breathing exercises designed by the newly appointed well-being coordinator and mental health adviser. The gadget will have an educational psychologist and school counsellor on speed dial. The child will be sent to special well-being classes, places that help students and staff with their relational neuroses and irrationalities arising from the system.

My partner of many years tells me she already has one but is yet to figure out that I'm the probable cause!

Remember, this book is not concerned directly with the teachers in the classroom but they are a direct beneficiary of an improved school climate. Because all teachers must be tutors, they take with them to their classroom a revived sense of self-worth and belonging inspired by their tutor group. They too will feel better about their role and value because of their tutor group, a bunch of crazy kids who embrace their teacher's need to belong.

The socially collaborative school arising out of the same-age ashes will be guided by research and decide the worthiness of any effect list. They will never believe, however, the untruth that class size doesn't matter, that relationships don't matter, and that social equity is unimportant.

So, what are some of the points we can take with us?

- Bullying manifests itself in peer groups formed by the school. (We have already started to appreciate that this construct is the cause of virtually all the challenges faced by schools.)
- Schools organized entirely on a peer-group basis lay the foundations for bullying. Intervention can only occur after such antisocial groups form (usually during induction day!). Schools then spend five years or so trying to fix what they broke.

- To cope with negative behavior, schools resort to add-ons and fixes (hand-me-down ideas used before); these massively increase complications, costs, and resources (failure demand).
- It is the school as an organization that needs attention and redesign, not the alleged character flaws in students.
- The school is resistant to change that it perceives isn't in its best interests. When it understands that change is needed, the school shows high skill and creativity in implementation. Schools embrace change which they see as helpful but have to be convinced.
- The school is best understood as a living entity, not a machine. Its behavior must be disturbed in some way (perhaps through provocation by heretics, mavericks, and others) to inspire any significant change.
- The solution is to create a different system, one that designs-in empathy through pro-school, in-group loyalty. This intervention requires mixed-age groups and remodeling of the school's management and leadership strategy. What makes schools so remarkable is the teachers who cope in a system that is so organizationally unsupportive of their efforts while claiming the opposite.
- A school must decide it has to transform. Ultimately, it must be the agent of its own disturbance, the complete opposite of what exists.

# Chapter 7

# Mental Health and Systems

Human systems require a high degree of consensus, interconnectivity, and agreed purposes to be called systems and in a system like a school so much of what happens is not readily apparent; it is assumed. A school can follow procedures and practices and act in a very rational way but still not achieve the results it hopes for. One reason for this is the difficulty to appreciate from inside the system exactly what is going wrong.

J. W. Forrester (1961) noted that everything that individuals do is done in the context of information feedback, and for schools this concept is critical. If the feedback loops between the many combinations of information and support sources (students, staff, and parents) fail because they are absent, assumed, or in any way deficient, problems occur. Over time, this causes a constant need for add-ons, fixes, and repairs (reform) that cause complications to burgeon. New bureaucracies are required to respond to regulation overload and soon the system starts to be bogged down by failure demand, the inability to deal with customer problems first time round. Costs increase, and further investment only makes things worse.

Errant analysis of systemic problems points to an issue with teachers and/ or leadership quality and a school unable to keep pace with demand. There is a failure to recognize connections, how the information feedback processes operate in the school, in favor of seeing what is visible; and what is visible are the people struggling to make the system work.

The effect of raising the assessment bar without thought for the system in use sets the school down a pathway of increased supervision, intense account-ability, and fearful inspection. Suddenly, all the ills of a separated system fall on the teacher's shoulders and hence to students and families. The system that claims to secure their safety and well-being is unable to match increased demand through support, training, and the social collaboration promised.

In this chapter, the focus is on schools, systems, and mental health issues. The aim is to show that joined-up and collaborative systems promote health and others (unrecognizable as systems) cause the health of participants to deteriorate. The same-age school is a partial system at best, and a strong case has been proposed that it is the root cause of the many mental health and well-being issues seen. So, it is helpful to look more generally at the bigger systems to which schools belong and see what might be learned.

## SYSTEMS AND CULTURE

Lucy Crehan (2016) explored the link between teachers, culture, and systems. She noted how education systems can be a force for good, nurturing potential and improving social mobility but warned that they can also demotivate, limit, and amplify preexisting inequality. The main conclusions from Lucy's book from a systems perspective are as follows:

1. Countries that approach system building by having adult conversations between government and teachers usually achieve buy-in, a sense of purpose that motivates those trying to make the system work. They build a better, more holistically equitable system, one where there is a consensus and recognition of system purpose and the difficulty of the school's task. To achieve this, there must be complete accord between political parties about what education is. Education cannot be the toy-box in which politicians squabble.
2. When teachers are given more time to share information and collaborate, they tend to perform better. Less isolation, more support, better mental health.
3. When school supervision is tempered with supportive work relationships, there is a greater sense of team endeavor. The teacher is never isolated and the school never ridiculed or forced into new ownership.
4. There is very little difference between teacher quality worldwide that cannot be improved by reducing workload and offering ongoing training and support. Teachers in the UK, the USA, Australia, and New Zealand (for example) are as good as any of their high-performing counterparts elsewhere.
5. There is a great deal of difference between cultures and the degree to which applied systems thinking is used to build holistic and integrated processes and (to repeat) very little difference in teacher capability.

Put bluntly, there is not a teacher problem; there is a systems problem.

In his blog, the political commentator Ed Straw (2016), talking about the UK, notes: "In no other country do politicians agree so little on how its school system should be managed." He reminds us how in Germany, "political parties entered the 2015 election with a shared commitment to a policy document they had worked on with teacher and head teacher unions, parent groups, and secondary school students."

Similarly, Finland and Canada have systems built on hard-fought consensus, both regarded as having high-quality teacher and student-oriented systems. All of these countries share another enabling system construct: they trust and respect teachers as professionals and understand that in living systems there is a need to work with people not control them. It doesn't require expertise on mental health to realize that poor systems will detrimentally affect the health of participants.

Decisions that occur in cabinet meetings behind closed doors, informed by errant consultants concerned with winning elections and scoring a mark on whoever is in opposition, are not consensual. They tend to glean information through biased and persuasive media platforms and whatever new favorite books they are reading. Their mind-set is formed by their own experience of school and they select research that best backs their latest whizzy fix (reinterpretation of a past failed project).

They then produce a major report of great reform significance with a compelling title (Every Child Matters, No Child Left Behind, and Race to the Top) as a sign of their endeavors. Shelves groan under their weight but little changes except that life gets tougher for teachers, students, and parents—the people who know most what's needed.

The reason Finnish teachers have higher qualifications is (in part) because teaching is such a popular and competitive career option. Psychologically, it is a healthy choice. Whether this necessarily makes for a better teacher is debatable (another heresy), but it does increase the knowledge base, authority, and credibility of both the task and the profession. Lucy Crehan noted that Finnish teachers tend to be very fixed on following high-quality subject textbooks—but building an equitable social system came first, one that ensures people and groups don't fall behind. In the UK, the curriculum is remodeled at such rate that great textbooks are hard to come by and too expensive to change.

Taking a neglected, patched-up system and adding on a research degree as a hoped-for fix as some authorities demand is unlikely to significantly change fundamentals elsewhere. Adding a mental health officer to every school in the UK is welcome but makes no system sense. It fails to deal with cause.

## UNINTENDED CONSEQUENCES

A system that often tops the PISA rankings is South Korea. It hasn't passed without notice that many "high-performing countries," a term used by PISA and McKinsey, also have the misfortune to have large and unpredictable neighbors, a factor that tends to focus the mind on using all available human resources. South Korea offers an insight into a system applying the same-age lever with full force.

Se-Woong Koo (2014) might be described as *a survivor* in today's parlance. Following the illness of his brother and ascribed to the South Korean education system, it was decided that he should be educated in Vancouver. Later he taught at a *Hagwon*, the crammer schools that form an essential ingredient of the South Korean education system where children can stay until 10 p.m. He describes education in South Korea in the following terms.

> Dominated by Tiger Moms, cram schools and highly authoritarian teachers, South Korean education produces ranks of overachieving students who pay a stiff price in health and happiness. The entire program amounts to child abuse. It should be reformed and restructured without delay.

Life in schools for South Korean students has one purpose: to pass the *suneung*, the high-stakes test that determines so much of their future. Schooling is tough, often seven days a week. There is a 99% literacy rate, and schools adhere to research-based learning models prone to direct instruction, including early learning intervention.

It is an irony that Andreas Schleicher, director at the OECD, talks of the need for problem-solving skills and of course has a standardized test to measure this. This relentless school system so lauded by the OECD/PISA for its *quick-learning, highly inquisitive, problem-solving students*, however, is far from perfect.

Two-thirds (66%) of South Koreans aged twenty-five to thirty four have degrees, compared with an average 39% in the OECD. But the downside damage is evident from high rates of suicide, depression, and stress anxiety among young people; this in a country where mental health issues are often regarded as a social stigma. There are an estimated three million graduates unemployed in South Korea, a figure dwarfed by the many students unable to get white-collar work who remain signed-on at universities to better their chances of employment.


## THE UK

So what of the underperforming UK with its low productivity? Let's look at what the UK, this nation of shopkeepers, produces. It is not often that the UK is given a complimentary *shout-out* for its schools and teachers, so here goes. Here are figures obtained from the Department for Small

Business, Innovation & Skills (2016) now called the Department for Business, Energy & Industrial Strategy. In particular, let's look at the data for evidence of lack of character, low resilience, unwillingness to take risks, and the absence of innovation, creativity, and a can-do mind-set—alleged school failure!

* 2014: 581,000 start-up companies formed.
* 2015: This increased by a further six hundred thousand.
* 2016: There were a record 5.5 million private businesses, two million more since 2000.

Small business accounts for 99.3% of all private sector businesses. Ninety-nine percent were small or medium-sized (SMEs). Total employment in SMEs was 15.7 million—60% of all private sector employment. The combined annual turnover of SMEs was £1.8 trillion. Not bad for a recession! A high number of start-ups were people (nonemployers) searching for a better life balance. In fact, more and more individuals are setting up their own businesses and learning the advantages of self-organization.

For South Korea, there are five main employing families. Here's the question: how on earth did the UK, this quirky little country so full of doubt and self-criticism, produce so many highly creative, gritty, can-do, resilient risk takers, innovators, and inventors? More importantly, what do our schools need to have (or not have) to help them produce more?

For schools that believe their purpose to be a much broader, ecological concept entailing moral leadership, a more holistic approach to the development of human potential, and the goal of goodness, the kind of examination and textbook regimes being lauded as the future seem both incomprehensible incompatible.

Nevertheless, it is the direction of travel. UK schools, for all their faults, have been a great success. But instead of recognizing gains made, they are being pushed in an ever more convergent direction, one already having unintended consequences. Copying your neighbor's work, as every teacher knows, is not a good way to promote learning and understanding. It is ironic that UK schools had already discovered the Google (chapter 15) framework for group endeavor and creativity if not the system to exploit it. The entrepreneurial schools advocated by the RSA (earlier) were already well on their way and so were the students and staff.

UK schools have done well. Now we are asking them to change over errant concerns about international league tables and misleading reports from consultancy firms and think tanks. Despite the limitations of their same-age structure, they produced people who understood what was needed to be happy and people able to create their own jobs rather than being tied to them for the long term.

Suddenly, it seems that we are in an imagined school crisis spooked by the headline writers. As Amos Tversky so famously said:

> It's frightening to think that you might not know something, but more frightening to think that, by and large, the world is run by people who have faith that they know exactly what is going on.

## MENTAL HEALTH AND SCHOOLS

And now to get to the point, one that concerns a serious issue lurking in the background throughout: schools and mental health. This is the heresy: the same-age system employed by schools is a major contributory cause of mental health disorders and general loss of well-being among young people and teachers today. The way we group students by age is a systems driver and all the while we persist in working around this obstacle to learning and well-being nothing of substance will change.

In complex Western cultures where the differences between haves and have-nots are close to unbridgeable, education systems are under constant scrutiny and always up for debate. As Ed Straw says, they zig-zag and are in a state of constant repair. The first page of Michael Fullan's book *The Principal* (2014) makes for depressing reading. It reveals a crisis in which "the conditions for mutual learning have been seriously eroding." Fullan states that two-thirds of kindergarteners are alienated from school by the time they reach grade 9 (Jenkins, 2013).

The Metropolitan Life Insurance Company, referenced by Fullan, adds to the gloom, reporting that teacher satisfaction has declined by 24% since 2008, with only 38% being *very satisfied* with their job; similar figure are repeated in the UK. Fullan further reports that 75% of school principals say their job has become overly *complex* (complicated in a systems sense) such that principals feel under stress *several days a week*.

In simple terms, schools in complex democracies are not only becoming increasingly difficult to lead and manage, but also dispiriting places in which to work. Where there should be professionalism and trust, there is fear and compliance. The UK schools that had started to be adaptive and produce a significant number of capable, risk-taking, self-employed entrepreneurs in search of an ecologically more balanced, happier life are now being forced to move in another direction. The New Public Management (NPM) campaign that began three decades ago is starting to kick in with all its unintended consequences.

In the UK, the Education Support Partnership (2016), a charity dedicated to support teacher well-being, conducted a survey of two thousand teachers that had contacted the group over two years and their findings are worrying. Around 84% said they had suffered a mental health issue in that time; 81% attributed this to workload. Only 25% had discussed their health with a line manager, while 77% were actively considering leaving the profession. What's more, 18% said they had taken occasional days off, and of these half felt that student learning had suffered as a result.

The statistics for mental health disorders among young people are equally worrying. Figures for the UK suggest one in ten young people aged five to sixteen suffer from a diagnosable mental health disorder—about three students in every class. Eight thousand children under the age of ten suffer severe depression (Young Minds, 2016). Data from the Mental Health Foundation (2016) indicate that for young people between the ages of eleven and sixteen, mental health disorders are rising sharply.

- 20% of adolescents may experience a mental health problem in any given year.
- 50% of mental health problems are established by age fourteen and 75% by age twenty-four.
- 10% of children and young people (aged five to sixteen years) have a clinically diagnosable mental health problem.
- 70% of children and adolescents who experience mental health problems have not had appropriate interventions at a sufficiently early age.

One noted area of concern in this report is teacher-pupil relationships; another is school bullying. The *Ditch the Label* (2016) report on the consequences of bullying showed that 31% of victims self-harmed (41,921 hospital admissions, the probable tip of an iceberg), 33% had suicidal thoughts, 26% skipped class, 15% developed an eating disorder, 15% developed antisocial behavior, 12% ran away, and 12% used drugs and alcohol. Meta-studies show that such effects often lead to depression and work problems in later life.

A national obsession in public services like schools is now data production, passing exams, hitting targets, and surviving inspections, itself the result of fragmented, disruptive, and piecemeal interventions. Mori Social Research Institute noted that students at university often struggle with work that requires independent thinking and making connections. Part of the reason suggested is modular courses; students taught to pass exams rather than think for themselves (Higton et al., 2012). This kind of approach is nonsystemic. When passing exams becomes the system purpose, almost everything of importance, including well-being, is sacrificed to the cause.

Peter Senge (1990) pointed out that structures and the underpinning decision-making processes determine so much of our behavior. Systems, especially the ones we work in, can be the cause of behavioral crises and dysfunction. Senge talks of *metanoia*, a shift of mind that enables us to see how our actions and the systems we build create the problems we experience.

The argument here is that underpinning the many health issues faced by system users and providers is the system itself and in particular the same-age structure and its high-risk assumptions about psychological well-being. While the NPM style of push management and the concurrent demand for higher academic pass rates are not causal matters within the remit of schools, a planned move to self-organization (the ability to create a better structure, learn, and diversify) certainly is. Schools can do more to help themselves through a greater understanding of their operational methodology. In the end, systems are all about people and how they work at their best.

The argument here is that the relationships that sustain living systems and human organizations become dangerously fragmented in same-age schools as external threats (pressures on performance and high accountability) increase. Schools in their current same-age management form are unable to adapt or wrest back any control, and many have been neatly folded up and packed away in school chains and academy trusts where they can do less self-harm and are more easily controlled.

## HAPPINESS AND WELL-BEING

The World Happiness Report (2016) published by the United Nations identifies factors that affect happiness. These include caring, freedom, generosity, honesty, health, income, and good governance. The UK is low on the list, while the USA failed to make the top ten and remains in serious decline. Topping the list of *happiest countries* is Norway closely followed by Denmark, Iceland, and Switzerland. The case for Norway includes descriptors such as high levels of mutual trust, shared purpose, generosity, and good governance. These system factors should be the guiding lights for school managers, but creating organizations that reflect these descriptors requires a very different direction of travel to the one schools are being asked to follow.

Same-age design leads to limitations on networking, fragility in support structures, and loss of belonging—separational risk factors not conducive to happiness, well-being, and learning. These impact directly on the classroom and make the lives of teachers and students considerably harder. Efforts made by schools to mitigate these negative factors using pastoral support subsystems are welcome but ultimately fortuitous and patchy in their resolution and fail to address cause. A single person like a year head, dean of school, mental health coordinator, or school counsellor cannot be responsible for mitigating the collective trauma caused by the system in use.

Only by changing the underlying structure and enabling a school to connect to more of itself can such risk factors be reversed. In other words, it is possible to design out many of the mental health issues that emanate from the school's same-age structure.

The next chapter shows how the application of existing systems theory can be applied to schools.

*Chapter 8*

# The School as a Viable System

At the risk of repetition, it makes every sense to design-in empathetic learning relationships, stable friendship groups, and quality learning support from the start. The same-age approach puts these relationships into immediate jeopardy and to then try and repair them when they inevitably break. These are relational matters and, although they might come under the umbrella of *soft systems management*, they remain among the most demanding challenges faced by schools.

In the absence of systems thinking, schools treat these important matters as add-ons and fixes; unfortunately, pro-social programs needed to handle failure demand can never replace the practical and everyday experience of genuine relationships. There is an important complementary place for PSHE-/ SEL-type programs but these should not be used to rectify problems caused by the system in use as they are now.

Having talked about VT as a system, it is helpful to place this model within the broad context of the viable systems models (VSMs). This model (discussed below) boils down to a simple idea and a complex change. In a service organization, it is far more important *who talks to whom* rather than *who reports to whom*. In management terms, vertical communications act as a constraint to those knowledge operators on the ground. Allenna Leonard (1999) describes the theory as follows:

> Viability is enhanced when the ground level operations have the maximum amount of autonomy consistent with their purposes because any intervention from above sacrifices some of the variety which the lower level can use. To justify intervention, there need to be good reasons for incurring the opportunity costs of not fully utilizing the lower level's greater familiarity with the immediate situation.

That's the simple idea; the difficulty is in making the complex change by decluttering the organization's assumptions and letting go of received management wisdom. For the school to survive and be viable, schools must relearn how to translate their values into working practices and understand that what happens at the base and edges of organizations is what really matters.

By now, the message about the shortcomings of same-age linear systems with their vast hierarchical power structures and endless complications and delays has been hammered home. An attempt has been made to show how nonlinear mixed-age organization can change working practices by connecting the school to more of itself allowing the learning process to become better supported, more effective, and fun. We need schools able to design-in emotional intelligence, empathy, resilience, grit, and can-do mind-set by default rather than through system apps.

## THE NATURE OF LEVERAGE POINTS

It is difficult to explain the practicalities of a system most secondary schools have never experienced, so in this chapter we'll turn to a model that demonstrates the fundamental requisites. But first a return to leverage points, those places in an organization where a small change can elicit a big and fundamental response. Donella Meadows (2009) noted the counterintuitive nature of leverage points and the time (sometimes years) it takes to discover them. She added, "When I do discover a system's leverage point, nobody will believe me."

Leverage points can remain hidden and be considered benign for years; in the case of schools, around 150 years! Managers usually have an inkling that they might be the cause of problems but can't figure out how they work and because there is no comparable model they try and force the one they have using adaptions (let's try doing it this way) and additions (let's add resilience to the PSHE program). The effect is to push the lever in the wrong direction making matters more and more complicated. Meadows (1999) suggested a dozen possible places to intervene in a system and set out below is an interpretation for schools (italics) of her top five. These are placed in an increasing order of effectiveness precisely as Meadows wrote them.

1. Information flows.
   *In a school, information flows via feedback loops in multiple directions via our players. If the flow is restricted, reduced, or absent, this causes delays to effective intervention and increases failure demand. The*

*mixed-age system is complex and increases flow and changes organizational structure to suit.*

2. The rules of the system (incentives, punishments, constraints).

   *The more rules, the more complicated the organization and the more restrictive and anti-learning it becomes. Removing impediments and replacing these with training and applied motivational psychology is beneficial. This means increasing trust and accepting responsibilities. Hence the VSM.*

3. The distribution of power over the rules of the system.

   *These too are limiting factors that prevent innovation and dull creativity. Power accumulates at the top (permission) levels rather than the level of system users. The VSM, like a mixed-age system, rewrites the system rules and allows power and decision-making to move to the base and organizational edge.*

4. The goals of the system.

   *The purpose of a system requires agreement to be a true system. Measures (test scores) have become purposes and values have become assumed. Revisiting purpose is a system prerequisite. Regaining values and purposes can be a strong leverage point.*

5. The mind-set or paradigm out of which the system—its goals, power structure, rules, its culture—arises.

   *The same-age design mind-set remains industrial and heavily influenced by the machine metaphor. The mixed-age design creates different power structures, rules, and culture. The former is now beset by complications, add-ons, and fixes and takes a dim view of people. Unlearning the same-age system is critical to any new dawn.*

From a child's point of view, it makes sense to be surrounded by a number of supportive personnel options and to have leadership, mentoring, and support on tap everywhere. The greater the number and availability of connections (nonlinear), the more stable, resilient, and adaptive the person and the organization. Being better connected and supported all the time is a better means of building resilience than attending a pro-social program some of the time.

At this point, we need to introduce a difficult systems construct. To make schools safer, relevant, and more effective, they have to become more complex, not more complicated. For schools, this means abandoning linearity and embracing nonlinearity, and this (as we all know by now) requires a mixed-age lever.

There is good reason for this. The external environment of the school is complex, and students bring a huge amount of variation into school, as do teachers. To cope, the linear school is obliged to place restrictions (limitation and separation) on how work is organized, what information is useful, and how relationships are expected to form. Managers seek to control complexity and are forced to make assumptions. Unfortunately, this leads to failure demand, increased workload, rises in costs, and slow improvement in outcomes.

Management becomes more coercive. As the same-age lever is tugged ever harder, another set of problems occurs; people start to feel disenchanted and unwell. The more complicated the school becomes, the less complexity it is able to absorb. In short, to deal with complex issues related to learning requires an equally complex organizational response, not one beset by complication. So, how to escape this nasty feedback loop?

## PURPOSE AND VIABILITY

All of the above has brings us to the work of Stafford Beer (1926–2002), founder of SIGMA (Science in General Management) and an authority on operational research and management cybernetics. Both Stafford Beer and Jay Forrester were interested in modelling systems and the feedback loops that sustain them. Beer's *viable systems model* (VSM) is an attempt to show how organizations (as living systems) can survive and adapt in a changing environment. This makes such an idea very relevant to schools.

For schools, and as part of systems thinking, there must be a purpose. Understandably, schools express purpose with grandiose aspirations and profound moral intention; more so, now they find themselves competing in the student marketplace. Unfortunately, like distributive leadership, this approach can act as a smokescreen. There is no point in saying, for example, that our school exists to develop the potential of every child if it is clear that this is palpably not what the school does.

In October 2001, Stafford Beer cut to the chase and made a statement of profound elegance and simplicity:

> According to the cybernetician the purpose of a system is what it does. This is a basic dictum. It stands for bald fact, which makes a better starting point in seeking understanding than the familiar attributions of good intention, prejudices about expectations, moral judgment or sheer ignorance of circumstances.

The purpose of a system is what it does (POSIWID)! If a school system separates and limits, then that is its purpose. It is easy to be hoodwinked by good intentions and our many biases, and it is a natural survival mechanism to be self-deceiving but all of this makes it difficult to face up to what is actually happening in a school and why it is happening in the way it is.

School purposes and intentions expressed in visionary statements are rarely as aligned to practice as schools like to assume. It is this kind of misalignment that systems thinking exposes.

Purpose is now connected to self-deceit; schools believe in the welfare and well-being of staff and students but exercise policies and practices which too often have an opposite effect. They then end up trying to fix what they've broken with new welfare policies and support staff but the cycle (the reinforcing feedback loop) persists. Making staff and students ill and then providing a mental health expert (the current strategy) to treat them again fails to deal with the issue. Beer's dictum is helpful; the purpose of a system is what it does (POSIWID), not what we think it does or what we hope it might do.

If the health of participants like teachers and students starts to suffer, if staff retention rates fall and recruitment collapses; this is what the system does! It may not be the intention of those running the system, but it is nevertheless the collateral damage of the system. It is what the system does and why it needs to change. Hence the difficulty in saying anything of a positive nature about schools organized on a same-age basis. The present school model, driven by same-age organization, is complicated, overly hierarchical, heavily layered, and relies on instructions cascading from the top. It is a very difficult system to operate even at its best. Add to this heavy accountability on staff for failures belonging to the system, and people suffer unnecessarily.

Not only is the same-age system cumbersome, but also it is unable to handle in a qualitative way the complexity it needs to absorb, and it is this inability that determines so much of the same-age system's behavior. The heresy is simple: the school in its hierarchical and same-age form is not a viable model. So what is?

## THE VIABLE SYSTEMS MODEL (VSM): THEORY AND PRACTICE

There is a deep fear that disaggregating and flattening a typical school management model will lead inevitably to chaos. Managers are reluctant to relinquish control, and concerns about loss of cohesion and direction underpin the paranoia of the management task. Besides, such a notion goes against everything (the received industrial wisdom) that larger schools are persuaded to believe is necessary management. But there is a high price to pay for such a system.

The work with hundreds of schools on system change (Barnard) reveals degrees of confusion at all operational levels. No fault is attached to school staff but the fact remains that players have very different interpretations regarding policies and practices. At the same time, attempts to hold the whole together with complicated job descriptions and endless line managers do little to alleviate the problem and can even make matters worse by causing border disputes and complications.

Much of the desire of teachers to go part-time (UK) stems from a need to seek a better life balance and escape the harmful effects of endless peripheral change, unnecessary paperwork, heavy accountability, and fear. It is a way of reasserting personal value and control that the school in its current form is no longer able to offer. However, these changes to working practices pose a risk to system integrity caused by a loss of attachment in student/staff learning relations. It returns us to the statement by Stafford Beer; the purpose of a system is what it does. It makes too many turn away.

The hierarchical, same-age, linear system is telling us loud and clear that it is under severe pressure and unable to cope qualitatively with the complexity it is required to absorb. It is cumbersome, slow, and error-strewn, and now causes as much harm as good to participants. Today, there is now sufficient knowledge, technology, and exemplars to provide an alternative approach.

The nature of these organizational issues is neatly interpreted in a paper by Raúl Espejo and Antonia Gill (2015) based on Beer's work (think school). This is where the "who talks to whom" comes from.

> It is becoming increasingly apparent that it matters much less who reports to whom, as who needs to talk with whom and how all the pieces of a complex interrelated jigsaw fit together to form a synergistic whole. Yet it is precisely this sense of the whole that is so often missing.

The VSM is able to improve functional capability through decentralization and improvements to communication while retaining complete coherence. It creates a framework of connected links able to form and reform wherever needed, and this makes such a model both flexible and adaptable. This describes the mixed-age approach to a tee.

Beer proposed that living systems (like schools) are *recursive* in nature. They are composed of myriad subsystems (people or living systems in essence) right down to a single cell. Whatever the level, each is autonomous and has the agency wherewithal and capacity to be self-organizing. It is this recursive nature that enables the organization to adapt in ways that generate sufficient internal complexity to balance the eternal complexity it needs to absorb.

Espejo and Gill describe five features that a VSM requires. Although the list (below) sounds like the organizational requirements we'd expect to see in any hierarchical structure, they are actually used to describe what we'd expect to see in a delayered structure or VSM. These can be interpreted for schools as follows:

1. Implementation. The school can be identified as an organization engaged in learning and teaching. To ensure that value is added, the organization requires all subsystems to work in a synchronized way (complex enough to handle and engage with the complexity it is there to absorb). It cannot be one-size-fits-all. These value-adding subgroups include parent partnership, mixed-age student networks, teacher and tutor networks, and include networking loops and interconnections between all of these groups. These occur wherever the system and the customer interact and wherever information is exchanged. The hierarchical system has to be sufficiently unfolded to allow these groups to connect and make decisions, to be agents of their own autonomy. All have parity of importance but each may be tasked to do more than the other to resolve an issue.
2. Coordination. To ensure the effectiveness of the relationships between subsystems requires coordination. However, this is not direction and control in the management sense we understand. Coordination stems from the need of subsystems to be mutually adjusting. The tutor might learn something from a parent that requires a change in another autonomous area like the classroom. The conversation between parent, tutor, and teacher leads to an autonomous intervention with a student. The system leans toward self-managing teams, and the more these units share the same values and intentions the better. They cooperate and join up to achieve the system's learning purpose.
3. Control. This must be achieved in a way that avoids top-down instruction likely to corrupt system integrity. Monitoring is still required, and the model suggests how communication with meta-levels can be enacted in a nonblame way. A preference here is for everybody in the school to become a tutor of a mixed-age group and, therefore, party to a value-adding subunit. When this occurs, leadership teams are able to learn firsthand what works, what needs tweaking, and what further support and training is necessary. It is a variation on servant leadership and embraces the idea that all change emanates from the points where value is added and complexity absorbed. This, and only this, brings distributed leadership into existence.
4. Intelligence. The VSM must be inextricably linked to its external environment. Intelligence doesn't emanate from the top (we all know that!) but from the interface between school and parents and the wider community. Parents are a key source of feedback because they are already part of a

key subunit (tutor, child, and parent) that contributes knowledge and support. The tutor in this respect is the central information and communications hub. This system ensures the school can monitor its environment, gather relevant information, plan, and then inform the community of its response. The school learns from the intelligence gathered and changes its modus operandi to suit. The authors offer a word of caution that unerringly describes the school situation:

These loops must operate in balance, to avoid either overloading the system with a swamp of external research data without the capacity to interpret and act on that data; or the alternative risk of communicating outwards in a strong fashion, without having a corresponding means to listen for feedback from the marketplace.

5. Policymaking. Policy exists not to overtly control but to provide clarity of direction and so needs to be very careful concerning the information and intelligence it uses. It ensures that units stick to agreed values and purposes. In some respects, the purpose of policy is to avoid making policy unless absolutely necessary. The preference is to ensure all organizational sectors are enabled to intervene, appropriately trained, and fully operational in the end-to-end learning process.


## SAME-AGE VERSUS MIXED-AGE SYSTEMS

Recursive structural change enables a living system to survive in complex times through an ability to absorb complexity (value demand). In short, Beer advises that organizations need to delay as much as they possibly can, a rewiring process that makes them more complex in themselves but also more interconnected. In simple terms, to handle complex matters like learning and child development, the organizational framework must of itself be complex. It must have the multitude of working pathways that Meadows advises. Herein is the unity of culture, systems, mind-sets, and behavior advised by Laloux (2014, p. 234).

Schools that have adopted mixed-age organization take a first step on the complexity trail. They create a nested system based on schools within schools with leadership, mentoring, and support on tap everywhere, and especially so in the tutor groups. This increases the capacity for intelligence gathering and system flexibility. It also frees up information flow by creating effective communications channels with the potential for rapid intervention and quality support. The system becomes complex enough to absorb value demand and prevent failure demand while its integrated support framework improves well-being.

To achieve this, mixed-age schools reduce the size of the tutor group, increase the number of tutors by using all employees, and rebuild the partnership needed with parents and students. In effect, schools recreate the network of intelligence units they need. What such schools have yet to do is to complete the process through a redesign of the existing leadership and management teams. Management has yet to change in ways that enable greater agency at the organizational base.

The same-age linear system fails to comply as a VSM in almost every respect. This includes the following:

- Information-light data sheets. These have replaced written reports (quantity replaces quality), making parents reliant on the creative explanations of their children for the information they really want. This damages key feedback loops besides being anti-VSM and leads inevitably to failure demand.
- Subject evenings restricted to annual occasions and five-minute slots. Parental engagement, support, and intervention are downgraded. The school has restricted listening and learning ability.
- Single-portal parental access to information via the school office (inability to cope with demand) creates delays and alienation.
- Tutors excluded from the information loop despite their job description.
- Paperwork and e-mails overwhelming participants.
- Information locked into hierarchical levels and difficult to access without permission.
- The student support systems on constant overload and designed for extreme events.

Such a list of system faults and obstacles to learning literally goes on for pages! The way schools manage and cope given the shortfalls of the same-age system in use is nothing short of magnificent. But staff working at the edge of the school in tutor time and in the classroom where value is added have become increasingly isolated, and when this happens protective silos start to form. The living subsystems react to their environment by protecting themselves as best they can in the haven of their offices, while those still trying to produce the goods lack the organizational support, relevant systems training, and information needed.

When working with same-age schools, these organizational issues and many more always arise. It is extremely courageous when schools choose to confront the challenges they face and embrace a systems solution. For the first time, they see the obvious faults, self-deceit, and the hold of an industrial machine metaphor staring them full in the face, and when such inconsistencies are exposed to the light of day, something Kurt Lewin called *unfreezing*, it becomes a Eureka moment.

Schools then say that they knew the answer all along; they just didn't quite see it. The fact is schools and those who work in them love to learn and especially so when the intention is to heal self-inflicted wounds and rebuild the school's circulatory system, something that only they can ultimately do.

*Chapter 9*

# Wicked Problems and Parent Partnership

Parent partnership has arisen many times as an area that is not as functional as claimed. Research suggests it should be an integral part of the learning and support process but there is sufficient evidence (below) to suggest that it is actually separating from the school and in decline. This diminution of this essential partnership acts to isolate teachers even more underpinning the false belief that it is the teacher who is solely accountable for student learning. Parents are important because they have information to share and are a means of support and intervention that offers significant help in the learning process and, when this is added to the school's contribution, learning improves. A working parent partnership is critical to the notion of a fully functional socially collaborative school as a viable systems model (VSM).

This chapter starts with the heretical statement, offers some background as to the nature of socio/organizational problems, and then return to the challenge of parent partnership. First, the challenge. How can a school engage with parents in their child's learning? Now, the heretical statement. A school organized on a same-age basis cannot develop viable parent partnership in any coherent and substantive way; this is because same-age schools are too complicated as organizations and insufficiently complex! Complicated organizations seek to simplify and in this case redefining what counts as parent partnership. They diminish and reduce channels of communication, and this always leads to failure demand and more complications, a kind of negative reinforcing loop! It is possible to see this process in the research.

A recent survey of 7,200 public schools by Rice University showed that only 34% of parents were satisfied with family and community engagement. A total of 46% of parents reported satisfaction with school communication, 45% said parent-teacher conferences suit their schedules, and 44% said that schools explained clearly how their child is graded. Parents rated family and community engagement as the main driver of satisfaction with their child's school. In fact, family and community engagement in learning outweighed the views of principals who assumed good teaching and extracurricular activities were highest on parent demands. The report concluded that parents are anxious to be actively involved and engaged, and their need for collaboration was high (Source: Collaborative for Customer-Based Execution and Strategy Benchmark. K-12 School Study, Rice University, 2017).

All schools can explain rationally how parent partnership works for them, and all schools can offer exemplars of successful engagement, usually a time when school and parents spotted a problem and intervened in time. Most same-age schools go further and claim to have *great* parent partnership but not one comes near when exposed to the scrutiny of systems thinking and any examination of customer demand.

This isn't because schools aren't trying; it's because the methods that same-age schools feel obliged to apply don't work in the way such schools assume. In fact, the work with schools transitioning from same-age to mixed-age systems reveals that partnership with parents and parental engagement in learning are in serious decline. The essential information networks on which learning depends are systematically closing down and separating out; as the workload pressures on schools increase, staff are afforded greater protection from what is seen as external interference. The school goes into protection mode.

Yet many schools have parent partnership certificates to validate their claims and some talk of the parent partnership training course that someone attended. Justifying assumptions makes no substantive difference. Same-age systems have a lumpy and lumpen quality; schools have to deal with large numbers of same-age students at critical times, and this causes organizational difficulties that cannot be overcome and this leads to self-deceit and assumptions. Remember POSIWID? The purpose of a system is what it does and the same-age system was designed with separation and limitation in mind. Set out here are examples of how same-age schools define and limit the partnership experience.

- The timings for parent consultation evenings have not been thought through. At subject evenings, parents may get a five-minute appointment limiting discussion and feedback.
- Given the high numbers at such events, the chance of lost or inadequate information is high and essential information easily missed.
- The information sent home (data sheet reports) is insufficient to provoke a meaningful discussion, again reducing any viable partnership.
- The partnership situations involve high numbers in classes and tutor groups effectively preventing parent partnership alienating relationships.

- There is an inadequate summative overview regarding learning and achievement by the school and subsequently by the parent and child. Tutors are invariable removed from the information flow and, therefore, the partnership.
- The back-up claim that all parents can contact the schools is really a cover story. Few take up the offer and those who do find the single-portal back office channel difficult to navigate.

Remember the words of Jay Forrester: a system is all about feedback loops, and this involves the movement of essential information between groups and individuals needed (in this case) to promote learning. All of the bullet points above denote broken, missing, and assumed feedback loops. This is not a criticism of schools but a description of the system at work, one concerned to maintain its identity and protect what it perceives to be its core teaching activity. Unfortunately, such a process is a direct route to failure demand, matters not properly resolved that require more work downstream and increased costs. Ultimately, the problem ends up with the teacher who has to work even harder, and this makes no sense at all.

## WICKED PROBLEMS

Having already mentioned *wicked problems*, the kind of problems so complicated and multifaceted that they become difficult to understand let alone resolve, it is useful to elucidate their nature more accurately. This is because the kind of problems that challenge schools are multifaceted and parent partnership is of this type. In essence, these are system problems and the nature of same-age schools dealing as it does with large numbers has almost no room for maneuver. Besides, living systems like schools are not going to listen to these strictures. From inside the system, energy is precious and cannot be expended on matters that seem only loosely connected with the school and which anyway seem OK (no one complains!), which means that any external disturbance has to be considerable if change is to occur.

Like bullying, parent partnership, or lack of it, arises from the system in use, the way schools go about organizing learning and teaching; system connectedness. Unless school managers understand why and how a learning system like a school relies on strong player networks, it will be prey to the kind of reform strategy fixated on a single element—trying to solve a nonexistent teacher quality problem rather than the system as a whole.

There are three goals in this chapter. The first is to briefly explore the nature of the problems (like parent partnership) that we might expect to find in systems that have remained unattended for a century or so. The second is to explain what schools should be trying to do with regard to parent partnership and why they find it so difficult. The third is to show how vertical tutoring, the kind of VSM approach outlined in the previous chapter, affords a high-quality solution. Russell Ackoff (1979) described the task of management like this:

> Managers are not confronted with problems that are independent of each other, but with dynamic situations that consist of complex systems of changing problems that interact with each other. I call such situations messes . . . Managers do not solve problems, they manage messes.

## THE NATURE OF THE WICKED GAMES WE PLAY

In the order of problems, messes come close to wicked problems. Like untangling Christmas tree lights, there is no obvious starting point as far as messes are concerned and it takes considerable time to ascertain any progress. You might get there in the end and try to be cleverer next time round but the process wasn't pleasant and took its toll. You vow next time not to make the same mistake but always do! Untangling people from systems is even more difficult and these, as Ackoff suggests, rarely get resolved. But messes are only one kind of problem. Beyond the mess and skulking in the background lurks the cause of the mess, the system in use, a higher category of challenge, or *wicked* problem. For Ackoff, wicked problems cannot be resolved; instead, they must be dissolved and a new system created.

The unattended system seems to delight in fabricating all kinds of issues for managers to resolve, and while managers busy themselves with their various reforms, fixes, and add-ons, the same-age system can be assured that no one will look in its particular direction. Managers cannot resolve the system problem, so they manage the complications (messes) created by the system they use; they manage the staff trying to make the system work and the behavior of students for whom the system fails in some way. The school system easily survives the managers' tinkering ways, shrugs, and continues on its merry way untouched and unaffected by any minor inconvenience.

The wicked problem is the same-age school's self-construction, the way the school works as a system and this always remains unscathed. It retains a low profile in the research literature; no one speaks of same-age organization as a concern, and it is doubtless delighted when teachers take the rap for the mischief it creates. Whatever the system outcomes, the system is the cause. If a system makes people ill, separates, limits potential, causes harm and makes reformers pull their hair out, undermines parental engagement, and causes student mischief, then this is what the system does; (POSIWID)—the purpose of a system is what it does, just as Beer said.

It is not what we might intend it should do, but few can argue that this is what the system actually does. It damages and heals all at the same time and is more concerned with its survival than our whims. No wonder politicians jettison schools to the private sector. Three of the five characteristics of wicked problems nominated by Horst Rittel and Melvin Webber (1973) follow, with brief comments (italics):

1. The nature of a wicked problem is never fully understood until after a solution is found. *As a high school principal, it was difficult to grasp the intransigent and complicated nature of the same-age school system until the idea of mixed-age tutor groups emerged. Only then could the school appreciate just how many obstacles to learning and teaching there were. The reason for going vertical was to involve parents more by turning data into information. Our view was that we needed parents inside the tent rather than on the outside. . . . You can only see systems from a distance.*

2. They have a no-stopping rule. *Once enacted the same-age wicked problem simply continues in motion using a combination of balancing and reinforcing feedback loops. The same-age system that began in industrial times continues unabated and uninterrupted. The solution, therefore, cannot be a teacher upgrade or curriculum add-on but a fundamental change to the way the system works and hence to the behavior it causes. Treating the current same-age system as benign and unworthy of attention ensures no systemic change, no resolution or dissolution.*

3. Wicked problems are not right or wrong. *They often arise from the best of intentions. No fault is attached. The problem, however, becomes more difficult to resolve whenever fixes (a toolbox approach) are applied and any new parts are added to old. At this point, the school is in full self-deception mode.*

One of the reasons given by same-age schools for changing to a mixed-age system is to improve parent engagement in learning—to bring the idea of family and individualism back to the school in a very practical way. Such schools take the view that it takes a community to both raise and educate a child and parents are critical to such a redesigned process. Parents have important immediate information to share and so do schools; each must act for and be the other. But students also hold vital information. Any school design in an age of information has to enable this complex multiplicity of learning relationships to form, if new learning processes and innovative strategies for improvement are to be realized.

Same-age schools have constructed data-driven student performance monitoring systems but are unable to turn this data into the useful information that really supports learning. Teachers are under such pressure that they rarely write written reports any more. What is seen as a protective time-saving activity actually makes the teacher's life more difficult. Simplification always leads to failure demand, added complications, and harder repeat work.

Only when parents and students are seen as true partners does the need for an improved partnership process become clear. Somehow, somewhere, sometime, there has to be a deeper learning conversation between school (tutor not just the teacher), student, and home that combines data and information. When this occurs, strategies for improvement to support learning can be agreed, monitored, and owned, and appropriate interventions made. Mixed-age schools call these occasions *deep learning conversations* or *academic tutorials*, and these take place at all critical times in the student's learning career.

## THE APPLIED VSM

The VSM outlined in the previous chapter is based on delayering the organization in order to make the subunits more effective and interconnected. The effect is to reduce management clutter and to prevent information and instructions cascading from the top. The idea is to open new channels (flow) between those doing the value work at the base and edges of the organization where learning in all its forms occurs.

The model predicts that if there are organizational problems, they are likely to be found in the consolidation of power and information at the top rather than at the point of delivery where significant agency needed to make decisions is critical. This will show itself within existing subsystems and how these connect or otherwise to other subsystems. Put simply, the static nature of the hierarchical model predicts that any inherent faults in the subsystems and their interconnections stem from complications in the school's design, its hierarchical self-construction.

What we are looking at is how a subsystem like parent partnership works and how it connects to other learning relationships or subsystems in the school. These learning relationships comprise teacher/student, tutor/student, parent/child, parent/teacher, parent/tutor, teacher/teacher, tutor/tutee/student, tutor/teacher/student, and student/mentor/tutor (figure 19.1, chapter 19). There are many, and all are important and need to be in effective working order. All of these are feedback and support loops connected by information, and all form part of assessment for learning (AfL). How these work and their effectiveness is dependent on the collaborative capability of the school as a system.

With information hubs seemingly everywhere, this makes the school complex and flow a challenge. Every subunit in a VSM has to work optimally if the connected whole (the school) is to be effective. The question that needs to be answered is this: What is the best means of releasing such a complexity of collaboration and distributed leadership? Pare it down to teachers alone and a whole set of quality support and intervention is discounted, and this is what is happening.

## BACK TO SYSTEMS

The intention is to compare the same-age system with the mixed-age system and so we need to start with the dominant same-age paradigm.

To lead us into this maze is another quote from the systems thinking philosopher and problem-resolving guru Russell Ackoff (2004). It is one that highlights confirmation bias and the idea that even the most rational of us rarely see the world with the objectivity we claim. Ackoff was making a general comment about having wrong policies and practices, ones that lead to complications and unintended consequence.

> The righter we do the wrong thing, the wronger we become. When we make a mistake doing the wrong thing and correct it, we become wronger. When we make a mistake doing the right thing and correct it, we become righter. Therefore, it is better to do the right thing wrong than the wrong thing right.

If the same-age means of organization used by schools is the *wrong thing*, a position this book proposes throughout, then any attempt to make the system work better by effecting change in a subsystem can only make matters worse (wronger). Parent partnership is a case in point. Throw all the eggs into a teacher-based system and energy and time for other learning relationships dissipates. A VSM requires synergy because the relationship between system elements adds value to the system as a whole (Betts, 1992). Everything must work together—as a system!

Schools value genuine parent partnership; it is an important subunit that should connect effortlessly to other school areas to support learning. If this is so, there should be a clear picture of how parent partner works to support learning—more precisely, how theory relates to practice. The expanded heresy proposed is as follows: no matter what the same-age school does and how hard the school tries, parent partnership cannot be made to work effectively in a same-age organization.

Before proceeding, a reminder of the words of Espejo and Gill commenting on the VSM. What matters is not who reports to whom but who needs to talk with whom, and how all the pieces of a complex organizational jigsaw fit together to form a synergistic whole.

## WHAT ELSE DOES THE RESEARCH SAY?

Janet Goodall and Caroline Montgomery (2014) call attention to a parent partnership *continuum* that ranges from cursory involvement with school at one end to engagement with a child's learning at the other. The latter, they suggest, is the best means to accrue real learning benefits. Parents, after all, are the first link with the world beyond the school gates and hold many useful insights into their child's learning dispositions and emotional behavior (and, most importantly, that of their friends!). In effect, they are a source of intelligence and a monitoring post, the external equivalent of the form tutor in the school.

Bill Lucas (2013) produced a clear partnership rationale and offers a number of useful digests covering partnership areas and strategies that schools might incorporate. Included are a host of tips and checklists. There is the usual caution required with any checklists; schools like them for all the wrong reasons. They are convenient and they make it easy to justify existing practice because exemplars can usually be referenced somewhere in the school, which enable the school to tick the relevant box. While tick-boxes create a picture of what needs to happen, they can also lead to self-deceit and so delay the process of redesign.

For Janet Goodall and John Vorhaus (2010), parent partnership involves improving home-school links, support and training for parents, and family- and community-based interventions. None of these are easy in the context of same-age design. In the USA, Joyce Epstein, a long-time proponent of parent partnership, proposed six strategies. These can be summarized as improving home/school communications, helping parents to be more involved in their child's learning, including parents in decision-making, and encouraging parents to be a resource for the school. This is fine until it comes to implementation and practice.

We know that parents play a critical role in learning (Desforges and Abouchaar, 2003; Lucas, 2013). Henderson and Mapp (2007) write:

> The evidence is consistent, positive and convincing: families have a major influence on children's achievement. When schools, families and community groups work together to support learning, children tend to do better at school, stay in school longer and like school more.

None of the above mentions age systems; otherwise, we are all on the same page. The stronger the collaborative relationship between home and school, the better, so the degree to which a school builds parent partnership is of critical importance and a vital component of the school's complete learning and support strategy. Such a learning relationship, however, is defined and determined solely by the school that controls time, place, discussion parameters, and what counts as valid or usable information. Sadly, what may be usable grade information to some is not user-friendly to others and especially so for students and parents.

## MORE PROBLEMS EMANATING FROM THE SAME-AGE SYSTEM

At a formal level, schools encounter parents using three approaches: subject meetings with teachers, tutor evenings, and emergencies arising in part from any failure or absence of the previous two. In between, there are occasional information evenings. Whole day closures when tutors meet parents throughout the day are completely inadequate. No organization would allow professionals to meet clients one after the other in a time-limited way using minimal information—one where so little can be achieved and one where no genuine partnership can be forged. Neither does an open invitation to visit the school help.

This is the question that schools have to answer. Is it possible for a child to go through the school without ever having a reflective learning conversation using the key requirements set out below?

- Parents and child present, plus someone from the school who knows the child well and sees him or her every day. Ideally, this is the child's tutor.
- Good information is available and preread. This includes a full school report that contains strategies for improvement and learning assessments, as a minimum.
- The learning conversation takes place at a critical learning time in the school year and at a mutually convenient time for all parties.
- The conversation lasts around forty minutes and is otherwise not time limited.
- From the meeting, broad improvement and learning development strategies are agreed by all parties, acted upon, and owned.

Instead of embracing complexity as in a VT or VSM system, the same-age school leadership team tries what it assumes is an obvious solution; it tries to protect staff and starts to minimize and simplify processes. Readers know what comes next; simplification causes important learning issues to be missed; this creates failure demand; failure demand increases workload and more repair work downstream; this increases stress on the system; this requires extra staff support; this means more bureaucracy; this increases the management function; this increases costs; this leads to more separation and limitation, and so the recurring cycle of failure demand continues.

## WHAT PARENTS REALLY, REALLY WANT!

The best approach to any system puzzle is to go back and find out what the customer really wants rather than to implant on the system an amalgam of ideas that appear to pass muster but ultimately pander to assumptions. The partnership purpose is to support learning and achievement, and the research says unequivocally that parent partnership done well has a positive effect. It is method that is the problem, the rules of engagement that social collaboration requires.

The research in many hundreds of schools during their switch from one system to another provided ten clear parental demands (Barnard, 2015). These included the obvious ones written into questionnaires such as good teachers, discipline, no bullying, and good communication. However, by drilling deeper into the demand list a descriptor formed that parents agreed met the partnership requirement. Parents often recalled their experiences at lower school, talking to other parents and school staff at the school gate.

What became clear for parents is that they wanted someone in the school they could talk to about their child—someone who would listen at critical learning times and someone who knew their child almost as well as they did, and who could intervene as needed. This means that such a partnership has to reach a degree of trust whereby either party can intervene without first seeking the approval of the other. There is no doubt that parents want to share a more complete learning picture and have a more genuine and collaborative partnership. They want to be good parents, and they want complexity, not complicated!

## PARENT PARTNERSHIP AND ASSESSMENT
## FOR LEARNING (AFL)

When a parent, a student, and a tutor engage in a learning conversation, they are reflecting on learning, reviewing what has happened so far, and strategizing for the next stage. They are engaging in summative assessment writ large, the child's big learning picture that needs coloring-in.

Schools tend to highlight the importance of formative assessment, the feedback process between teacher and student. It is a highly technical area where research reveals so much that can go wrong. The idea is that a teacher can modify pedagogical approaches to maximize learning effectiveness based on the interaction between teacher and student. Formative assessment seeks evidence that learning has occurred and can be improved.

Less discussed is summative assessment, the kind of judgments arrived at over time; both kinds of assessment can result in feedback interventions and strategies for improvement, and both are linked. Assessment cannot be the domain of the teacher alone, and summative assessment can be so much more because it offers an overall perspective like a systems thinking view.

It need not be just an overview of performance conducted by a child's subject teacher over time, but can embrace a critical examination of learning across all subjects to seek out any commonalities and obstructions to learning. This is where the deep learning conversation between child, parent, and form tutor comes into its own by providing a time to formulate different and more qualitative overall improvement strategies. This is the purpose of the academic tutorial or deep learning conversation—an occasion when student, tutor, and parents take on a high degree of agency and responsibility in the learning process. This is the active engagement of parents, child, and tutor in the learning process.

When parents attend a subject evening and meet with a number of teachers, they are gathering information, making a summative assessment as they go. But this is also the tutor's role. At some point, the overview of parents and their child's tutor needs to coalesce and be further advised by the student involved. In turn, this requires a much longer and more detailed meeting or academic tutorial and better, more detailed information on the table.

## HOW MIXED-AGE ORGANIZATION WORKS

In a mixed-age setting, the numbers problem has a novel solution. A tutor rarely has more than four students from a single-age group and because each age group has different critical learning times, this flexes time over the academic year and this flexibility changes everything! When school and home (parent/child/tutor) are engaged in learning, there is a better chance of growing the child's resilience, grit, and a can-do mind-set besides ensuring the child's wellness. Carol Dweck (2006) offers this further advice:

If parents want to give their children a gift, the best thing they can do is teach their children to love challenges, be intrigued by mistakes, enjoy effort and keep on learning. That way they will have a lifelong way to build and repair their own confidence.

But this isn't easy if players are uncertain what the challenges are or what mistakes they may be making. However, when child, parent, and tutor engage in a deep learning conversation based on information gleaned from expanded reports, clarity and support are provided. All parties can agree on what action to take and make a monitoring commitment to effect improvement. In effect, all parties can pull down from the system the resources needed to perform the support function required. Everyone becomes a teacher and a learner, including all students as the school moves from being complicated to being complex.

The mixed-age school provides information in reports that is more user-friendly and is able to flex time; all parties in the subunits are in a better position to share, analyze, interpret, and strategize; here is the synergy of the mixed-age model. From this holistic summative perspective, tutors, parents, and students can conspire to formulate and agree broad strategies for improvement. This is what parent partnership is, and this is the kind of systems thinking that makes the school self-organizing, able to learn and innovate.

The organization then makes certain that information gathered at the edge flows to the next teams and so the connectedness grows and the VSM forms. Therein, the school creates the complexity it needs to absorb the variety of demand on the system. This is precisely what Stafford Beer advises in the viable organization. If any further underpinning is needed, this is what Dylan Wiliam (2016) said, describing the *secret of effective feedback*.

> In the end, it all comes down to the relationship between the teacher and the student. To give effective feedback, the teacher needs to know the student—to understand what feedback the student needs right now. And to receive that feedback in a meaningful way, the student needs to trust the teacher—to believe that the teacher knows what he or she is talking about and has the student's best interests at heart. Without this trust, the student is unlikely to invest the time and effort needed to absorb and use feedback.

This may not always be possible in lessons where it may take considerable time for a relationship to form but it is omnipresent in tutor time where the child is known immediately. Think what happens when the teacher is supported by invisible hands that together design a collaborative system based on trust and empathy from tutor group to classroom and beyond. Think what happens when we apply Wiliam's advice to the academic tutorial—the learning and support relationship between tutor, parent, and child.

In summative situations, feedback is necessarily delayed but the same conditions apply. Now, it may or may not be that a student has a great relationship with all her teachers, but the school can certainly provide tutors whose single undying concern is the well-being and progress of tutees. The key is to manage the school in a way that promotes trust and designs-in empathy. As most schools know, it is the form tutor who is the key player; this is the person who sees the student every day.

## THE MIXED-AGE RESOLUTION

It is now possible to set out the arrangements for a partnership whereby parents, students, and staff are all engaged in the learning process. So the guidance for systems management in building partnership is as follows:

1. Identify critical learning times in a child's school career. These may occur (a) early on for students settling into a new school, (b) at times when important decisions need to be made, and (c) at times when a block of work (mock exams) has been completed and data (information) produced. These are the times when parents, students, and the tutors need to meet to review and plan summatively. Key strategies for improvement are agreed (see point 5).
2. Make sure usable information is produced (reports) at such times. Such information cannot be data sheets alone but must contain written reports usable by participants (staff, students, and parents). These tend toward dispositional descriptors regarding EQ, the way a child learns, plus strategies for improvement—a complete picture of a whole child.
3. Allow information to flow via a communications system. A full report sent home is a starting point not the finish. The feedback loop must be completed by ensuring that information is used as a means of assessment, intervention, and support, one that creates a strategy for individual and system improvement. Everyone is a learner and so is the system.
4. Make the tutor the information conduit. Deal with the numbers issue by adopting mixed-age organization. Tutors should have only four students from any year group to deal with at any critical learning time. Because critical learning times are peculiar to year groups, these times will vary across the academic year. In effect, the tutor is then ideally placed to engage with parents.
5. Organize academic tutorials or deep learning conversations. The report home starts a feedback loop. While subject evenings still take place to add substance to the report and explain what is happening in class, it is the meeting between parents, child, and tutor that is the game changer. This may take about forty minutes per student annually (four students). From that meeting and the discussion about learning (using the full report

as a guide), participants agree more general strategies for improvement. Remember that building in relational quality reduces workload and costs.

6. Allow a week for the tutor to conduct the four academic tutorials. These conversations need time and shouldn't all take place on the same evening. All participants need to be present. Offering a single occasion and time slot is not the way to treat learning partners.

7. Build a self-organizing management structure with the tutor as the key player and information hub. Hopefully, this book and previous ones offer a primer on mixed-age systems and their construction. Teachers are important, and in this model all are tutors too. When the tutor role is fully realized and the school is fully networked, the teacher role will be so much easier.

## COMPLICATED TO COMPLEX

The key to a VSM is who talks to whom not who reports to whom, a design imperative of the mixed-age system. Set out above is the partnership required, and it can only be applied in a school that is vertically tutored. In this model, groups bring resourcefulness and innovative responses to solve learning issues. The idea is to release the creativity within the school and among players.

The process above is the school connecting to more of itself; it complexifies. As such, it strengthens the school's identity and designs-in leadership, resilience, and empathy. As a living system, it does so much more. The school starts to move from self-construction to self-organization. It changes its behavior in a way that enables it to adapt and innovate by exploiting what systems must always do; encourage information flow and enabling power and decisions to move to the edge, in this case to the tutor/parent/student interface, where it matters.

The danger for schools that change to mixed-age groups (VT) is to think of it as another add-on, a pastoral change rather than the transformational lever intended. VT is not another appendage to the school's pastoral care system but how the school operates as a viable learning system; it is how it understands itself. Edwin Nevis, Joan Lancourt, and Helen Vassallo (1996) put it like this:

> To transform something is to change its fundamental external form or inner nature . . . In the world of nature, a caterpillar is transformed into a butterfly; its DNA remains unchanged, but its form and properties are fundamentally different. A butterfly is not a caterpillar with wings strapped on its back.

It is bad form to quote yourself, but as a kind of homage to the great systems thinker Russell Lincoln Ackoff (1919–2009), rules can be broken! This is the situation (Barnard, 2015).

> The problem we see, is not the problem there is. If we try and solve the problem we think we see rather than the problem there is but don't see, we create more problems than there are; this means that the original problem, the one we didn't see as a problem, becomes an even bigger problem. If the problems we see were the problems that need to be resolved, we would have resolved them by now. The fact that we cannot resolve the problem we see means that the real problem, the one we can't see, is still a problem and remains unresolved. So the real problem is not just the problem we cannot see or even the ones we think we see, but is the way we see the problem. If we can change the way we see the problem, there is a better chance of *dissolving* the problem that causes all of the other problems.

It seemed to make sense at the time and, hopefully, still does!

## Chapter 10

# Distributed Leadership, Psychology, and Collective Teacher Efficacy

Reducing three enormous topics to a single chapter is foolish but necessary. Like most things in systems thinking, the concern is more how these topics are organizationally linked and whether they can actually exist in a same-age context. The heresy here is simple; distributed leadership in a same-age system is nonexistent whether it be an individual school or multiacademy rust. In other words, the same-age schools have the same inherited leadership structure they have always had. Some titles may have changed but not the tasks.

Today, we are confronted with an increasing array of leadership models from which to choose and their various descriptors. These include *behavioral, situational, transactional, transformational, participative*, and so on. In schools, we might add *instructional (increasing), pedagogical (popular with the research community)*, and *learner-centered (declining)*, and among recent additions are *systems leadership* and *distributed leadership*. There are many more.

An alternative is to describe leaders by traits and habits that their followers believe they should have; *visionary, heroic, moral, positive, purposeful*, and *charismatic* spring to mind. Such shopping lists are incredibly long, and their use is questionable. We tend to notice their absence more than their presence, but they make us realize we are dealing with a complex topic.

Different leverage points create very different systems. By now, readers are aware of the structure of same-age schools and how these depend upon hierarchy and instructions cascading from the top, and how this model gets more and more complicated over time. Such schools separate the pastoral and academic functions and exhibit layer-cake structures, places where information is locked away or difficult to access. Such organizations tend to be slow and cumbersome and often frustrating places in which to work, and tend toward a model where one-size-fits-all.

Schools that have adopted mixed-age systems have made the first move to delayering but still find themselves locked into a pyramidal organization. These schools have significantly improved learning relationships, are more aligned to motivational psychology, and have started to develop their leadership structure in the distributed way that a viable systems model (VSM) demands. They have moved sufficiently to envision better processes and practices but not far enough to fully realize them but they are evolving.

## LEADERS AND MANAGERS

Keith Grint (2010) proposes that leadership is not about competencies but relationships and is best understood in terms of followers, probably the most useful statement we are likely to hear on the subject given its implications. Grint makes a useful distinction between terms like *leadership, command,* and *management* according to the context in which each is applied.

*Managers* deal with *tame* problems that have arisen before and use standard procedures to resolve issues. *Command* is used when a crisis occurs and an urgent decision is required. *Leadership* comes into its own when the organization faces problems that take on a *wicked* form (discusses earlier), one so complex that no solution is evident, let alone likely. A head teacher turning around a failing school or one undergoing reorganization is often confronted with a wicked problem that can take years to dissolve and fully resolve. This is where the term *leadership* can be more aptly applied. This head is dealing with relational issues, and these are always tricky.

Of course, it helps to know that a problem exists and what the nature of that problem is and having the courage to confront it. There is little to be gained developmentally by training leaders to manage a bad same-age system better; yet, this is exactly what is happening. Separating (that word again!) leadership from the system as though the two are unconnected seems odd. Leaders at a minimum should understand the system they are leading but this doesn't seem to be the case. System reality is swapped for system vison as the attainable is swapped for the unattainable. Grand vision has by far the greater chance in ending in disaster in the absence of systems thinking. Otherwise, such leaders are really managers of messes.

Robert Greenleaf (1970), founder of *servant leadership*, explains the concept as follows:

> The leader-first and the servant-first are two extreme types. Between them there are shadings and blends that are part of the infinite variety of human nature . . . The difference manifests itself in the care taken by the servant-first to make

sure that other people's highest priority needs are being served. The best test, and difficult to administer, is: Do those served grow as persons? Do they, while being served, become healthier, wiser, freer, more autonomous, more likely themselves to become servants? And, what is the effect on the least privileged in society? Will they benefit or at least not be further deprived?

This *pull* leadership model has many attractions, not just because it is enabling and respectful of others but also is one more likely to lead to self-organization and the kind of viable systems model discussed earlier. The servant is also a follower and so recognizes the followers' needs, a relational matter in Keith Grint's terms. When senior staff return to the role of form tutors as mixed-age schools demand, they are better able to understand, practice, and serve the needs of those doing the value work by absorbing system demand. Then, and only then, can the school begin to understand the concept of distributive leadership as practice.

## DISTRIBUTED LEADERSHIP

The hierarchical command structures in schools promoted by same-age systems are basically the same as they ever were. The advent of school chains and multiacademy trusts changes this not one jot. Given that the old command model is the same as before, why is it that so many suddenly think that leadership has somehow changed and become distributed? The opposite (as ever) is the case. The answer may lie in the need to hold those at the base of the system highly accountable for failures not of their making.

Servant leadership should be the perfect description of *distributed leadership*. Within its remit is the possibility of decisions and interventions being made when and where needed by those closest to the action where value is added and learning occurs. These are the many places where our players interact and are readily identified by mixed-age schools. Distributed leadership in a mixed-age school is what it says on the tin; everybody, including every student, parent, and member of staff, is a leader, so we can discount such an idea in a same-age system marked as it is by separation and limitation.

Alma Harris (2003) noted, "Despite a substantial research base, a singular, overarching theory of leadership has proved elusive." Not only is there no consensus, but also it appears there are "as many perspectives on school leadership as those who research and write about them."

The basic theory of distributed leadership is sensible; we need leadership and support to be on tap everywhere in a learning organization and especially so for every child when direction is uncertain. It cannot be the prerogative of static permission layers where information is locked away and difficult to access, neither should teachers shoulder sole responsibility for system failures not of their making. The onus is on schools to create the conditions where all players take on responsibility and contribute, and this means changing leadership as practice.

Alma Harris and James Spillane (2008) describe the distributed leadership model as follows:

> A distributed model of leadership focuses upon the interactions, rather than the actions, of those in formal and informal leadership roles. It is primarily concerned with leadership practice and how leadership influences organizational and instructional improvement.

It is a fine concept and describes perfectly the flat organizational features of Stafford's VSM, where running a successful ship depends upon the interactions of the crew and how they work together for a common cause. In this definition, leadership is freed to form and reform wherever needed according to context. In a deep learning conversation, the child or parent may well assume the leadership role and take on the responsibility. It depends on the context and who is best suited for the task.

Given the pressures schools face, this is where schools should ideally be. Power should be redistributed to allow decision-making wherever needed; it should be recognized that the old heroic, competency-based style of leadership is no longer sufficient in a joined-up world. The challenge, Harris and Spillane suggest, is how to maximize the potential of distributed leadership in a way that leads to organizational improvement and transformation. It actually works the other way round. The system's structure has to change first; otherwise, no redistribution can occur.

Trying to apply distributed leadership to the current same-age model is close to futile. There is no evidence that transformation and organizational improvement describe the current direction of travel—quite the contrary. So, there really is little point talking about distributed leadership, no matter how desirable, because without system change it simply cannot happen to the extent that warrants such an accolade. There are always limits to what is allowed in terms of responsibility and agency. Heads busy themselves managing failure demand, bureaucracy, and system fallout, not transformation and innovation. Schools are then required to apply inappropriate management tools (we'll come to these later) borrowed from the market and the kind of arbitrary measures that lead them to convergence and sameness. Such organizations require no redistribution as they shuffle along.

One of the better descriptions of distributed leadership emanates from the three characteristics described by Bennett et al. (2003). These are broadly described as the following:

- An emergent property of a network of interacting individuals;
- Operating within undefined boundaries;
- Having widely distributed expertise and leadership opportunities.

This is a precise description of the direction of change being adopted by mixed-age schools. While the same-age model has no requirement for leadership distribution, it does have a requirement for compliance and keeping to the NPM script. The reaction of these school leaders (not staff) to lofty ideas like distributed leadership is notoriously indifferent and often described in the research as *a smokescreen* for maintaining the status quo. We can appreciate this as the living system absorbing a concept, waxing lyrical about it, but totally ignoring it in any practical change sense! This is not the kind of identity change schools easily take to.

Schools assimilate ideas by redefining them in ways that often describe what they already do; they tick the box. Schools never stray far from what Maturana and Varela describe as their evolutionary biology, while their capacity for proxy-assimilation of educational concepts knows no bounds; they maintain their identity and seek stasis. There is no fault attached to school leaders, but there is confusion. The old industrial model with its accompanying mind-set based on separation and limitation is deeply ingrained.

It is the schools' wonderful ability to manipulate language while continuing to do their own thing that explains why there is so much to be admired in their formidable leaders. Grit, a can-do mind-set, resilience, and more have all been tacked-on with ease, so claiming distributed leadership is not a problem. While stubbornness and self-deceit are understandable in living systems, this can only get them so far as survival is concerned. To be true systems, schools have to be driven by values and connected to more of themselves and their community of parents. This removes the need for self-delusion and enables a school to reclaim a better sense of identity and purpose.

As things stand, schools do what they always do as living systems. They convince themselves that they conform to the educational menu of the day. They claim distributive leadership but at the same time are *commanded* to implement management ideas from the market that are hierarchically dependent. No substantive change occurs or can occur in a same-age system. They happily assume the mantle and describe themselves both as practitioners of distributed leadership and believers in the new ways of management, a wonderfully ambivalent contradiction in terms that only our amazing schools and their high-caliber leaders can rationalize. This is praise, not sarcasm—there is no shortage of leadership in our schools!

Heads will, however, happily demonstrate how they practice distributed leadership by allowing others to share and make decisions; they will use terms like *delegation* and *empowerment*, which ensure that nothing of substance changes. They will always maintain identity and prefer managing tame problems rather than the wicked ones gathering at the school gates. Let me remind readers that this is not a criticism of schools or those in them who try so hard to make schools work. In desperate times, survival is the sole aim of a living system.

## DISTRIBUTION AND *IMPLEMENTATION*—RESEARCH

Despite these concerns, distributive leadership is already a descriptive part of the policy framework in places like Malta, Spain, England, and Wales and is likely to have a contagion effect worldwide. Quasi-experts like to convince themselves that this new design tool is current in schools and changing practices, though the evidence is spurious. Unfortunately, while distributive leadership (DL) has potential, it lacks the organizational restructuring on which it depends but cannot, of itself, create. The organizations stay the same, making DL an overlay that has little impact on relationships or how organizations like schools actually work.

The problem is not so much that nothing will change but that systemic change will be delayed. DL as practiced in a same-age school system is no more than the recycled, bureaucratic, Weberian command model that already exists, one more likely to prevent change than drive it. The transformational imperative contained in the definition proposed by Harris and Spillane is absent by design in a same-age school.

In the new breed of school chains, there will be more meetings for the top leaders, more costs, more missing and broken relationships, more delegation, and more empty claims of collaboration. There will be more compliance and some temporary improvement.

## MALTA

Malta is an example where experts conceived theoretical structures bound by fine words and loose theory without the faintest idea, other than assumption, about how such a concept might work in practice. Part of the confusion lies in the belief that leadership style changes once schools are linked in a trust or school collective; recursive evolutionary systems theory suggests the opposite.

Strangely, as intimated, the system has to change fundamentally before the distribution (DL) can occur, and the mixed-age change lever is the only one available to do this. If, for example, distributed leadership were given full reign and simply set free, it would create the kind of chaos likely to resolve itself by recreating the conditions prior to any random distribution. Similarly, if such a distribution is granted from the center without any system change, the same center is able to reclaim what it designfully distributed inferring that the existing system was never actually dismantled in agency terms in the first place.

This make distributed leadership another Internet sensation, one that has attracted a sufficient volume of high-level traffic needed to be considered laudable. Like grit, resilience, character, and a can-do mind-set, the basic supporting ideas for distributed leadership are sound. But when school leaders get hold of them, predictable things happen that can only be explained by an absence of systems thinking and through the concept of living systems.

In Malta, collegiality has been *mandated* (a command style that recognizes a crisis but rarely works well as a transformation tool) through a document (2005) called FACT (For All Children to Succeed). Schools have been divided into cross-phase colleges or networks. To *mandate* (some might use the term *empower*), change in this way seems anathema to the very notion of distributed leadership. One of the lessons of such an approach is that top-down change invariably means that nothing of substance actually changes!

Research by Denise Mifsud (2017) reveals that head teachers in Malta have a mixed response to distributed leadership to say the least. It is invariably described by participants as a leadership style they already practice (no change) or something that appears to make no substantive difference (again, no change). In fact, reading between the lines of her research lurks a certain system resentment: living systems dislike unnecessary disturbance!

What schools dutifully do is follow the criteria set out in the FACT operational manual. Mifsud describes this reaction as "tantamount to 'imposed' distribution." The pointed question Mifsud poses is the important one. Can distributed leadership and hierarchical leadership coexist? The systems answer is no, it can't! It is a simple contradiction in terms despite the valiant efforts of schools to make something of it. To appreciate why requires experience of systems in which it does work. In fact, VSMs or VT schools in our case are dependent on DL in order to operate at all.

Distributed leadership cannot transform insecure organizations reliant on hierarchy into something they were never designed to be, a matter confirmed in general research. When attempts are made to implement DL, it seems it surreptitiously acts to maintain existing hierarchies and power bases common to same-age schools.

Megan Crawford (2012), quoted by Mifsud, said that distributed leadership serves as "a smokescreen for authoritarian practices." The literature search on distributive leadership conducted for this book is not encouraging, which means that the UK is likely to insist that it happens! It sounds good but when applied to a same-age school or community of schools, it changes nothing of substance and flatters to deceive.

Strangely, the search for validating evidence leads to Barcelona and an interesting study by Jordi Diaz-Gibson et al. (2017) involving eighteen educational collaborative networks (ECNs). ECNs are school/community partnerships, and the study sought an answer to one overriding question: What are the key leadership conditions necessary to enhance ECN outcomes? Put another way, what are the important factors needed to build a community response (health sector, neighborhoods, schools, families, etc.) that act to remove barriers to learning?

From a systems perspective, the question seems odd. It infers that DL changes systems and relationships, but this doesn't appear to be so. These networking ideas are attractive but they are also time-consuming, uncertain, and reliant on considerable enthusiasm and energy to maintain. They can easily die under the weight of their own increased bureaucracy and costs. The overall idea, however, is attractive; it involves moving from the existing professional school culture to networked leadership—itself a major disturbance!

As ever, the problem is implementation. From a systems point of view, the process described by Diaz-Gibson is upside-down. We continue to be drawn to complicated industrial design when it comes to creating networks rather than the kind of organic, relational approach that living systems need. Our organizational thinking has been badly damaged over time by our reductionist ways. Later, we'll look at Buurtzorg as a community model that is entirely dependent on distributed leadership and design a Buurtzorg school.

## THE WAY OUT

The concept is right; power should be distributed; people should be enabled to shoulder more responsibility, have greater agency, be trained accordingly, and thereby trusted to make decisions; but the implementation problem has to be resolved. Schools will not and cannot break away from their own self-construction and machine metaphor while the same-age lever is operational. Neither is empowerment and delegation an answer because these require and maintain power within a set hierarchy.

Distributed leadership as a concept can only be viewed as something that is already the case and same-age schools know it! DL will lead to a situation where leaders will attend more meetings, be on new boards, and accumulate even greater power and pay than before as they remove themselves ever further from the value work. More managers will be required, not less, along with more admin staff. These structures start out with the best of intentions but rebuild themselves just as King and Frick (chapter 3) said.

Those doing the work at the edge of the system should be leading the changes needed. Mandating distributed leadership in a hierarchy cannot work. The hierarchy has to be dismantled, or, in Stafford Beer's terms, made viable by removing layers and allowing people greater agency in an environment of trust, better training, and ongoing support. To achieve this redistribution in a school requires a process of reconstituting working relationships and partnerships and for this to happen there has to be a (mixed-age) starting point, a point where the first domino leads to a system-wide response.

## PSYCHOLOGY

The powerful influence of psychology on leadership and learning relationships cannot be ignored. There is a direct connection between the way leadership operates throughout the school, the way the power of leadership is handled, and the learning that results. In this section, the focus is on psychology and the guidance it offers to the kind of systems schools operate.

Helena Marsh (2015), a teacher conducting research as part of the Cambridge University SUPER schools project, noted, just as many of us do, the degree to which students attribute their own enjoyment of learning and success to their teachers. "The response to almost every question about their engagement in their studies was, *it depends on the teacher*."

Here is the important part of Helena's analysis:

> While I acknowledge that the perceived quality of teaching, experienced or reported, is a factor in such engagements . . . their perception of the relationships they had with their teachers was of paramount importance. (p. 17)

If this is the case, it is fair to conclude that learning relationships are integral to the success of the learning process. In schools organized on a same-age basis, learning relationships between our players are overly assumed and too often disconnected and left to chance. Given this is the case, a major challenge to a large school rests in its ability to promote and maintain quality within the many combinations of learning relationships on which learning depends, including the time it takes for any necessary attachment to form.

In a mixed-age setting, due diligence is paid to psychological well-being and this approach enables pro-social programs to be complementary rather than the compensatory add-ons and fixes we tend to see. The two have to work together rather than one being a cure for the failings of the other. In a mixed-age model, the basic design spec starts with the idea that the learning relationships that drive and support learning have to be in place immediately the child starts her new school and before the child even reaches the classroom. In short, any school design must be informed by child psychology not assuming of it.

Leadership has to be distributed all the way down to students as mentors. It starts at the base, not the top. When older students are leader servants and are supportive and empathetic to younger ones, the younger ones not only feel safe but also that they belong. The younger ones learn how to behave through such attachment experience, not through a delayed program. John Bowlby (1969) said this:

> Human beings of all ages are happiest and able to deploy their talents to best advantage when they are confident that, standing behind them, there are one or more trusted persons who will come to their aid should difficulties arise.

Urie Bronfenbrenner said the same, as did Abraham Maslow. While there is no dispute about the importance of the teacher as an enabler of learning, any learning relationship between pupil and teacher can take a long time to develop if at all. In the interim, there is much that can go wrong in a student's career, and schools rightly provide a pastoral system to catch the fallen. But the better strategy and more sensible design approach is to prevent a child falling out of the system in the first place. This is achieved by ensuring that all learning relationships work optimally from day one in ways that promote pro-school behavior and any rapid intervention required.

The mixed-age lever changes practice to do just this and is dependent on leadership and power being distributed to the organizational edge. It ensures that all players (parents, students, and staff) play their part in the leadership required in all its different forms. The underpinning psychology is attachment theory. When a child enters school, that child joins a small mixed-age group that has her back and is empathetic and supportive toward her.

## (BIO)ECOLOGICAL SYSTEMS THEORY

It is worth spending a moment on the work of Urie Bronfenbrenner (1977/1979) whose focus on child development concerns environmental impact, more specifically, context. As the child develops and physical and cognitive structures mature, the interaction with the environment increases in complexity. The big question that Bronfenbrenner asks is this: How does the world that surrounds the child help or hinder continued development? For 'world' read 'school'.

Bronfenbrenner points out the massive disruption to the child's immediate home environment (the microsystem) and, like Bowlby, he notes the child's search for affirmation and belonging, including the need for a sense of life-long care from a primary caregiver. While same-age systems perform a reactive secondary role, what is really needed in complex and uncertain times are schools flexible enough to provide a more primary support role.

It cannot be a matter of serendipity whether or not a child forms healthy learning relationships with a teacher and other students as exemplified by the same-age system. This is an abdication of care based on assumptions about what is best for young people. Just as schools are perfectly capable of managing a system that separates and limits—one likely to exacerbate inequity (family background–determined outcomes)—so schools are equally capable of designing a safer, more secure, and holistic approach to learning, one more supportive of child development.

Bronfenbrenner talks of nested systems, and this is exactly the model that mixed-age organization provides. Perhaps the bigger question is this: do schools in their current separational form result in emotional disengagement from learning, and do they inadvertently contribute to social disintegration and what Phillip Blond (2010) calls *atomized societies*?

> Look at the society we have become: We are a bipolar nation, a bureaucratic centralized state that presides over an increasingly fragmented, disempowered and isolated citizenry.

Before returning to the management arena, let's take another glimpse at schools and how students see them. In his seminal work *The Social Animal*, David Brooks (2011) uses his character *Harold* to describe how high school is "structured like a brain."

> There was an executive function—in this case, the principal and the rest of the administrators—who operated under the illusion that they ran the school. But down below, amidst the lockers and the hallways, the real work of the organism took place—the exchange of notes, saliva, crushes, rejections, friendships, feuds and gossip. There were about 1,000 students and therefore roughly 500,000 relationships, the real substance of high school life. The people in the executive suites believed they fulfilled some socially productive process of information transmission. But in reality, of course, high school is a machine for social sorting. The purpose of high school is to give young people a sense of where they fit into the social structure. (p. 73)

The purpose of school identified by Brooks has a certain honesty, a hint that schooling is not really all we think it is. It hurtles along within a confusion of social interaction, a chaotic blur forever in movement. For Harold, the school seemed hyperactive, while the classroom became a place of relative peace and calm, respite care from the social demands of school life.

A character from the 2004 film *Mean Girls* illustrated a similar point. The screenwriter Tina Fey describes school life through the experiences of Cady Heron, a child who has been home-schooled but suddenly finds herself having to attend public high school.

> The first day of school was a blur. A stressful surreal blur. I got in trouble for the most random things—"Where are you going?" Oh, I have to go to the bathroom. "You need a lavatory pass." "Okay, can I have the lavatory pass?" "Nice try. Have a seat." If not that, "Don't read ahead!" "No green pen!" "No food in class!" I had never lived in a world where adults didn't trust me, where they were always yelling at me.

Exactly who is the person who knows Harold and Cady well? Where are the older students who should be on hand to help them through? They seem absent in the chaos of the social whirl when the need for stability and affirmation is critical. The bottom line from parents (chapter 9) is the desire to have someone in the school who knows their child almost as well as they do, someone they can talk to who will listen to their story, and someone able to share information and intervene and support as necessary.

The psychology of child development is unambiguous and signals the essential design requirements for schools, in particular the child's need for a secure base from which to explore the world (Bowlby, 1988). That secure base in a school requires particular design features.

The very first meeting with tutors on day one needs to be brief, small-group, and lasting. The second part of induction involves older students from their vertical tutor group, trained to look after the newcomer's best interests and supportive of them (empathy and leadership designed in). The child can now go to the classroom. In this model, practice has changed; leadership has become distributed.


## BACK TO LEADERSHIP

The message is clear. Leadership should be distributed and, when this happens, students, staff, and parents will feel more secure and psychologically attached to the school and each other. But practice has to change first; otherwise, distributed leadership can go nowhere other than be usurped by the same-age system. A century ago, Mary Parker Follett (1868–1933) said this:

> Leadership is not defined by power but by the capacity to increase the sense of power among those being led. The most essential work of the leader is to create more leaders.

The great lady didn't stop there. She understood the importance of systems design and the weakness of add-ons and fixes. In 1918, she wrote the following design specification:

> The training for the new democracy must be from the cradle—through nursery, school and play, and on and on through every activity of our life. Citizenship is not to be learned in good government classes or current events courses or lessons in civics. It is to be acquired only through those modes of living and acting which shall teach us how to grow the social consciousness. This should be the object of all day school education, of all night school education, of all our supervised recreation, of all our family life, of our club life, of our civic life.

Warren Bennis believed that just about everything written today about management and leadership emanated from the words of Mary Parker Follett. She probably never used the phrase *systems thinker*, but this is undoubtedly what she was. She clearly understood distributed leadership.

> A large organization is a collection of local communities. Individual and institutional growth are maximized when those communities are self-governing to the maximum extent possible. (1924)

To exploit its considerable potential, distributed leadership requires a very different kind of organization. The mixed-age setting requires all personnel, including members of the school's leadership or admin team, to return to tutoring for twenty minutes a day. This single courageous and flattening act enables the leader to understand the system she leads, the information needed, any obstacles to flow that must be removed, and identification of the training and support our players require to do the value work. This delayering within a collaborative framework where all subunits play their part builds the trust needed for distribution to work effectively.

## COLLECTIVE TEACHER EFFICACY (CTE)

High on Hattie's effect list (1.57) is CTE, is a concept touched on previously. The idea is that by working collaboratively, teachers are much more effective. Hoy (2000) described teacher efficacy as the confidence of teachers to promote students' learning.

> Teachers who set high goals, who persist, who try another strategy when one approach is found wanting—in other words, teachers who have a high sense of efficacy and act on It—are more likely to have students who learn. (Shaughnessy, 2004)

Craig Jerald (2007) defined CTE as a collegial approach. Teachers in such schools (we are told) plan more, are more open to ideas, and persevere against the odds of socioeconomic status. This definition may be accurate but is open to misinterpretation. A same-age system may interpret this in ways that lead to increased paperwork and bureaucracy, so reducing time for the collegiality needed. Besides, it is unusual despite reform fatigue to find schools not engaged in extensive planning.

And that's the problem. Here we have a statement that has always been the case one directly associated with organizational improvement. The problem, however, is not teachers and any apparent failure to plan sufficiently, nor is it a failure to go the extra hard yards in challenging circumstances; the real problem is organizational implementation and context—the system in use. CTE is not designed in but added on, and this is problematic. It shouldn't appear toward the top of Hattie's effect list because it should be the way schools work.

The fact is that the direction of school travel in complex societies (ones low in social mobility and high on inequity) asks less creatively of teachers, not more, and acts directly on them in ways that are not conducive to collaboration and innovation. High efficacy and agency are the stuff of learning organizations, not teaching organizations. The strategy advised in the literature is to *empower* middle leaders to concentrate less on admin and more on building the CTE needed. Amber Carter (2017) sees the middle leader as ideally placed in the organization.

> An important characteristic of effective middle leaders in cultivating CTE is they are able to develop professional networks throughout the school and beyond through collaboration, sharing of resources and participation in both in-school and external professional learning.

Unfortunately, this approach is yet another attempt to make the system in use work better. Carter has set out the correct design attributes but this is not the way same-age systems work. The connectivity is too weak. This makes CTE a big ask and schools might typically respond by removing the middle leader almost entirely from teaching (a risk) or introducing another layer of enabling management. Carter builds on the six enabling conditions for CTE proposed by Donohoo (2017).

- Advanced teacher influence: providing opportunities for teacher leadership;
- Goal consensus: seeking teacher involvement in decision-making;
- Teacher's knowledge about one another's work: providing opportunities for teachers to learn about each other's work;

**Table 10.1.   Expanded System Descriptors**

| Same-Age Grouping | Mixed-Age Grouping |
|---|---|
| System 1 thinking | System 2 thinking |
| Theory in use | Espoused theory practiced |
| Complicated | Complex |
| Lower-order consciousness | Higher-order consciousness |
| Machine metaphor | Living systems metaphor |
| Reductionism | Holism |
| Self-construction—closed | Self-organizing—open |
| Command and control management | Leader/servant/distributive designed in |
| Professional collaboration desirable | All collaboration designed in |
| Ineffective parental engagement | Parent engagement/partnership designed in |
| High potential for bullying | Bullying designed out and empathy in |
| Psychologically errant | Psychology designed into blueprint |
| Weak collective teacher efficacy | CTE designed—the way the system works |
| Add-ons and fixes needed | System designs in all it needs |

- Cohesive staff: encouraging a sense of team within and between faculties and stages;
- Responsiveness of leadership: leadership that protects the work of teachers and is aware of the challenges that teachers face in their day-to-day work;
- Effective systems of intervention: teachers working together to recognize and close gaps in student achievement.

There is nothing wrong with such a list, and many schools will readily tick each and every line not realizing that the list describes a completely different model. The aim is to somehow make the system malleable and like all reforms it has an understanding of what is needed but lacks the means of implementation. It describes in part the viable systems model (VSM) DL and CTE are seeking to achieve, one that goes beyond collaborative professionalism to include collaborative networks at all levels and by all players (the socially collaborative school based on mixed-age organization).

In the end, it is easier to build this model by levering mixed-age change than it is to apply DL and CTEs as add-ons and fixes—an approach that will require everyone to work harder and in more complicated conditions with increased costs. So, we have all the right ideas but none of the organizational conditions needed! We can end part 1 by returning to table 1.1 and adding some of the areas discussed (table 10.1).

# THE LONG AND WINDING ROAD TO THE SOCIALLY COLLABORATIVE SCHOOL

We need to walk gently into the mess of organizational and managerial assumptions. To do this, we need to sketch in the past and look at the connections. We learn from the past, so any visit there should be familiar.

Remember, the purpose is to take the school as an organization and make it into a system that better supports learners and teachers. This is a design change from horizontal to vertical, linear to nonlinear, complicated to complex. So, we need to know more about why schools organize themselves in the way they do, and this means looking again at the received wisdom of the school and its penchant for repeating the mistakes of the past. To avoid mistakes, fresh thinking is required.

Gradually, we'll explore other systems and ways of working and thinking. The final chapters offer insights into more soulful organizations and the design spec needed. It is a world painted in the color, teal. Particular attention should be paid to Buurtzorg. It may be helpful to read the chapter on complicate versus complex first if that distinction has proved a problem!

We end by looking at systems thinking and the advice it offers for systems design and living systems.

# Chapter 11

# A First Management Trawl

It is humbling to hear the words of Mary Parker Follett echoing down the years, and glancing back we can only wonder at her disappointment. She would undoubtedly urge that schools be given back to students, parents, teachers, and community.

The examination of schools as systems in the first section of this book offers a telling picture of how our industrial mind-set pervades management and leadership. This is a good time to look at the influences on the thinking that have got us to this point and judge whether anything has really changed over time. If we understand why we think about organizations like schools in the way we do rather than the way advised by Mary Parker Follett, there is the possibility of changing our approach.

The best place to start any talk of change and management theory is with Frederick Winslow Taylor (1856–1915) and his *Principles of Scientific Management* (1911). For someone often harshly criticized, his ideas continue to be a major influence today; but first, let's get a flavor of the great man's ideas in his own words—for workmen, think teachers!

Under the old type of management, success depends almost entirely upon getting the "initiative" of the workmen, and it is indeed a rare case in which this initiative is really attained. Under scientific management the "initiative" of the workmen (that is, their hard work, their good-will, and their ingenuity) is obtained with absolute uniformity and to a greater extent than is possible under the old system; and in addition to this improvement on the part of the men, the managers assume new burdens, new duties, and responsibilities never dreamed of in the past. The managers assume, for instance, the burden of gathering together all of the traditional knowledge which in the past has been possessed by the workmen and then of classifying, tabulating, and reducing this knowledge to rules, laws, and formulæ which are immensely helpful to the workmen in doing their daily work. (chapter 2)

It seems that Taylor was also a futurologist describing accurately how schools today are required to operate! At the core of Taylorism are four management principles Taylor called "duties." Taylor was considering things like how pig iron could be efficiently handled to improve productivity, rather than teachers—but you'll get the idea! A tongue-in cheek (in part) interpretation to his original wording has been attached to each management duty below.

- First. They develop a science for each element of a man's work, which replaces the old rule-of-thumb method. (*Study what works and follow the latest effect list. Only use evidence-based methods. Ensure all training is about pedagogy and a study of the evidence. Become masterful.*)
- Second. They scientifically select and then train, teach, and develop the workman, whereas in the past he chose his own work and trained himself as best he could. (*Choose only the right people to be teachers. Make sure they have a research degree. Train staff to work to maximum efficiency and follow the guidance given. Make sure they keep to the work script outlined in the first duty. Make sure the training offered is regulated and standardized as per the Teacher Training Agency. Teach to the test.*)
- Third. They heartily cooperate with the men so as to ensure all of the work being done is in accordance with the principles of the science, which have been developed. (*Try and make sure teachers are happy following instructions by encouraging staff throughout. Remind them they are accountable for their work which will be measured for efficiency, judged by appraisal and rewarded by productivity. Get rid of those who don't heartily co-operate or are unproductive; reward those who comply.*)
- Fourth. There is an almost equal division of the work and the responsibility between the management and the workmen. The management takes over all work for which it is better fitted than the workmen, while in the past almost all of the work and the greater part of the responsibility were thrown upon the men. (*Remember, managers have a tough job given all the thinking they have to do. This enables the teachers to concentrate entirely on their work. Separate practices division by division. Teachers don't need to know everything and need protection. Remember, it's really all about the teacher in the classroom. Managers are there to make you great! We need to keep the various tasks and groups separate.*)

Taylor's ideas about recruitment (an HR issue), developing competencies, collaboration (the kind that maintains work distinctions), rewards and punishments (carrot and stick), standardized measures of success, and so on all exist as *modern* practice today. It seems questionable whether there has been any substantive managerial or organizational change to date. It also seems that deeply held assumptions about people and the degree to which they can be trusted to do their best persist. Hence the need for controls.

It is basic *command* management, also known as *Alpha theory*, sometimes described as an *industrial mind-set*. Taylor breaks work down into its constituent parts (reductionism): efficiency is improved by analyzing the work using functional, social, and time controls. While many argue that Taylorism is returning to schools with a vengeance, others argue it never left. In fact, most of the problems and challenges faced by schools in part 1 are symptoms of a system (same-age) unable to evolve.

Taylorism is a simple idea and easily applied. Bring people together, and train them well to perform set tasks; managers do the thinking and organizing, while everyone else does the practical graft using scientifically proven methods. In this way, work can be easily standardized and output measured, inspected, and rewarded. Had Taylor been around today, there is no doubt he would either be in charge of a government delivery unit or be the chief inspector of schools. Taylor was a Quaker whose motives were very much of his time and well intentioned. He believed that if workers worked more efficiently, work might have more meaning and accrue greater benefits for everyone, something few would dispute.

Most are familiar with school management, so nothing that follows should be a surprise. A brief look at organizational theory reveals that school managers might see their role as a list of activities:

- Planning—thinking and reflecting before acting.
- Organizing—policies, practices, and procedures that regulate employee behavior.
- Staffing—recruiting a suitable workforce to do the work.
- Controlling—motivating workers to pursue the goals of the organization.

Feel free to tick the statements if you agree. In organizations short on time, everyone is engaged with box-ticking! A narrative is constructed from the list that assures organizations are systems compliant and inspection proof. The list above should be immediately familiar to schools and all too obvious. It appears completely valid, and schools can easily say that these are the key management activities in force. But our biology is urging caution. Teachers know that schools are engaged in so much more.

We might add to the list above *Forecasting* and *Commanding* to form a comprehensive description of what school managers and administrators do from day to day. It all sounds very familiar. These are the six management functions identified by Henri Fayol more than one hundred years ago. It seems that age doesn't render such functions invalid. Fayol (1916) also promoted fourteen principles of administrative management that continue to influence thinking today. It is worth comparing these with the fourteen systems thinking points nominated by Deming (1986), which provide a far more heretical and useful update.

Unfortunately, what works in a time of predictable industrial markets and abundant labor fails when organizations become more complicated and outcomes less predictable. Let's try something more familiar, like designing some kind of blueprint and drawing up the guidelines needed to run a school:

• Define the work that needs doing and who's in charge of it.
• Create a hierarchical structure of offices.
• Provide written guidelines and performance criteria.
• Recruit staff to various posts based on specialist expertise.
• Ensure tenure of office as a career or vocation.
• Attach duties and authority to positions, not people.

This is the bureaucratic management model nominated by the renowned sociologist Max Weber at the start of the twentieth century. Weber was all too aware that his methodology was likely to have unwanted side effects (collateral damage) but felt the existing model of business management based on family was ineffective. Important features of this model include loyalty to the organization (not the boss), supervisory power based on position, professional competence, and compliance to set rules and regulations.

The fact is schools today pass on to students more than they think. The way a school operates as a system teaches our students much about how work is done, ordered, organized, judged, and rewarded. Operating beneath the overt school is a secret school with a hidden curriculum, one which ensures that young people leave with a clear idea of how the world is ordered, how they are likely to be judged, what their limitations are, and how complicated and obstructive it is to navigate a way forward.

Perhaps we should consider the comparative "X" and "Y" theory of Douglas McGregor (1960), then a professor at MIT. For McGregor, managers hold two distinct views of workers that determine how an organization works. Theory X is an authoritarian style of management often referred to as *command and control*. (Readers must judge which theory is the more relevant.) Theory X takes the view that people dislike work and avoid it if at all possible. Unsurprisingly, they often mess up! Workers lack ambition, cannot be trusted, and are only in it for the money, preferring security above all. Because of these perceived negative dispositions, they require coercion, supervision, and direction. Testament to these negative dispositions is work hemorrhaging to other locations within the system (failure demand) and gaming. When people inevitably respond by gaming the system they feel is devaluing them, it confirms the manager's opinion (another negative and reinforcing feedback loop).

Theory Y has a more optimistic view of people, a view shared by systems thinkers. Here, work is seen as fulfilling and more like play. It was the Dutch historian Johan Huizinga (1938) who saw play as a vital form of culture, one able to combine freedom and order. Theory Y managers regard workers as people who are reliable and can be trusted. As such, this group works better with less control, an approach that encourages more innovative ways of working and one that appeals to knowledge workers (like teachers). These people willingly accept responsibility and don't need the threat of punishment or the counterproductive lure of rewards—something Alfie Kohn (1993) consistently argues.

The more enabling management style of Theory Y releases human potential such as ingenuity, an ability to solve problems, and to want to solve problems. It increases productivity and work quality.

The assumptions contained in both systems X and Y are true because in both cases the manager's thinking is validated. Put simply, you reap what you sow. If people are seen as lazy, untrustworthy, unreliable, and unproductive, the work environment will be plagued by rules, policies, practices, inspection procedures, intense accountability, supervision, targets, and punishments. People will start to game the system, and productivity eventually falls; recruitment and retention become difficult. When people are assumed competent and trustworthy, they return that trust and accept responsibility.

In his book *Drive*, Daniel Pink (2009) noted how organizations continue to use extrinsic motivational means ideal for training animals (Pavlov's dogs come to mind). Teachers rarely salivate at the thought of their annual performance review and the hope that a reward might come their way—quite the opposite! Teachers tend not to be rewards-driven in an extrinsic sense; neither do they improve performance when threatened with punishment or required to work in a climate of unrelenting accountability and targets. People work optimally (Pink's motivation level 3.0) when engaged in the kind of meaningful work that provides them with intrinsic satisfaction.

If schools operate best using the intrinsic motivation inherent in Theory Y, then using the extrinsic motivation of Theory X is not going to work! The problem is this: teachers rightly think of themselves more as Y, while school managers are encouraged to think and behave as though they are more like X. At the learning interface where fast, creative solutions to complex problems are needed and where value is added, Y thinking is the operational management style needed. We end up with two broad management theories to bear in mind, *Alpha* and *Beta organizations*, simplified in tables 11.1 and 11.2.

**Table 11.1.  Characteristics of Alpha and Beta Organizations**

| Alpha Organizations | Beta Organizations |
| --- | --- |
| Repetition of the past | Principles-and values-led |
| Theory X assumptions about human nature | Theory Y assumptions about human nature |
| Formal command structure | Decentralized, team-oriented, collaborative |
| Rules, specifications, and permissions | Flexible, informal; everyone can make decisions |
| Complicated | Complex |
| Simple purpose—extrinsic motivation | Sophisticated purposes—intrinsic motivation |
| Relies on *Push* theory | Relies on *Pull* theory |

**Table 11.2.  From Niels Pflaeging (2014)**

| Alpha | Beta |
| --- | --- |
| Dead | Alive |
| Repetition | Surprise |
| Rules | Principles |
| Formal structure/command | Value creation structure/flow |
| Mechanistic | Systemic |
| Centralized | Decentralized |
| Economies of scale | Economies of flow |
| Technology: management | Technology: leadership |
| Theory X human nature assumptions | Theory Y human nature assumptions |

*Push* theory (table 11.1) is the model that schools in the UK and elsewhere are required to reestablish using industrial practices like rewards, appraisal, inspection, and intense accountability. It is a basic command structure whereby *can-do* leaders drive change from the top, and a new breed of focused and forceful managers use rewards and punishments, inspection, and targets to make painful changes to achieve narrow performance outcomes in a short time. The *Pull* method is about value creation from the customer's perspective and how people work best. It requires shared purpose and collaboration, and an empathetic approach to the resolution of complex matters. Teachers are familiar with both styles.

Niels Pflaeging offers a helpful distinction. Alpha theory organizations are characterized by the whole being the sum of its parts (e.g., same-age system), while Beta is characterized by the whole being the sum of its interactions (mixed-age). The two archetypes create very different systems: one based on separation and limitation and the other reliant on collaboration and networking.

## OLD PAJAMAS

An early example of Alpha versus Beta stretches back to 1939 and the *Harwood Studies*. Readers are reminded to "think school" and reflect on the problem of staff recruitment and retention in jurisdictions like the UK and the USA. Harwood, a US textile company, specialized, among other things, in making pajamas. During the 1930s, it moved its plant from New England to Virginia, where it set about the task of training new workers. Despite initial enthusiasm, output remained poor and staff turnover high. The factory responded by using more abrasive techniques to meet production targets, including new incentive schemes; despite these efforts, things went from bad to worse.

Industrial relations declined, worker turnover increased, and productivity remained low. The owner, Alfred Marrow, tried everything he knew but had no idea what was causing the high staff turnover. At a loss to turn things around, he hired Kurt Lewin, an early specialist in organizational psychology. Lewin devised a series of experiments at the plant that later led Marrow to appoint a full-time organizational psychologist, Alex Bavalas, to continue the work.

Lewin realized that the push/command style of the factory managers was having a demotivating effect. To prove the case, he introduced a different way of working with selected teams, one that changed the relationship between *managers* and *subordinates*. This included a number of different strategies:

- Collaborative approaches to work
- Team building
- Sharing of responsibility—enabling teams to decide and set production targets
- Leadership training at all levels

The results were encouraging. Teams using the new format accepted more responsibility and became more involved in the work process; turnover decreased, job satisfaction improved, and productivity started to rise. Work became meaningful. Lewin showed that when people have more control over their work, they tend to innovate and become interested and active participants in the operational process. A recognition grew that the purpose of leadership was to ensure work had meaning. The *empowered* groups set higher targets and significantly outperformed control groups, and, when the scheme was rolled out, the problem of retention melted away and output improved.

There are many advantages to Beta approaches. Not only is collaboration designed into the model as a necessity, but it also turns out to be a more efficient and more effective way of doing the work. It is the same for the service sector, as John Seddon (2016) observes:

> Involving all service providers in understanding the true nature of demand enables the development of services that are truly person-centric. Costs fall, lives are speedily put back on the rails and most telling of all, demand falls. Happier people, stronger families and communities, shouldn't this be the purpose of public services? (p. 13)

For Lewin, any change in the workplace requires a change of heart, an emotional dimension based on human relationships and feelings. Stray too far from organizational and social psychology, and things go awry. For effective change, Lewin proposed three constructs: *unfreezing, cognitive restructuring,* and *refreezing*. It is the best way to train schools in system change, and this book is loosely based on Lewin's model. Lewin famously said, "If you truly want to understand something, try changing it!"

Edgar Schein (2006) pointed out important features of Lewin's change process and the challenges that need to be overcome:

> Key, of course, was to see that human change, whether at the individual or group level, was a profound psychological dynamic process that involved painful unlearning without loss of ego identity and difficult relearning as one cognitively attempted to restructure one's thoughts, perceptions, feelings, and attitudes.

To put it bluntly, change is not as easy and can be painful given the risk to ego and identity. The purpose of this book is to encourage *cognitive restructuring* in a practical sense, but to achieve this there have to be compelling reasons why and how schools should move from a system based on same-age groups (unfreezing) to one based on mixed-age groups (refreezing). Any cognitive restructuring midway must protect identity and ego and minimize risk. At the same time, the school must feel sufficiently disturbed to be open-minded to change and to want to change.

The ideas of Mary Parker Follett were never enough to outweigh the rise in scientific management theory, the dominant discourse of her time. Schools never did become the kind of civic community centers she envisaged and the learning organizations advised by Senge. For Follett, our sense of *belonging* to such places is of the highest civic importance. While schools will claim to be followers of the philosophy of Mary Parker Follett and Kurt Lewin, *using the group to change the group*, they are increasingly required to be practitioners of Taylorism.

When the new change lever is activated and a mixed-aged system adopted, the school as a living system starts to unfreeze and is able to connect to more of itself, to the relational support and learning ties it needs. The school learns to embrace complexity and abandon complicatedness. If only such a transition were so simple. As Kurt Lewin said, "There is nothing so practical as a good theory."

And all of this takes us now to the past thirty years and the age of New Public Management (NPM).

*Chapter 12*

# From New Public Management (NPM) to Public Value Management (PVM)

Following the brief management trawl, it is time to consider the management epoch schools are now in (NPM) and to see what if anything has changed this time round and what has been learned; or, as Oliver Hardy might have put it, to see if we have created *another fine mess*! It is important that schools understand the management epoch they are in and have some idea of how it works and, more crudely, what is going on! They will then be in a better position to consider a different option (PVM).

NPM really began in the Thatcher years. Previously, public services maintained a fairly low profile operating in the background barely disturbed by major changes. They oscillated between governmental ideologies maintaining their identity with dignity and were fairly untouched with regard to the use of performance data. This is not to infer governments didn't take outcomes seriously.

In the UK (and elsewhere), a mix of economic stagnation, strikes, low productivity, and old bureaucracy (*stagflation* was the term used to describe what was termed the *British Disease*) led to a growing realization that government departments were ill-equipped to run any service competently, and this fueled the idea of business-style alternatives. Margaret Thatcher famously described the public sector as "bloated, wasteful, over-bureaucratic and under-performing." That being the case, it seemed sensible to change things; hence the birth of NPM.

## DEFINING FEATURES OF NEW PUBLIC MANAGEMENT (NPM)

NPM is characterized as postbureaucratic with a dominant focus on results. Christopher Pollitt (2007) described NPM as a two-level phenomenon:

> At the higher level, it is a general theory or doctrine that the public sector can
> be improved by the importation of business concepts, techniques and values,

133

while at the more mundane level it is a bundle of specific concepts and practices. (p. 110)

Schools will be all too familiar with the kind of NPM descriptors set out
by Gruening (2001). These include budget cuts, voucher or choice systems,
accountability for performance (sometimes interpreted as culpability), performance measures, and privatization including the formation of new kinds of
schools as part of a marketization process. The credo of NPM is that managers should be allowed to manage, to push system improvements rather than
to pull!

The concepts and practices now include new performance measures,
the creation of markets (including performance-related pay, league tables,
tendering and contracted services), structural changes (disaggregation into
delivery units), and viewing service users as quasi-customers. Unfortunately, an amalgam of ideas borrowed from the business sector doesn't
necessarily make for an effective user-friendly and people-centered school
system. Neither, it seems, does it have more than a marginal effect on
outcomes.

When examined closely, NPM is little more than a dressed-up form of
Alpha management ideas. Hands-on managers are responsible for planning, organizing, staffing, directing, coordinating, reporting, and budget-
ing. Measures of performance at all levels rely on standardization and key
performance indicators (KPIs). Markets are the preferred contractual means
of delivering services, and economies of scale are seen as the best means of
controlling costs; the bigger the better, hence the multi-academy trusts.

Our original management trek indicates that we haven't come far in
terms of organizational practice. The ideas of system renewal promised
by NPM were really born one hundred years ago. In fact, schools have
been frog-marched into a management paradox. If we think like system
X that teachers are lazy, underperforming, and unwilling to change, then
NPM appears to be the solution, one that commands change by coercion
and incentives. However, if teachers are actually hardworking, perform
as well as they can, and are open to ideas but are subjected to NPM strictures, higher accountability, rewards, and punishments, many will *game
the system* and adopt the kind of negative dispositions that validate NPM
thinking.

If this is so, we should expect to see signs of this—more cheating in exams,
manipulation of results (in part by excluding students unable to achieve the
required levels), teaching to the test, manipulation of data, curriculum convergence, high leadership turnover, retention and recruitment difficulties, and
loss of well-being. And we do!

## A BRIEF LOOK AT THE NATIONAL HEALTH
## SERVICE AS A SISTER ORGANIZATION

Sometimes, it is easier to appreciate what is happening in schools by looking at a sister organization enduring the same NPM process. Dunleavy et al. (2006) characterized NPM as "disaggregation + competition + incentivization." It is a wonderful encapsulation and reveals a Pandora's Box of assumptions and loose theory dependent on a negative view of how people work, including what motivates people (rather than incentivizes them) to work in public services.

In 2007, Christopher Pollitt wrote a paper to make sense of what was happening in the UK's National Health Service (NHS). For Pollitt, things started to change following Margaret Thatcher's 1989 white paper, *Working for Patients*. This introduced the idea of internal markets. Hospitals became *providers* that sold their services to district health authorities that became *purchasers* (disaggregation). Hospitals also became trusts just as UK schools have, with their own governance and budgets. The reforms began at such a pace that even the reforms were reformed.

Pollitt notes the following:

- The fourteen regional health authorities were reduced to eight regional offices.
- In 2001, these eight were reduced to four regional directorates of health and social care.
- Two years later, these were replaced by twenty-eight strategic health authorities.
- In 2006, these twenty-eight were reduced to ten.
- During 1997–2006, the Department of Health underwent three major reorganizations.

This process hasn't stopped. In 2006, David Hunter (quoted by Pollitt) wrote this:

> The NHS has been in a state of permanent revolution. Its managers have become "change junkies"—able to deliver whatever structures or systems their political masters and mistresses demand. Yet, for all the frenetic, testosterone-charged activity over this period, paradoxically many of the problems to which these successive reorganizations and policy fixes have been directed stubbornly persist.

Little has changed since. Like schools, a host of new bodies, regulators, consultancies, training groups, software providers, and think tanks have emerged all thriving on the fact that the UK is to reform what Hannibal Lecter is to healthy eating. To describe the top-down approach, Pollitt coined the phrase *redisorganization* and the pace of redisorganization shows no signs of slacking.

## SCHOOLS

Pasi Sahlberg calls the equivalent process in schools GERM (the Global Education Reform Movement), which comprises standardized tests, standardized teaching and learning, test-based accountability, control, and a focus on core subjects. It is a business system constructed for survival and profit in a highly competitive marketplace where predetermined competencies are required. It is in essence a means of separation and limitation posing under the banner of collaboration and distributed leadership, and borrows from the "operational logic of private corporations." Ethical asides have been ignored in this mass takeover. Glatter (2017) advises:

> If publicly funded schools can be conceived as civic institutions, with citizenship at their heart, then it becomes questionable whether the ownership of such an institution can legitimately be transferred from civil society to a third party by means of a commissioning and contracting process. For example, the issue arises of whether such processes delegitimize citizen stakeholders, including parents and pupils, who are not party to the contract.

It seems stakeholders are being slowly written out of the new corporate script once any school choice is made. Those jurisdictions that have avoided copying the English tradition of public reform and the messes that invariably follow have relied far more on consensus making the passage to reform far easier. The UK serves as a lesson in how not to do reform; even the OECD notes the importance of stakeholder engagement in any reform process. It may be that the whole purpose of UK Education plc and its many acolytes is merely to serve as a warning to others.

The problem with NPM is people; people do not come in standardized form and yet are required to conform to a one-size-fits-all system. The belief underpinning NPM is that innovation and efficiencies needed to improve performance are driven by targets, accountability, economies of scale, choice, and market forces. Such an idea may seem *modern* and schools may even feel more business-like, but NPM always fails to provide the conditions that enable people in the public sector, especially creative ones like teachers, to be their best. Very few workforces are faced with the wide variety of challenges and degrees of complexity that public sector services have to absorb.

At the heart of NPM are two assumptions about human nature. The first is that we all belong to a species called *homo economicus*—people who can make the right rational decisions in their own self-interest and so are ideally suited to the NPM way of doing things. The second is described by Charlotte Pell (2016); at the heart of what many call neoliberalism is the belief that individuals are *perfectible . . . digital by default and service-shaped.*

NPM has seen the development of charters, multiacademy trusts, colleges, and community systems. These new school networks claim advantages like increased collegiality, innovation, improved results and reduced costs, and of course distributed leadership. None are particularly evident but there is an opportunity for flexible use of staff. John Seddon (2016) puts the problem of costs and efficiencies succinctly:

> Economies of scale as promulgated by NPM, means services designed as factories. It means the separation of front and back offices, monitoring activity, specializing and standardizing work, inspection, service levels and standard times. All of these are thought to reduce costs as they did in early manufacturing factories. But they don't. These things cause costs to rise.

This might explain in part why schools are always in the position of pleading poverty. It is an expensive failure demand system that increases costs both in school and far beyond the school's gates. No blame is attached to teachers.

## PURPOSE, MEASURES, AND METHOD

During the past few decades, business practices in schools have become *de rigueur*; schools have moved from being data light to data heavy. The effect of this change has negatively influenced our understanding of school purpose. All systems must have a purpose, and schools are not shy in stating them. It is not unusual to see school purposes related to academic performance, international citizenship, developing individual potential and character, and others to do with what we might call the goal of goodness.

Deborah Kenny (2014), founder and CEO of Harlem Village Academies, strikes the right balance describing the purpose of her schools in the following way:

> Of course, we all want our children to be well-prepared to attend fine universities and to enter the world of work. But that is not our goal. We see the purpose of schooling as the nurturing of a strong, skeptical mind, a kind heart, and an abiding interest in advancing the greater good.

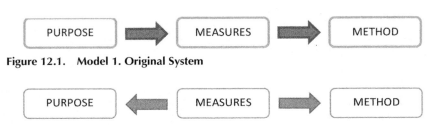

**Figure 12.1.   Model 1. Original System**

**Figure 12.2.   Model 2: The Revised System**

Kenny believes in authentic practice, the idea that citizenship is very much about how schools operate rather a taught program. This way of expressing purpose emerges from the identity of the school and what it sees as its ecological role in the great scheme of things and what the world is asking of it as a living system. Identity has a spiritual dimension, and, for a living system like a school, identity is based on shared values and purpose and what Myron Rogers calls "a sense of what it believes it knows." While a school's identity is rooted in its history, it also governs how it thinks about the future.

For Edgar Schein, a school's identity is formed from its tacit assumptions and is not something to be taken lightly where change is concerned. But things have changed (figures 12.1 and 12.2) since the introduction of neoliberalism and NPM. Purpose has been replaced by measures! Originally, the model looked like this:

- Purposes were broad, moral aims and aspirations based on values. They are derived from what the school thinks the world is asking of it. The school has always tried to see its purposes from the point of view of parents, students, staff, and the community at large (civil society). There was a goal of goodness and being a good citizen.
- From these purposes, measures were derived. The school ascertains how well it is doing with regard to its purposes. It develops an understanding of itself.
- Based on the measures, how well the school thinks its purposes are being achieved, the school changes or liberates the methods it uses to meet its purposes. It adapts and innovates around learning and teaching and wider social collaboration.

This is the way schools have tended to operate with values omnipresent. However, schools have never really measured their purposes fully, in part because local authorities (back in the day) logged all kinds of information from exclusions, examination success, to student career destinations and more; these were fed back to the school as measures of school performance.

As these old bureaucracies disappeared and schools started to manage their own affairs, much of this information became assumed and devalued, a net loss to identity. The arrival of NPM changed the model in a subtle but insidious way.

- In this model, a new *de facto* purpose has been created to improve test scores and this remains the only measure of significance. In effect, measures have become the *de facto* purpose.
- This constrains the method used by teachers and the school; it encourages teaching to the test and gaming. The moral tiller is no longer present nor is the need for innovation.
- The school holds on to old purposes and values by assuming them to be still operational in some way. This self-deceit is the school's covert way of coping with loss and protecting identity as collateral damage to well-being, resilience, and a can-do mind-set accumulates.

The first model relies on connectivity, common human purposes, and the kind of ecological thinking that benefits all. This model is sophisticated, caring, and less harmful but *tinkers its way to Utopia*. The second model relies on basic command and control. It adopts a single set of standardized measures based on league tables to judge school and teacher performance (compliance and system convergence). The school teaches to the tests it is measured by.

To survive, the school aligns itself to the new target culture by focusing on the *de facto* performance measures. Suddenly, teachers find themselves in the middle of a pedagogical debate about the methods they use in the classroom, while the school is accused of being stubborn and unable to promote collaboration or follow the latest effect lists or *what works* (as if what works, works everywhere!). When the school is in full survival mode like this, it retreats and tends to shut down incoming calls.

Model 2 (above) relies on incompatibilities. The school has to delude itself into believing that such a system works for all and that its caring nature still shines through. The staff try and support the students as best they can using what's left of the old system. The system in use, however, is far from the system espoused and is forever moving further away. Unjust comparisons are then made between schools to bolster compliance to the new cause.

Donald Cambell (1979) was concerned with internal and external validity. He observed that the use of quantitative social indicators for making social decisions has unintended consequence; "the more subject it will be to corruption pressures and the more apt it will be to distort and corrupt the social processes it is intended to monitor." *Cambell's law* states that as soon as test scores become the goal of the educative process, they lose their value and "distort the educational process in undesirable ways."

Rebecca Boden and Debbie Epstein (2006) examined the so-called *evidence-based policy* followed by the Blair government. Making policy in a way that appears to follow academic rigor seems completely rational but the process becomes fundamentally flawed (corrupted) when governments control the knowledge-producing processes and determine what counts as evidence in ways that reflect their own bias. Today, schools are locked into the resultant testing and inspection loop, one riven with irresolvable paradoxes.

We might set these out as follows. Model 1 follows attachment theory and model 2, separation theory; model 1 is about democracy and freedom, and model 2 is about coercion and compliance; model 1 is about diversity and innovation, and model two is about convergence and sameness; model one is about creativity and innovation, and model two is about scripts and sameness; one is safe and the other harmful; one follows the goal of goodness, and the other leads to corruption and despair. One is more Beta theory and system Y thinking, while model 2 is Alpha theory and system X.

Mixed-age organization is the escape route should schools wish to make a break for it! It cannot stop the folly of model 2, but it can ensure that every child and every teacher matters and halt much of the collateral damage caused.

Very few head teachers have any idea that what passes for school management today comes under the umbrella of New Public Management, yet NPM has been around for the past three decades. With NPM came a brand new management toolbox supplied from the business world, one that has maintained old management ideas just at the time when new ideas were needed.

NPM comes with a new breed of consultancy whose main delight and means of income rest in the knowledge that there is considerable profit to be made by prolonging the existing problems rather than dissolving them through system change as Kerstein (2005) suggested.

Within a living system there is only so much room for maneuver, which means the drivers and the underlying design principles have to be chosen with care to avoid unintended consequences. A system driven by contracts, specifications, and compliances creates a very different school culture from one driven by professional trust, support, and collaboration. For countries like the USA, the UK, New Zealand, Australia, and elsewhere, the option of democratic system renewal and an adult conversation between providers and users has been largely superficial.

## FROM NPM TO PVM

John Seddon (2016) nominates the key areas where NPM fails. These include economies of scale, marketization, targets, and concurrent increases in regulation and inspection. All of these have a stultifying impact on schools.

There is no cost saving, paperwork increases, system demand escalates, and people end up working dangerously close to overload. As in Lewin's pajama factory, recruitment and retention both suffer, targets become unrealistic, and the carrot-and-stick management style backfires.

The flaws of NPM are many and almost impossible to repair. This book promotes mixed-age organization because it reconnects the learning relationships that NPM seeks to regulate, separate, and limit.

Beyond NPM is a different paradigm called PVM, and, although this is a safer model, moving from the former to the latter will not be easy. PVM is, however, the natural home for school systems and the learning society we need our schools to promote rather than the one that seems to be content throwing plastic in the sea. Mixed-age tutoring, because of its ethics, emergent nature, and dependency on a collaborative learning system, is the model best able to take schools there.

Janine O'Flynn (2007) constructed a helpful guide reproduced in part below. Table 12.1 should be of considerable importance to schools and the reflective discipline Peter Senge noted in *The Fifth Discipline* (2006). The point is not to glibly tick the PVM boxes but reflect deeply on the reality of school.

**Table 12.1.  Paradigms of Public Management (from O'Flynn, p. 361)**

| | *New Public Management* | *Public Value Management* |
|---|---|---|
| Characterization | Postbureaucratic, competitive | Postcompetitive |
| Dominant focus | Results | Relationships |
| Managerial goals | Achieve agreed-upon performance targets | Multiple goals, including responding to citizen/user preferences, renewing mandate and trust through quality services, steering network |
| Definition of public interest | Individual preferences are aggregated | Collective preferences are expressed |
| Performance objective | Management of inputs and outputs to ensure economy and responsiveness to consumers | Multiple objectives are pursued, including service outputs, satisfaction. Outcomes: trust and legitimacy |
| Dominant model of accountability | Upward accountability via performance contracts: outward to customers via market mechanisms | Multiple accountability systems, including citizens as overseers of government, customers as users, and taxpayers as funders |
| Preferred system of delivery | Private sector or tightly defined arms-length public agency | Menu of alternatives selected pragmatically |

Table 12.1 is very clear on cause. Schools yearn for a values-led paradigm (PVM), one where trust relationships are reestablished and success measured not only on examination success and value for money but moral purpose, equity, and value; these are the kind of soulful organizational matters we'll return to later. The route to PVM for schools is nonlinear, complex, and requires a design like mixed-age organization that enables learning relationships (socially collaborative schools) to form in a more complete and community-oriented way.

As expressed earlier, Stafford Beer coined the term POSIWID; the purpose of a system is what it does. The claimed benefits of new economies of scale that (for the UK) began with the mass closure of small and special schools, and the arrival of multiacademy trusts and school chains, have yet to materialize and progress seems marginal at best (NFER Blog, February 2018). This is because school chains are not transformational but a reshuffling and reinterpretation of the past. Costs have risen not fallen; parents, students, and teachers (our players) are less collaboratively involved in producing better outcomes, not more; equity and social mobility have barely changed. The Seventh Report from the House of Commons into multiacademy trusts was similarly lackluster to say the least (February 2017).

To put a price on education requires acceptance of standards that can be measured and what Flynn (above) calls an *aggregation* of demand. Ultimately, it is not competition that drives improvement in public services, but collaboration between players on the ground at the base of systems, and this requires a very different approach to management, one that is more PVM than NPM.

As for targets, these will always lead to distortions in behavior. It is all too easy to concentrate on targets rather than the variety of student need. These, perhaps more than anything else, have kept school management largely the same and prevented its evolution. The myth of targets, the false hope of long-term plans, and even a compelling vision for the future are insufficient to produce system change and serve only to prop up failing self-confidence. None are system levers.

## SYSTEM REACTIONS

Australia is trialing a number of initiatives, including *Learning Frontiers* based on "an education worth having." This seems to assume that the one in use is not worth having! The current system strategy that entails an intense focus on exams and a disconnection from the real world has been recognized as detrimental to learning and motivation. To encourage better practice and increase motivation, "design hubs" have been initiated by the

Australian Institute for Teaching and School Leadership (AITSL) to trial other approaches to learning.

It seems wherever we look (Japan, China, British Columbia, Finland, Canada, and even New Zealand), there are new learning initiatives in operation that stem from a dissatisfaction or reappraisal of the road traveled; perhaps, these are early signs of a move from NPM to PVM. Unfortunately, none will lead to systemic change. There does appear to be a growing consensus that testing has gone too far and needs reconsideration.

In the next chapter, we move from this big picture of management theory to the actualité of the teacher's annual performance review or appraisal. This is the point where the system interacts with those trying to make the system work, the interface where judgments are made, aspirational targets set, and incentives applied.

We start by looking at a management concept called *deliverology* (the driving force behind NPM and the work of the PMDU (Prime Minister's Delivery Unit) that began in the Blair government (1997–2007) and has spread (deliverologists claim) far and wide. According to David Runciman (2016), in his review of Tom Bower's book *Broken Vows: Tony Blair-Tragedy of Power*, it is a scheme Blair continues to peddle around the world in his adopted consultancy role.

# Chapter 13

# The Problem of Deliverology

Let's take a moment to recap on living systems (chapter 5). The school is a social system, a gathering of individuals who work together to achieve a common purpose. The greater the agency and collaboration, the more effective the learning system. But the school is also a biological and ecological system (Maturana and Varela), one that behaves like any living organism. Its many attributes (individuality, self-construction, self-referencing, autonomy, and its closedness as a system) combine to ensure its survival and make it resistant to any changes (reforms) it perceives as a threat to its identity and ways of working.

The metaphor in current use is the machine, one that is designed to limit, separate, sort, and batch. Speed up the machine or ask it to do things beyond its design capabilities creates a high likelihood of detrimental effects on operators and users, especially teachers and students. Changing the metaphor from machine to a living system allows the voices of those working in the school to be heard more clearly. It affords a much clearer picture of learning relationships and interconnectivity, one that can be examined and better understood. These relationships keep the living system informed, and stories arise from interactions that create a narrative that enables the system to better understand itself. This understanding of itself (identity) is based on past experience and involves juggling with its sense of purpose, what it thinks the world is asking of it.

As its identity grows stronger, the school will only entertain changes that fit its understanding of how it sees its role. Over time, like any system, it develops its own culture, including how it deals with any disturbances to its usual way of working. Without an appreciation of how the living system operates and what it holds dear, any reform-like disturbances will be given short shrift or be compromised to lessen any effect on the way the living system goes about its work.

A school will only consider change it deems meaningful. The annual performance review (APR), for example, is unlikely to be seen as particularly meaningful by staff, but the school will still comply in its way. Had the APR in the UK, for example, not been mandated from government, it is unlikely that schools would ever use it as a management tool. School have to comply but will seek to justify the process and effort expended by rationalizing any perceived benefits and meshing it to any common purposes. It will be absorbed into the school's narrative. Of course, some (insecure) school leaders will believe passionately in the APR while others will go with the NPM flow.

Any substantive change in the school's system (a disturbance) requires a collective response. Everyone has to believe in the change to make it work and ensure successful implementation. Problems arise when these social rules of engagement are broken by incompetent leadership, external imposition (especially), or misapplication of research that treats the school like a machine, something that can be speeded up in the hope of making it more efficacious. The school as a living system will do all it can to lessen any disturbances of this kind.

A school can easily change its behavior superficially. For example, the school can introduce an APR scheme with no problem whatsoever, adapt to new curricular demands, wax lyrical about parent partnership, and more. It can engage in self-deceit, adopt a front whereby it shows compliance, and is seen to be doing the right thing; it can tick all the boxes on a questionnaire without so much as a blink and game to its heart's content. But the organism decides the real relevance and extent of any change; it exercises control on variation including the how, what, who, when, and where, ensuring that its fundamental form and identity are never compromised. It does whatever it takes to survive.

How the system is approached, treated, and engaged is everything as far as change is concerned, and this brings us to deliverology and the annual appraisal. But first, the delivery unit!

## THE DELIVERY UNIT

Governments are always well intentioned, often poorly advised, and easily duped by talk of reform, targets, change strategies, and plans. It is their karma to suffer a kind of political ADHD (attention deficit hyperactivity disorder), to be seen to be forever active in their drive to be considered competent. Government, after all, is a living system and as such is dependent on the past (its machine mind-set) to make sense of the present; and this means repeat errors and an inability to understand the living systems it continually frustrates. To be seen to be doing nothing isn't an option.

Blair's difficulty was his inability to motivate change in the civil service (another living system) and make government more proactive. His idea was to sidestep the problem of inertia and create a *delivery unit* to get on with the job of translating policy into action—to deliver on the NPM promises claimed. To do this, he drafted in Michael Barber, a former science teacher and special adviser in the education department.

The Blair government took up the NPM mantle with ease creating a delivery unit to promote better public services, one described by its proponents as a means of turning political aspirations into reality—a model that *can be applied to most organizations*. Although it was scrapped in 2010 and transmuted into the *Implementation Unit* under Cameron's government, the model and its effects remain.

*Deliverology* is a results-led management model designed to improve performance by aligning performance with targets. It is a basic command-and-control approach to change and as such it increases complications; like Taylorism, it seems to be largely ambivalent to motivational psychology. What deliverology recognized was the frustrating gap between policy and implementation—in effect, the rate of improvement. It begins as a process by asking government four questions, very similar to those asked by school inspectors:

- What are you trying to do?
- How are you planning to do it?
- How will you know you're on track?
- If you're not on track, what action are you going to take to get back on track?

The questions seem simple but get more and more difficult to answer as the relationship between each becomes clearer. The trick is to keep aspirations simple by formulating measurable targets. The purpose behind the approach is laudable, and, like Holland and Finland, the intention is to make public services like schools and health so good that few would ever wish to go private. The model tries to make the mechanistic system in use work more efficiently rather than to recognize the school as a trustworthy and complex living system.

The concern here is that the model contains a number of assumptions and job creation schemes (cost increases) that have little impact on customer service and the capacity to resolve complex challenges (absorb system demand). So, let's play spot the assumption! Stay alert! In the deliverology model (below), a delivery unit (Barber et al., 2011) is established that is responsible for implementing "the six elements of best-in-class performance management"—the first six assumptions!

The model (think school) has two recurring themes: first, define measurable targets, and second, hold managers to account for their delivery using carrots and sticks. Here is the model:

- Set direction and context. There has to be a clear idea of what success looks like across the organization and with relevant partners.
- Establish clear accountabilities and metrics. Accountabilities are clear; key performance indicators (KPIs) and scorecards are balanced and cover both performance and health; metrics cascade where appropriate.
- Create realistic budgets, plans, and targets. Targets stretch employees but are fully owned by management and supported by appropriate resources.
- Track performance effectively. Reporting gives a timely view of performance with appropriate detail, and it does not burden the organization.
- Hold robust performance dialogues. Performance reviews are both challenging and supportive and are focused, fact-based, and action-oriented.
- Ensure actions, rewards, and consequences. Actions are taken to improve performance, and there are consequences for good and bad performance.

This is precisely the NPM model schools are required to apply today. Unfortunately, at every stage, staggering assumptions and extensive bureaucracy are built into the model. A great problem with education is consensus about purpose. If the school's purpose is to pass tests and enable the country to climb the PISA league tables, then deliverology via *a target culture* is an ideal tool—but only for incompetent managers unable to fathom how this might otherwise be achieved.

If this same management plan was given to an organization like Apple or Google, it is unlikely that it would be well received, so why should schools fare any better? Readers may like to flick to chapter 15 where Google's own extensive research revealed a completely different perspective on the nature of organizational improvement, one more in line with living system theory than the factory.

Many thoughtful school leaders balk at prescriptive scientific models like deliverology, even though their job tenure depends on the end-of-year examination passes and achieving targets agreed with governors. They prefer to use wisdom and trust and only accept such management methods under duress. Others, perhaps less secure, readily endorse such methods and are keen to show their NPM push management credentials. Even though schools are now geared to a target culture, it is still possible to have a system driven by relationships, values, mutual support, and fun; paperwork and judgmental bureaucracy always gets in the way of these.

Deliverology finds trust issues difficult and maintains hierarchical separation and line-management structure and ultimately takes what John Seddon calls *a dim view of people* and their capability. It induces fear and reduces innovation. This is not a system to encourage risk.

As a former teacher, Barber may have found this model fairly easy to envisage. It is in its way what schools used to do as a matter of course but without the intense rigor. Later incarnations of the deliverology model emphasize the need to build good relationships (at last!) and the way these are built is described as a *critical thread*. Unfortunately, this kind of push management is unlikely to result in good relationships and more likely to make them far worse. Managers, we are told, should ensure they have a good relationship with other employees. As F. W. Taylor said (earlier), "They heartily cooperate with the men so as to insure all of the work being done is in accordance with the principles of the science which has been developed."

Barber is adamant that the school structure debate is over; the fact is there never was such a debate, at least not one to which teachers were invited. Besides, structure is not about the label applied to a type of school or any club it has been invited to join, but to the operational system a school uses to facilitate learning and teaching. The mixed-age system is self-organizing and handles the work very differently and just as rigorously in its way.

The existence of deliverology is a paradox. It comes into its own when the system in play fails to produce the goods despite increased investment. Instead of changing the system, however, it seeks to fix it by acting directly on participants using targets and incentives. It makes the usual Alpha management mistake of assuming people are the problem and so tries to manage them rather than the system that is the real cause of any problems. Proponents of deliverology can only really maintain the status quo and contribute nothing to systemic change—quite the opposite. This approach accepts unthinkingly that the basic school system in use (the industrial same-age model) is organizationally OK and so acts on staff very directly in a vain attempt to make the system work better.

The revised deliverology model continues. It advises construction of a small team focused on performance, *a delivery unit* (presumably the admin or leadership team) that pushes a no-excuses system, "knowing full well that the tendency of any system is towards inertia." But if a system tends toward inertia as a same-age system surely does, the answer is to design a self-organizing system, not one that embraces deliverology and ensures the inertia it seeks to avoid.

Above all, deliverology is a push model. One of the things very noticeable when working with schools is that most leadership teams are already working at full capacity given existing system demand. To take on the deliverology model requires an even larger team, more bureaucracy, and increased costs and the risk of increased disaffection and ill health. It is an approach to management that makes little sense and is largely unworkable.

## THE LADDER OF INFERENCE

Any organization (and UK schools are so obliged) sad enough to attempt the deliverology model in its pure form will quickly find itself climbing what Chris Argyris called the *Ladder of Inference*. The ladder starts with misguided assumptions about human nature and motivation, and implausible cognition of reality and facts. The ensuing process of decision-making involves a climb that starts on the first rung with *selected reality*. This is followed by the second rung that is *interpretation*, then *further assumptions*, followed by *misplaced conclusions*, then *beliefs and actions* (Argyris, 1990).

Using the Ladder of Inference means the higher you climb, the wronger you get. On glancing down from the fifth rung, the school *leadership* team will observe that most of the school's staff have walked away, staff well-being has gone into meltdown, and those left have become compliant, disillusioned pen pushers. More worryingly, there's no one holding the ladder!

Deliverology is a model that politicians love: it is loaded with misleading management assumptions, completely impracticable, time-consuming, and psychologically incoherent, but provides a whole tranche of administratively pointless tasks, described accurately by David Graeber (2013) as "bullshit jobs." It will, however, lead to temporary improvement but at a cost to morale, health, and innovation. According to Graeber:

> Huge swathes of people, in Europe and North America in particular, spend their entire working lives performing tasks they secretly believe do not really need to be performed. The moral and spiritual damage that comes from this situation is profound. It is a scar across our collective soul. Yet virtually no one talks about it.

This brings us to the lynchpin of deliverology, the teachers' annual performance review or appraisal, the point where feedback data are supposed to drive performance and staff development.

## THE ANNUAL PERFORMANCE REVIEW

Seddon often said that targets distort behavior, and Barber agrees but with a twist! Barber argues that the introduction of competition, league tables, and targets is an intentional distortion intended to align behavior throughout the system. This seems a foolhardy and dangerous strategy and one likely to result in all kinds of unwanted gaming. One place where this distortion or realignment to the organizational cause occurs is the annual performance review, a statutory exercise in teacher evaluation (UK) used to assess capability, inform staff development, shore up accountability, and decide any reward.

This book started with a simple heresy: the same-age or year (or grade)-based system doesn't work, has never worked, and cannot be made to work no matter how hard schools try. We can now add another heresy to the growing list. The APR or appraisal system doesn't work no matter how brainwashed schools are persuaded into thinking it does. In effect, it causes more individual and organizational harm than good and especially when linked to rewards. The research says as much.

In an organization like a school, the results achieved are never the result of individual performance but arise from a complexity of teams and teamwork. Pflaeging goes further (p. 27): "Individual performance is not just overrated. In organizations, it simply doesn't exist." The same-age model is destructive to the idea of teams from the word go; appraisal is a classic example of a basic management error whereby a clumsy focus on the individual leads to unintended consequences.

Unfortunately, NPM spurred on by effect lists is obsessed with individual teacher performance as both cause and effect, and this makes the idea of appraisal attractive to managers. It cannot work without line management. Work with schools changing from one system to another reveals a healthy ambivalence to the practice, and there tends to be more talk around the competence of the appraiser than the appraisee. As David Marsden (2010) suggests, this makes performance appraisal a paradox. Marsden asks why we keep adopting such schemes when the evidence from attitude surveys suggests they fail to motivate people who neither like them nor believe in them.

## PROFESSIONALISM AND APPRAISING APPRAISAL

As ever, the UK is one of the first out of the traps and convinced that this process improves results—other jurisdictions will doubtless pile in. The question is one of cost-effectiveness in the widest sense. Any study of the rocky and checkered history of appraisal reveals that it has never been a satisfactory tool. It certainly cannot motivate and is signally unlikely to improve performance. The question that proponents must answer is this: Upon what assumptions about human nature are appraisals based? Theory X or Theory Y? (Pflaeging, 2014, p. 27).

No matter how prevalent the formal school APR is, its existence is impossible to justify psychologically or managerially. It can rarely be as hard-edged as deliverology demands in part because the line manager has a high dependency on subordinates to perform well, while implementation in its current form prevents the development of better ways of assessing, supporting, and improving performance. It is in essence a systems blockage and attempts the kind of feedback that is too fragile and ill-conceived to affect performance and stimulate the intrinsic motivation that drives teachers.

This is not to say that feedback is unnecessary, but there two features of feedback learned from teachers and their students worth noting. The first is immediacy; the quicker it is given and the more regularly, the better. The second is direct from Dylan Wiliam; there has to be a bond of trust to enable feedback to work, or what is termed throughout this book as a learning relationship. The process can never be completely clinical and will always have an emotional underpinning.

The idea fed by deliverology is that teaching and learning work can be easily measured with the right data, evaluated against given criteria (standardized test results and ultimately international test scores) and *stretch targets* set to change behavior and achieve even higher targets. At the same time, support and training may be agreed and the appraisee rewarded or otherwise. It all seems so logical and such a simple concept; after all, everyone can get better at what they do, and most teachers want to perform well and be part of a team. At the same time, there is no question that people unsuitable for teaching should be humanely *set free*. There's just one problem; the evidence says it doesn't work!

The examination of the biology of a living system reveals that the school will readily acquiesce to changes that don't threaten the system's identity, and this enables life to stay largely the same. The formal APR far from supporting an improvement agenda, therefore, tends to maintain the sameness it seeks to remove. Such a process and its apparent acceptance by the teaching profession are explained beautifully by Peter Taubman (2009) in a critique of neoliberal ideology (effectively NPM) as follows:

> The rhetoric of blame and fear and the promulgation of heroic narratives of exemplary teachers, which, coupled with the wide-spread use of tests, render teachers and teacher educators susceptible to the language of policy and the lure of business practices and make possible teachers' psychic investment in various aspects of the transformation. (pp. 12–13)

The rhetoric of the need for a great teacher in every classroom and the difference this individual makes is part of the reason teachers feel they must acquiesce to the direct importation of business practices and controls that NPM demands, together with the narrow measures used to judge performance. It makes hardworking teachers feel devalued, unworthy, and ripe for self-flagellation. The fact is that behind the great teacher is a team and a system and if these fail, so will the teacher.

Mockler (2013) describes the subtle difference between *teaching* quality and *teacher* quality. Appraisal lends itself to narrow measures of teacher quality and so endangers or fails to recognize teaching quality as a craft.

> Embedded in a focus on teaching quality is a desire to support and foster teacher professional learning, to encourage pedagogical and curricular innovation and risk-taking and to collaboratively determine and pursue good teaching practice. Conversely, embedded in the ensuing focus on teacher quality is a desire to narrowly measure and quantify teachers' work (usually represented simply in test scores), to standardize practice and attribute blame to teachers where their students fail to "measure up." (pp. 6–7)

If there is to be appraisal, it needs to focus as much on the team, the capacity of the school for social collaboration between players, and professional learning—a systems approach. It is after all the system that needs to be managed more than the staff trying to make it work. What is interesting is the thinking behind the APR, which is often *sold* as the employee's *right* to receive feedback on performance. There is such a right but the APR or appraisal is not the way to meet such a need.

Those who work in schools value and willingly accept feedback but this particular management event implanted on schools from the marketplace remains an unworkable, ineffective, and counterproductive oddity. It is built on misguided assumptions about human motivation in public life, one likely to have negative and unintended consequences and the potential to go very wrong. There are much better ways of giving feedback, enabling people, and improving performance.

As it is, the APR is essentially command-control thinking, System X thinly disguised as System Y. It relies on a kind of received managerial wisdom using control, compliance, arbitrary standards, and external regulation stemming from an unworkable reform agenda, one which sees individual teachers as both the cause of all ills and the single solution. Its effect is to downgrade collegiality, reduce autonomy, and damage motivation, the very attributes on which professional life and staff development depend.

Rather than teach children, the teacher's redefined role is to meet externally set corporate goals, and document student progress to satisfy purposes of public accountability (Brennan 1996). If we believe that teachers are an important and professional part of the solution to the challenges a country faces, then surely we need to stop seeing them as the problem and seek better ways of ensuring their support, professional development, and engagement with work.

## DISCONNECTIONS AND RESEARCH

As things stand, schools are obliged to spend considerable time, effort, and cost in a people-management exercise, one likely to have a demotivating and demoralizing effect and one likely to diminish learning. Rob Lebow and Randy Spitzer (2002) write:

> Too often, appraisal destroys human spirit and, in the time span of a 30-minute meeting, can transform a vibrant, highly committed employee into a demoralized, indifferent wallflower who reads the want ads on the weekend . . . They don't work because most performance appraisal systems are a form of judgement and control. (p. 208)

Many will argue that the problem here is that the appraiser isn't good enough; but that's the problem; this chain has far too many weaknesses, too many opportunities to go awry.

In Teal organizations (discussed later), new approaches involving peer discussions provide a better way of developing, supporting, and training staff. Meanwhile, the APR tells us much about the appraiser's capability as a line manager and much about the frailties of the school as an organization, but almost nothing about the appraisee's real potential! After all, the appraisee's performance is more a reflection of the school's organizational effectiveness, the system in operation (McGregor, 1960).

It is no surprise that many sensible companies have abandoned the APR and sought better alternatives. In 2016, Accenture decided to grant 330,000 employees an enormous favor and scrap its annual appraisal scheme and replaced it with a fluid feedback process related to ongoing work. Companies like Microsoft and Deloitte have also lost faith in the extravagant waste of time, paper, and money involved in appraisal and are experimenting with other approaches.

According to the HR practice leader at the giant research company Gartner (formerly CEB), employees who did best in performance management systems were also the most narcissistic and self-promoting. "Those aren't necessarily the employees you need in order to be the best organization going forward." According to their research, an average manager spends two hundred hours a year on process bureaucracy related to APRs, which translates to $35 million for a company of ten thousand people.

Ann Fisher (2012) states, "Not even the HR people in charge of overseeing yearly appraisals think they're worth doing." She quotes a poll by *Achievers Intelligence* (2012) where a survey of 2,677 people across the USA, including 1,800 employees, 645 human resource managers, and 232 CEOs, found that only 2% of HR people thought that their process of review accomplished anything useful! The survey reveals a discrepancy between the CEOs who assumed employees received regular feedback and the 24% of employees who actually did. Around 95% of managers surveyed are dissatisfied with the way their companies conduct performance reviews.

It seems that more and more organizations are beginning to realize that annual appraisal systems are an aberration and are more likely to create inertia than increase productivity. It is estimated by Forbes that around 90% of companies are rethinking their approach. Appraisal, it seems, is another obstacle to transformation not a means.

The fact is the APR process maintains hierarchy and status and ensures control. It is in essence a theory X view of how people operate. Fred Nickols (2010) sums it up as follow:

> A perhaps less typical but more candid executive might add a final benefit: the formal performance appraisal system shores up an organization's hierarchical authority system. It gives the supervising manager control over the carrots and sticks in what is essentially a carrot-and-stick management system.

The counter arguments are powerful.

- A once-a-year meeting is insufficient and should be replaced by ongoing feedback, coaching, and support. The APR works against positive and constructive feedback given in a timely way; it demotivates.
- It is not possible to make judgments based on a year's work, and this creates an uncomfortable situation for both parties. You cannot base the future on the past.
- In a school, a teacher may have many line managers all of whom need to contribute to validate any feedback and support.
- Schools are forced to build a line-management system that propels them straight back to hierarchical structures and to management sameness and organizational inertia.
- A school runs on a shoestring. Any activity that absorbs time, energy, and costs for uncertain gains and unintended consequences is not viable.
- APRs create individual and system anxiety. The introduction of fear into the system is contagious.

Today's schools have to be agile organizations, and as such, they are superbly equipped to manage such matters meaningfully, including regular feedback, personnel development, realistic goals, and pay. Unfortunately, they are prevented from doing so by excessive regulation and a view that the organizational structure in use is benign and somehow immutable. The fact is the beliefs we have about people shape how they behave. Simon Caulkin (2016) put it like this:

> If managers believe that individuals will only work under a regime of sticks and carrots—controlled by hierarchy and incentivized by money—and design companies accordingly, that is what people become.

As Simon Guilfoyle (2016) so neatly says, "The performance manager emperor has no clothes." But the last word must be left to the great management guru W. Edwards Deming (1986), who described the system by which merit is appraised, rewarded, or otherwise, as, "the most powerful inhibitor to quality and productivity in the Western world." Never one to mince his words, the great man went on to say:

> The idea of a merit rating is alluring. The sound of the words captivates the imagination: pay for what you get; get what you pay for; motivate people to do their best, for their own good. The effect is exactly the opposite of what the words promise. (p. 27)

Here's the message for schools: never be tempted to fix your appraisal system. Scrap it and see if you notice a difference in the school. When obstacles to learning and collaboration are removed and replaced by enabling feedback, the energy that was previously tied up with waste is released back into the system. The living system starts to feel better about itself and is able to learn more. For individuals, fear and anxiety dissipate and wellness starts to return, increasing what Deming called joy in work.

There is one last reason that supporters of APRs offer. The APR is essential for recognizing and rewarding talent. And this brings us neatly to the idea of talent management, a notion creeping back into unsuspecting schools.

Abandoning the APR, schools are required to use it to set targets and decide pay issues. This comes under the guise of personal development.

*Chapter 14*

# Talent Management and a First Look at Teams

From a systems perspective, an organization like a school should prioritize connectedness, an area it still controls and described by Betts (1992) as "open, organic, pluralistic, and complex." Motivation belongs to individuals; system leaders, like teachers, create the conditions conducive to its being. The motivation is in the work being done, the difference to lives the work creates, and the comradery of the team—the complexity of learning relationships that comprise the school. The mixed-age school is dependent on such conditions and designs them in from the outset.

Given these *conditions* and ongoing training and support, people enjoy work, direct themselves to any targets they feel they can endorse, take on responsibility, and take risks—all sound theory Y attributes. These are unique, admirable, and much-needed qualities embracing attitude, motivation, and creativity. If participants are wrongly diagnosed with resilience, character, and well-being issues, the problem isn't one of individual flaws and failures but with disconnection issues caused by the system in use (Barnard, 2018).

The purpose here is to enable the system to understand itself more than it does so that it can be driven by the shared values and goals that define it. As a system, it sometimes requires an infusion of new blood to reenergize the system, and this raises the concept of *talent management*.

## TALENT MANAGEMENT AS MUDDLED THINKING

The Chartered Institute of Personnel and Development (CIPD) suggests that talent describes those individuals who can make a difference to organizational performance. They go on to say (CIPD, 2006):

Talent management is the systematic attraction, identification, development, engagement/retention and deployment of individuals with high potential who are a particular value to an organization.

People who think in systems often find statements like these not only odd but also objectionable. Besides, talent management and talent spotting are clearly something none of us are much good at: every few years, we elect a bunch of politicians, the most talented, who immediately start to make a mess of things and so we remove them at regular intervals. Talent is strange; it comes in different forms and can have very different effects (disturbances) on organizational improvement.

Davies and Davies (2011) believe talent management is critical for the development of successful organizations, including schools. But is this true, or just another cheap NPM import from business land not properly thought through? The focus of Davies and Davies is to show schools how to define talented individuals, develop talent and leadership, and build a talent culture. But making this into a management strategy within a living system that thrives best on the strength of relationships rather than individuals may be a difficult proposition. If there are such people, many would argue that their talent must relate to enhancing common purpose of the living system and building consensus. This is not to limit their input but to give it full reign.

Strategic direction is important and the Hay Group (2008) envisages a change from the *formal management* of the twentieth century to the *connected leadership* of the twenty-first century. It is a move along continuums from hierarchy to collegiality, constraint to flexibility, accountability to reciprocity, information to communications, and so on. But this movement is not necessarily what we are seeing. It is questionable whether there can be any such thing as *managing* talent. Talent can be nurtured, released, grown, discovered, and all kinds of things, but *managing talent* seems a strange idea and out of kilter with the strategic direction nominated by the Hay Group.

## LESSONS IN TALENT MANAGEMENT FROM BUSINESS

During 1997–2001, McKinsey and Company conducted a survey of companies, many from their own *talent indexed* client list, organizations regarded as highly successful. They claimed to have interviewed thirteen thousand executives from 120 companies. The result was a book by Michaels, Handfield-Jones, and Axelrod titled *The War for Talent* (2001) "intended for any leader in any organization, who manages people."

The theory tells us how successful companies are able to spot and attract talented individuals and build a great management pool. Companies are advised to *hoover up* the most talented people, retain them, and cull those who aren't up to the mark. It is the kind of push management idea central to NPM thinking, and the annual performance review is an essential ingredient in the talent management mix; recognize the talented and reward them. In schools, this too often involves removing the best teachers from the classroom where they are most effective.

Following the theory, it would not be unreasonable to expect such companies to thrive and still be around today but sadly, this isn't the case. Many of the *talent-driven* companies that were the source of the survey are no longer with us, while others are no longer regarded as excellent. One of the largest and most successful companies, Enron, collapsed spectacularly, existing as it did on self-deception and misrepresentation. We don't have to look far down the road traveled to realize that many other companies have met with a similar fate. Richard Foster calculated that company lifespans declined from sixty-seven years in the 1920s to fifty years today (BBC News, January 19, 2012). Some school chains and trusts have already suffered a similar fate.

Stanford University's Jeffrey Pfeffer (2001) deemed such a *war for talent* to be hazardous to an organization's health.

> This war for talent imagery overlooks the fact that it is often the case that effective teams often outperform even more talented collections of individuals, that individual talent and motivation is partly under the control of what companies do, and that what matters to organizational success is the set of management practices that create the culture.

Collaboration and teamwork will beat so-called talent pools every time. Leicester City F.C. winning the English Premier Soccer League without any player being recognized as world class is a case in point! The B team versus the A-listers. In the next chapter, this kind of seeming anomaly has been examined by Google researchers with surprising results!

Of course, we all want our schools to be populated with talented teachers, but great teaching is grown and nurtured over time, and such a process depends on a mix of organizational factors such as training, support, context, time, collaboration, and connectedness. There is never a time when every teacher is great, but there is a time when every teacher is getting better at what they do if the system conditions are right; and of course, it depends on the particular talents of the school leader to create such conditions. Any system that undermines the intrinsic motivation on which the organization depends and lays too much importance on extrinsic motivation and overbearing accountability diminishes all that teachers bring to the table.

The Stanford professor did not stop there. Not only is the *war* metaphor wrong, but it is also one likely to lead to other problems.

> Companies that adopt a talent war mindset often wind up venerating outsiders and downplaying the talent already inside the company, set up competitive, zero sum dynamics that makes internal learning and knowledge transfer difficult, activate the self-fulfilling prophecy in the wrong direction, and create an attitude of arrogance instead of an attitude of wisdom.

In an article for *The New Yorker*, Malcolm Gladwell (2002) wrote this:

> At the heart of the McKinsey vision is a process that The War for Talent advocates refer to as "*differentiation and affirmation.*" Employers, they argue, need to sit down once or twice a year and hold a "candid, probing, no-holds-barred debate about each individual," sorting employees into A, B, and C groups. The "A"s must be challenged and disproportionately rewarded. The "B"s need to be encouraged and affirmed. The "C"s need to shape-up or be shipped out. Enron followed this advice almost to the letter, setting up internal Performance Review Committees.

The rest, like Enron, is history. We tend to manage people because we think we understand them and can control them and have the wherewithal to change their behavior with spurious stretch targets and carrot-and-stick management. Our System X thinking is never far away, and such a notion presupposes that other organizational factors such as the way learning relationships and feedback mechanisms work are all OK. Such processes tell us more of the arrogance of those implementing such practices than those suffering because of them.

## TINKER, TAILOR, SOLDIER, SPY

The fact is different people have different talents and different ways of seeing a problem. In a fascinating study by the Centre for High Performance, Ben Laker and Alex Hill (2016) examined the impact of different leadership approaches on 411 schools that needed to be *turned around*. The researchers were looking at the talents needed for the job and the effect these had on successful outcomes. They called these talented head teacher-type philosophers, surgeons, architects, soldiers, and accountants.

The surgeons (33 out of 411) adopted short-term fixes that led to a rapid change in fortunes. Their priority was to improve examination scores fast and to do this required the removal of any obstacle that prevented their patient from recovering. This involved excluding up to 25% of students from school and/or not entering weaker students for examinations, while making sure the examination group had the best teachers (a gaming strategy). This was the most rewarded group in terms of salaries.

The soldiers cut costs, trimmed what they perceived as excess staff, and expected everyone to work harder. Examination results didn't improve but finances did. When the soldier was reassigned for another battle, the staff who were *let go* had to be reemployed to enable exhausted staff to recover. Costs then increased, and it seems that everyone was left to wonder just what happened as the school slowly returned to its previous state!

The accountants tried to grow their school out of trouble. They market their school well and create revenue streams to boost funding. It seems, however, that this kind of management approach creates an imbalance with less focus on student achievement. Examination results remain static because this particular area is not prioritized in the same way.

The philosophers formed the largest group (51%), many of whom were former teachers of English literature. They focused on trying to promote better teaching rather than the connectivity between staff, improvements to the working environment, and funding. Philosophers were convinced that teachers held the answers to improvements in behavior and tests. Unfortunately, these schools tended to coast or decline. It seems that these heads talked a good game but had no real understanding of systems leadership and the many other factors needed to make a good school. This soon resulted in low morale and frustration.

This group was the most rewarded in terms of public honors despite being the worst performing group both during and after its tenure.

The architects turned out to be the highest performing group. (This book is all about design after all!) The architects believed that schools fail because of design issues. This group adopted a design strategy (or holistic systems thinking style) where all the parts of a school have to work together, an approach that takes time (in a hierarchical same-age system!). Notably, many of these architect head teachers started their teaching careers later and so were less contaminated by the school's organizational practices. Their tenure saw no marked improvement to results over the first three years. Instead, they focused on building good relationships and provision for underperforming students. This group received the lowest salaries but its schools continued to improve even after its tenure.

Sadly, many architect heads have been removed for failing to apply the skills of the fast turnaround surgeons! It seems that turnaround is expected to be very short in NPM terms despite the long-term cost. The architects' approach was to design a system that connected people in a way that grew their leadership capabilities and releasing whatever latent talent existed in their schools. It seems that they intuitively understood the nature of failure demand and the importance of being able to absorb complexity. Their priority was not to manage talent but to design a system sufficiently connected to give existing talent the full reign it needs.

Schools believe that the world is a competitive and paranoid place and consultancies and experts often prey on the illusion that they see the world more clearly than their clients and can prove it! Architects didn't fix parts or rely on add-ons; they designed a system which they viewed from 1,000 meters; they needed to see the whole school working as one.

Schools are awash with the kind of reform thinking that seeks to influences policy, speed up the system, and parachute in push managers like soldiers and surgeons rather than the architects who design networks, enable flow, grow leadership, and understand social collaboration.

Even planning is problematic. Much as it is comforting to have a ten- or even a five-year plan; the bits of the future needed to write such plans are unavailable. School organizational improvement isn't easy but being values-led and designing empathetic relationships in rather than trying to add them on, is the safer, long-term bet. The architects who did this were found to be modest and insightful. They designed an enabling system, one that connected to more of itself, and that same system grew its own talent.

Sooner or later, architects (the most likely group) will discover mixed-age groups; it will be in their design somewhere! We need to leave the management aberrations of deliverology, NPM, and so-called talent management schemes and end with a few wise words. Simon Caulkin (2016) calls for better management theory, one applicable to all organizations including schools.

> Without being po-faced, it needs to incorporate more rounded assumptions about human nature, allowing trust and intrinsic motivation to become as self-reinforcing as greed and suspicion currently are; recognition of the need to nourish the unique properties of the company; and the obvious and observable notion that a company thrives when it simultaneously pays attention to the interests of employees, suppliers and shareholders and thereby those of the wider community too.

In 1990, W. Edwards Deming responded to a request from Peter Senge, whose own seminal work, *The Fifth Discipline*, was about to be published. Senge had asked Deming for a comment for the book's jacket. Deming, who had spent a lifetime trying to change management thinking, wrote this:

> Our prevailing system of management has destroyed our people. People are born with intrinsic motivation, self-respect, dignity, curiosity to learn, joy in

learning. The forces of destruction begin with toddlers—a prize for the best Halloween costume, grades in school, gold stars—and on up through university. On the job, people, teams, and divisions are ranked; reward for the top, punishment for the bottom. Management by Objectives, quotas, incentive pay, business plans, put together separately, division by division, cause further loss, unknown and unknowable.

Deming was in his ninetieth year when he wrote these words. It is a quote we should all return to again and again.

# Chapter 15

# Google and Emerging Thinking

The corporate evaluation exercise used at Enron was known as "rank and yank" and has probably already arrived at a school near you! Having a *talent mind-set*, one that fawns over the best, is not the way to go and should be avoided. For schools, the real challenge is to get the very best out of staff, students, and parents (team school) and create a connected system able to recognize that everyone has talent and a contribution capable of being nurtured.

The better way of developing people is through the learning relationships that teamwork, mentoring, and collaboration bring to the party and to stop assuming that the pyramidal organizational architecture and the same-age system in current use are either benign or sufficiently able to do the job. Schools have teams and team potential everywhere but too much is either unexploited or inaccessible because of the school's operational structure. It seems strange to ask schools to abandon a complicated system for one that is more complex and one that turns management and leadership on its head—a process it seems that only architect leaders seem willing to take on.

It is easy to illustrate how same-age structure limits and separates so many aspects of school life, and how reliant on assumptions, rather than research, managers have become. The real challenge is persuading schools to engage in a conversation about how schools work as systems. Most are now in a state of constant flux and persuaded that it is only the classroom that matters, not realizing that learning and teaching are effected by learning relationships throughout the school; everyone has a part to play in the school's success and teamwork is critical.

Today, schools are drifting further away from being the self-organizing places we need them to be. Never before has there been so much supervision, so much exercise of control, so much unusable advice, and so much mistrust. League tables and intense accountability have introduced fear into the system, undermined the confidence of a profession, and set schools on a single convergent strategy toward set competencies. At the very point where complexity and diversification are needed, the preference is to retreat to the past.

## DOMINANT THINKING AND EMERGING THINKING

We arrive at a point where it is useful to broadly classify organizational thought. *Dominant* thinking tends to replicate our industrial past. It is this hand-me-down thinking drilled in at business schools that has made schools compliant and prone to NPM business ideas. Ian Burbidge (2017) explains it like this:

> Public services remain largely based on outdated models that assume a linear relationship between inputs, outputs and outcomes and that change is best achieved by pulling the big levers of central government: legislation, tax and spend, and earmarked funding streams. The legacy of this deeply ingrained thinking is the idea that if only we can properly understand an issue, and perfectly design a response, the problem will be solved. These responses are too rigid, path dependent and pre-ordained and consequently do not readily enable a systemic view of a particularly challenging social issue to be taken.

Emerging thinking brings about desirable change from within and throws most of the NPM management rulebook away. Banathy (1991, 1996) argues the need to move beyond the traditional paradigm, where inquiry is dominated by reductionism, objectivity, and determinism. This approach, he says, is unable to cope with the "complexity, mutual causality, purpose, intention, uncertainty, ambiguity, and ever accelerating dynamic changes that characterize our systems and larger society environment."

Table 15.1 is not an either/or model but one that indicates the kind of mind-set and organizational arrangements in use at any one time. It indicates a direction of desirable change more suited to putting the *service* back into public services including living systems like schools. By being more aware of the management thinking in use, it is possible to identify when we are using a fixed mind-set response rather than the more challenging, can-do growth mind-set that Carol Dweck advises. But this requires managers to learn alternative systems approaches, and there is little evidence of this happening in leadership programs, courses on system repair, and teacher training.

The linear same-age system is driven by dominant thinking. It seeks to control complexity and in so doing creates a complicated organization unable

**Table 15.1.  Dominant Thinking and Emerging Thinking**

| Dominant Organizational Thinking (Positional Authority; Build Hierarchy) | Emerging Organizational Thinking (Shared Responsibility; Build Connectedness) |
|---|---|
| *Linear: Same-Age* | *Nonlinear: Mixed-Age* |
| Power through hierarchy | Power/leadership distributed (interconnectivity) |
| Mission and vision | Shared values and purpose |
| Rational argument | Making sense through emotional connection (EQ) |
| Leadership driven (top-down) change | Viral (grassroots driven)/creative (viable) |
| Tried and tested ideas (handed down) | "Open" approaches, shared ideas, coaction |
| Transactional | Transformational |
| Permission levels and knowledge dumps | Decisions and interventions taken where needed |
| One-size-fits-all | Individualized as far as possible |
| Managerial leadership | Leadership enabled as needed |
| Complicated | Complex |

to absorb value demand and unable to control costs. It has no alternative other than to create add-ons and fixes in the form of pro-social programs and to employ an army of ancillary staff to deal with complications arising from failure demand and complication. This makes such a model self-perpetuating until it reaches a point where the investment in and the outputs achieved no longer correlate. In systems terms, this approach acts like a kind of negative reinforcing feedback loop likely to lead to collapse.

The complex nature of mixed-age organization provides a very different management scenario. Its collaborative structure reduces the need for add-ons and fixes by absorbing the variety of demand on the system with greater ease; by building in quality from the outset, costs reduce. Because the organization is of itself empathetic and supportive of learning, this reduces (failure) demand and the heavy reliance on pro-social programs and ancillary support to fix kids who don't need fixing.

It requires leadership and management to be everywhere but always close to the student; this means that everyone, including every child, has to adopt a leadership and mentoring role; the organizational structure flattens as a VSM demand. When this happens, complex issues are dealt with at source before they become difficult and expensive failure demand issues.

The next section takes us to Google, one of the world's most successful companies, and two pieces of research and two (perhaps) surprising results. Both have implications for schools, the curriculum, and how schools should operate, and provide a further endorsement for mixed-age groups.

## FUTURE SKILLS, GOOGLE, AND PROJECTS
## OXYGEN AND ARISTOTLE

Throughout, mention has been made of competencies, something the OECD seems obsessed by, including trying to predict the workplace needs of 2030. The advice to schools is to improve the areas measured by PISA and get the core STEM subjects (science, technology, engineering, and mathematics) right. This is the conventional wisdom but while these hard skill subjects are rightly very important it seems they are far from all that is needed, and as such their status in schools may be overly simplistic in terms of workforce readiness.

The OECD's recommendations for global competence are of a different order and invite consideration of the knowledge, skills, values, and attitudes needed to do the following:

• Examine local, global, and intercultural issues.
• Understand and appreciate the worldview of others.
• Engage in open, appropriate, and effective interactions across cultures.
• Take action for collective well-being and sustainable improvement.

So how does this connect with schools and education? The immediate response of educationists might be to take these concepts, build a program around them, and apply a test that measures the teacher's effectiveness of delivery. This is a mistake and a weakness that publishing companies are all too willing to exploit. Most schools have already devised better methods and know that the best approach is real life—to make them authentic through travel, twinning, and openness to diversity.

The beauty of mixed-age organization is its dependence on these concepts for the learning, knowledge, skills, and attitudes needed in an interdependent global world—an ecological mind-set. The real answer is to ensure that these concepts are designed in using social collaboration (the authenticity of the way the school works) and not be reliant on courses and add-ons.

In the world of business, companies are anxious to maximize productivity, something called *employee performance optimization*. It's happening in schools coerced into believing they have a teacher performance problem, a matter that dominates reform thinking. It seems, however, that such an idea is far from simple and not necessarily the way to go. More and more, a team approach is required and this requires collaboration, an activity estimated by the Harvard Business School to occupy around 50–75% of an employee's time in knowledge industries.

There are many advantages to collaboration: mistakes are seen earlier, better solutions materialize, productivity increases, and people are happier.

For schools too, collaboration is important but schools are poorly positioned to afford the time and collaboration is far from the direction a high-stakes environment encourages. The business of teams, how they are formed, and why some are more successful than others became a puzzle for Google, a company renowned for seeking out talented individuals with STEM expertise.

Google set about analyzing decades of research into teamwork covering education, background, gender, social activity, and more. Despite considerable effort, Google was unable to pin down any obvious success factors among its own teams. Eventually, researchers noticed how groups started to develop cultural norms of behavior that seemed to be of particular benefit. When the researchers drilled deeper into the groups that seemed more successful, the patterns became clearer. Cathy Davidson (2017), writing in the *Washington Post*, described the research carried out by Google.

> In 2013, Google decided to test its hiring hypothesis by crunching every bit and byte of hiring, firing, and promotion data accumulated since the company's incorporation in 1998. Project Oxygen shocked everyone by concluding that, among the eight most important qualities of Google's top employees, STEM expertise comes in dead last.

Google's hiring policy involved tracking down the best STEM expertise around, but when Google looked at group success the results were not as expected. The characteristics of success all turned out to be soft skills:

* Being a good coach;
* Communicating and listening well;
* Possessing insights into others;
* Having empathy toward and being supportive of colleagues;
* Being a good critical thinker and problem solver; and
* Being able to make connections across complex ideas.

If this is related to schools, the success characteristics and social skills set out above are not only given full range in mixed-age groups but also practiced every day. Google's research shows the vital importance of soft skills in a high-tech environment, perhaps any environment.

Following on from *Project Oxygen* came *Project Aristotle* that looked at inventive and productive teams employed at the company. The A teams consisted of Google's top scientists, while the B teams were a general mix of personnel. Once again, the results were a surprise. Analysis showed that the B teams came up with more important and productive ideas than the A teams. As the Google researchers again drilled down into this curious turn of events, they discovered that the best teams also exhibited a range of soft skills.

The list below starts with a question mark for readers to guess the top placement!

• ?
• Equality;
• Generosity;
• Curiosity toward the ideas of teammates;
• Empathy and EQ (emotional intelligence).

Topping the list (above) is emotional safety, a psychological notion that can be interpreted in a very simple phrase: No Bullying! Emotional safety requires that everyone is heard, everyone is allowed to speak, and everyone feeling free to make mistakes. For schools, the same-age peer environment is unlikely to have sufficient listening skill and empathetic dispositions to be safe, while the mixed-age group has all the dispositions needed.

Cathy Davidson calls attention to similar findings from Chevron, IBM, and elsewhere. These are companies that understand how their survival and identity are dependent upon connectedness, the sharing of information and ideas among those that make the organization work. As a living system, Google understands that it has to listen, be generous, be safe, be curious, and be equal—and being recursive, so must all of its teams and individuals.

Google has done what Google always does. It gives us the information we need (in this case, how to design schools as systems) fast. In very clear terms, it answers questions that the school as a living system has been asking for three decades. What is it that the world of work is asking of us? What are the design requirements of a learning organization? Schools, of course, have known the answers all along but have been battling with the obstacle of the same-age system as far as any realization is concerned.

Of course, it is important that students engage systematically and practically with the hard-core STEM subjects but it is equally important that students develop the soft-core skills, dispositions, and traits more likely to lead to the goal of goodness, happiness, and increased human productivity. We might call it an ecology of mindfulness. All have a contribution to make and to do this children need to feel safe if they are to practice the cooperation and connectedness so essential in life.

## THE DANGER

Schools will look at the list and tick the boxes. Then, they will start to develop teaching programs based on the lists above just as they did with resilience, grit, well-being, and mindfulness to the chagrin of the original researchers.

If they do, this would be a terrible mistake just as Mary Parker Follett said. These are matters learned when the connectedness of the organization is designed in and authentic. This is the essence of the mixed-age tutor group. No pro-social programs are needed, but the lessons needed to live a good and productive life are still learned. The school has to show, practice, and redefine what it is to care, and the students the same. The school has to become pro-social and socially collaborative by design.

When this happens in a mixed-age tutor group, the hidden curriculum is rewritten. This is the safe place and the means of laying the foundation for innovation, creativity, and risk. And from this complex place, the design of the school emerges and is rewritten.

The natural home for schools rests with emerging thinking, and this is where many schools delude themselves into thinking they are. Linear thinking seeks simplification but ends up with complication; nonlinear thinking tends to be complex but ends up with a simpler and better connected system. Linearity requires heavy supervision and is intolerant of error; nonlinear is more democratic and learns to expect and predict mistakes as the price for higher achievement. Good leaders who understand these distinctions also have the humility to seek change. Seddon (2008) set out a table (table 15.2) to highlight the difference.

## MAKING THE MIXED-AGE TRANSITION

Supporting a school wanting to make the transition from same-age organization to one that is mixed-age requires unfreezing accepted practice, but it isn't wise, when working with a school, to attack school culture head-on or

**Table 15.2.   Command-and-Control versus Systems Thinking (from Seddon)**

| Command-and-Control Thinking | | Systems Thinking |
| --- | --- | --- |
| Top-down: hierarchy | Perspective | Outside-in system |
| Functional | Design | Demand, value, flow |
| Separated from work | Decision-making | Integrated with work |
| Output, targets, standards: related to budget | Measurement | Capability, variation: related to purpose |
| Contractual | Attitude to customers | What matters? |
| Contractual | Attitude to suppliers | Cooperative |
| Managing people and budgets | Role of management | Act on the system |
| Control | Ethos | Learning |
| Reactive, projects (reform) | Change | Adaptive, integral |
| Extrinsic | Motivation | Intrinsic |

to point out all the things that are wrong. The biological reaction of the living system is to react and resist, and politely get rid of such an irritant.

The skill is to promote change by enabling the school to look again at what is really happening during the child's school career, looking at what is happening through the eyes of other players. Rather than challenging thinking outright, such critical reflection allows the school to reformulate its mind-set and think anew. In this way, the school starts to realign with its values and this makes the shift in thinking from one system to another easier. Mistakes occur when a mixed-age system is introduced without the necessary changes to the school's management structure needed to make it work. It is always management that has to change.

Many head teachers and school staff instinctively know that changing from the limitation and separation of a same-age setup to a mixed-age system (vertical tutoring) has considerable advantages. However, some are dubious because of tales about schools that have tried and failed. Such schools say, "We tried VT but it wasn't for us." In fact, these schools never fully considered the implications of change and assumed VT was a simple alteration to their pastoral system. Even today, there are schools that struggle with VT because they have yet to rid themselves of old management ideas.

Research into schools where transition failed indicates the kind of leadership failure that can only be described as a mix of arrogance and naivety. Few, if any, of these schools made an effort to seek advice or receive expert training. Collaboration with staff, students, and parents was poor; ignorance of systems high; and understanding of the change process low. Many introduced systems where senior staff avoided being tutors, where groups were too large, where tutors were required to teach PSHE, and tutor groups had a single tutor. Successful schools have already written a template of how such a transition occurs (table 20.2).

All are system errors derived from the past, the living system's initial reaction to disturbance. Around half the schools that attempt the change to VT do it well; such schools do their research, seek training and advice, visit schools, and avoid making assumptions. For others, the dominant management mind-set returns, and, when it does, the school as a learning system becomes worse, not better. Simply mixing students by age is insufficient; management has to change along with the end-to-end learning and teaching process, a domino effect. The school must unfreeze, learn, and refreeze (unlearn, learn, and learn anew).

The process of unlearning is the painful part. The rest, cognitive reframing, growing, and embedding a new system of learning relationships is common sense, but difficult to get right without referencing support and understanding organizational culture and to understand this process more, it is helpful to look at the work of Edgar Schein.

## Chapter 16

# School Culture

Google's original hiring policy along with many other companies' was very much STEM-dominated but having learned about itself as a system, that policy is now better balanced and more in line with the emerging thinking needed to ensure synergy and balance.

Unfortunately for our schools, they exist within a larger governmental system so disturbed by PISA league tables and consultancy reports that there is a constant return to the past and to a litany of old assumptions. The reestablishment of the dominant thinking over the past thirty years, courtesy of NPM, has taken schools back to their original industrial design spec. As Pasi Sahlberg (2015) said:

> It has become clear everywhere that the schools we have today will not be able to provide opportunities for students to learn what is necessary in the future.

It would be remiss not to connect the previous chapters and this without a heretical statement or two! The current direction to multiacademy trusts and school chains reduces leadership, increases compliance, feeds convergence, and legitimizes old management practices. Further, the school CEO is increasingly separated from the system base and overreliant on second- or thirdhand information plus metrics derived from examination results. Such an approach has a temporary stabilizing effect because organizational risk and innovation are no priorities; this enables schools to continue with same-age structure with all its incumbent disconnectedness.

Schools do and can collaborate to a limited extent but they are not the socially collaborative enterprises needed and are prone to sameness, not innovation. Neither are they less expensive. As ever, no fault is attached to such organizations or those trying to make such NPM systems work. We all pay the price of governments unable to embrace a systems thinking approach.

Heretical statements need justification, and if countries are to have chains of schools, great care must be taken in enabling them to work without harming participants directly or indirectly by limiting individual achievement. Their single asset seems to be staff flexibility. The rest of this chapter references the thoughts of Edgar Schein and his work on organizational culture. To try and understand the school, we need to go beneath the surface into the school's culture, the way it works and thinks; insights gained from the previous chapter are given substance by Schein.

## THE NATURE OF CULTURE

Schein offers an explanation of culture, loosely interpreted and adapted here for schools. For Schein, culture is not only how an organization (like a school) goes about its work, but also how it makes sense of the world in which it finds itself, and how it survives internal and external threats. It is very much in tune with the evolutionary biology that started this journey. Schein's (1992) definition of culture underpins much of what has been discussed so far, and much that follows: note the evolutionary metaphor.

> A pattern of shared basic assumptions that the group learned as it solved its problems of external adaptation and internal integration that has worked well enough to be considered valid and, therefore, to be taught to new members as the correct way to perceive, think, and feel in relation to those problems. (p. 9)

Unsurprisingly, there are striking similarities to the definition of systems. Schein (1996a) later defined organizational culture as:

> the basic tacit assumptions about how the world is and ought to be that a group of people share and that determines their perceptions, thoughts, feelings, and, their overt behavior.

Implicit to the idea of culture is a sense of belonging to a like-minded group; the challenge to culture is its capacity to learn and evolve over time. We know that the school's culture like all public service organizational cultures is concerned with two important aspects. The first is to survive and maintain identity as it adapts external pressures, and the second involves the internal relationships it uses that enables it to function on a daily basis and to learn.

Schein (2016) makes an important point about cultural assumptions as follows:

> After a set of assumptions has come to be taken for granted it determines much of the group's behavior, and the rules and norms that are taught to newcomers in a socialization process that is a reflection of culture. (p. 22)

The same-age assumption is not only a powerful builder of school culture, it is the original leverage point—the design blueprint that determines how and why the system operates in the way it does. Same-age groups do not and cannot exhibit the list of traits and dispositions derived from Projects Aristotle and Oxygen; they are not safe, there is bullying, they are not the best places to listen and speak freely, let alone grow empathy and resilience. Because of this, learning behavior is put at risk and the school has to compensate using pro-social programs, fixes, and add-ons. Everywhere, there is failure demand, escalating costs, complications, and endemic cognitive dissonance.

According to Schein:

> The bottom line for leaders is that if they do not become conscious of the culture in which they are embedded, those cultures will manage them.

And this is precisely what exists. The assumptions used by schools to solve problems and manage situations are now deeply entrenched, and few will believe that the same-age structure is the cause. It is now possible to find similar management structures worldwide. This kind of *theory in use* is rarely debated or considered as a research topic except by a handful of schools, and so it remains forever under the research radar. But like a black hole, its effects are very apparent.

## CULTURAL LEVELS

Culture, Schein suggests, has three levels that become increasingly difficult to decipher. First, there are *artefacts* composed of visual processes and organizational structures. Most of us understand how schools are run and have familiarity with this level. Second come *espoused values*, the philosophy and aims claimed by the school. Finally, there are the *basic underlying assumptions*, largely unconscious beliefs that determine values and action (figure 16.1).

These can be interpreted for schools as follows:

- Artefacts: A visitor may notice student behavior and dress codes and gain an immediate impression of the school, how the place *cares*, and what seems to be of value. People instinctively gauge whether or not they feel comfortable and safe.

  The artefacts are a manifestation of the organizational culture, a means of self-identification. (Remember, schools as living systems are big on identity!) While artefacts offer a first impression, no conclusions can be drawn. Much goes unseen, so care is needed when making assumptions.

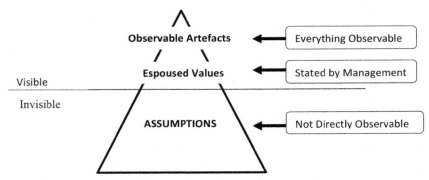

**Figure 16.1.   Organizational Culture (from Schein, 1996a)**

In Schein's words, the artefacts are the *manifestation of the organiza-tional culture*.

- Espoused values: Here we note the work of Chris Argyris and Donald Schön (1995). What the school *espouses* (the organization's beliefs and what it claims to do) may not be compatible with practice on the ground but remains the official explanation of the school's culture. Espoused values are the means a school uses to explain its culture, *the official view* to the outside world. We might look at the artefacts alongside what is espoused to confirm initial impressions of a school. It is easy, all too easy, to accept the espoused view without question. These are the stated strategies and philosophy of the school, the school's explanation of why it works in the way it does. When these explanations are interrogated (checked for validity by systems thinking), they often prove to be less than watertight. A strong belief in par-ent partnership, for example, may not accord with parental opinion or any definition of *partnership*. Similarly, developing the potential of every child may not be what is actually happening. Something else is happening deep in the school, invisible to observers.

- Tacit assumptions: Beneath the artefacts and the espoused values are the real drivers of the school, the parts of the organizational iceberg not easily seen—a place that officialdom cannot reach. These are shared organiza-tional assumptions, ways of being, doing, and understanding that become accepted over time. This is the culture formed at the base and edges of the school that is forever trying to make sense of it all—the heart, memory, soul, and brain. This is where it matters. This is the place that holds the collective school history and determines attitudes to work, relationships, change, success, and failure. These are the largely unconscious, taken-for-granted beliefs and emotions that inspire action, the real determinants of how the work is done and why it is done in the way it is. Dormant here, and seemingly benign, is the same-age assumption. This is a place where staff talk about philosophy and meaning and where the school's memories are stored. This is the place where ideas emerge and die.

Schools have learned to be wary of change. The message from Schein to those involved in organizational (school) improvement is this: any attempt at changing the way an organization works that is contradictory to the deep-seated tacit assumptions of the school is destined to either fail or have damaging consequences for players. The effect of NPM management practices and the creation of a single *de facto* purpose is contrary to the tacit assumptions that schools have developed over time. Instead of supporting staff development and student learning, its approach is evaluative and judgmental. Hence the problems of well-being, low morale, recruitment and retention, and more as unwelcome additions to the perceived performance problem.

Successful change requires that deep-seated assumptions are brought into the open in safe ways that enable participants to look at them afresh and so understand where and why any misalignment has arisen. From an NPM (System X) perspective, there is a people fault problem. People cannot be trusted and, unless they are heavily supervised and rewarded, they fail to perform. At the risk of repetition, the people problem is actually a systems problem and it is this that needs attention.

In Einstein's words, problems can't be solved using the same level of consciousness that created them, something Peter Drucker called acting with yesterday's logic. The aim of this book is to persuade schools to consider a fundamental change to their tacit assumptions and move from one system (linear, complicated, separational, and same-age) to another (nonlinear, complex, integrated, and mixed-age) at a cost of twenty minutes per day.

Cultural theory suggests that such a task is simply tilting at windmills because it questions basic assumptions and is viewed as a major disturbance. But, as ever, the opposite is the case. This is because the invitation to make such a transition is different in two respects. First, the change suggested is fully aligned with the tacit assumptions and values of schools. It is in teachers' terms caring and able to make a big difference. Second, it frees the school from the shackles of dominant NPM thinking and promotes self-organization and agency rather than coercion and compliance. Mixed-age structures enhance partnership and learning providing the binding glue that the same-age system takes for granted.

The effect is to stabilize and reconfigure the school in a way that enhances the organization's connectedness and aligns it with the school's tacit assumptions. Schools must be aware that they are no longer values-driven as organizations; they have undergone a deep disturbance to their identity that has taken many to a very soulless place, and most seek a way back while they still possess the memory of past possibilities.

Like their many counterparts worldwide, they have experienced turbulent organizational change but have yet to find genuine ways of living the values they hold dear. Each wave of change has left them searching for a means of surviving the new conditions in which they find themselves; they have never fully been masters of their own destiny. Mixed-age methodology gives schools the opportunity to take back control of how they work. In particular, it gives schools the opportunity to self-organize (to create a different relational structure, to learn and diversify). It also wards off suboptimization, which occurs when the organization shifts into full testing mode at the expense of other purposes.

## THREE OCCUPATIONAL CULTURES AND ORGANIZATIONAL LEARNING

The fact that so many schools are oblivious to vertical tutoring as a management concept, just as they are seemingly unaware of the term NPM, indicates a deep-seated learning problem not of their own making, a challenge that reform and research often sidesteps. If an organization like a school is unable to learn and adapt, there has to be a cause. Schein (1996b) explains why this is in a unique way. Culture exists not only in the schools but also across occupational communities. Head teachers are a classic example, so are politicians.

Schein starts by rejecting *resistance to change*. It is fair to say that schools have never shown anything other than compliance and endeavor to make change work, albeit in their own inimitable and sometimes wonderfully subversive way. Schools know their limitations and have an excellent sense of what works and what doesn't.

Schein then moves on to reject *leadership failure*. The heresy used earlier stated that schools do not suffer from a deficit of good leaders. Leaders may be poorly prepared, reliant on self-help books, attend inappropriate leadership courses, and may not all designer architects, but more often than not they do make a disconnected system at least appear to work at an operational level.

Finally, Schein rejects *human nature*. Schools are packed with dedicated and hardworking people who want to learn more but are prevented from doing so through misdirection and battle fatigue. At heart, people are Beta, not Alpha, and respond accordingly. Schein proposes that the reasons why organizations fail to learn are caused by differences pertaining to three distinct cultural and occupational groups. Understanding these groups and the cultures they represent is the key.

1. Over time, a school develops a way of working based on past experience and success, something Schein calls an *operator culture*. The operators

(teachers and school workers in this case) are the people who actually do the value work at the public interface. They always manage to get the work done despite the other two groups (below). They use ingenuity, collaboration, whatever it takes to complete the task, and the organization depends on this group's commitment, collaboration, and skill. They often work around management processes and technology they know can fail at any time.

Schein thinks of the operational culture as virtuous and pragmatic, one where experience is important and trust essential, in part because this group is closest to reality. This is where learning ability, agency, skills, and collaboration come to the fore. This group is smart enough to question change and so has to be approached on an equal footing. If operators reach a point where they start saying, "Just tell us what to do," severe damage has been done. When surprises occur, this group has to have sufficient agency to deal with them.

2. Beyond the school is an *engineering culture*. The engineers seek a perfect world preferably without the complications of human intervention. Theirs is the world of the pilot and the ferocious dog. The pilot is at the controls of a highly computerized aircraft; her task is to watch the dials. The dog is there to attack the pilot should she touch anything. The engineers are curriculum designers and experts who have influence at the highest levels. We might include government consultants, the inspectorate, and bodies like the OECD that advise jurisdictions and states.

Engineers seek to build a well-oiled machine and are always cautious. They believe in a single curriculum, a great teacher in every classroom, standardization, and convergence; they even believe they know what the future demands and confidently nominate the competencies needed, knowing they won't be around to pick up the pieces.

The engineers aspire to systems thinking and even steal its words, but they cannot break from the shackles of linear thinking and are unable to master human nature. Their karma is command and control and making the industrial legacy work. They see education and schools as a jigsaw puzzle with few straight edges. Not surprisingly, this group uses data and league tables to influence governments by inducing fear with a smiley face. Operators are expected to learn the abstract language of the engineer, who in turn sees the operator as subversive and resistant to the school change agenda.

3. Finally, there are the CEOs who manage schools, the *executive culture*. This group has trust and control issues they can never fully work through.

Like the engineer, they see operators as *human resources*, more Alpha than Beta, who generate problems and need carrot-and-stick management.

Their culture focuses on finances, pay, contractual obligations, and competition. These are the Knights Templar of New Public Management, forever fighting in an imagined war zone for the wrong reasons often using nasty methods. Some see the system ripe for looting. Their subordinates are unreliable and so they build hierarchies around their chosen bunker. They avoid risks and any loss of control and like to be seen colluding with engineers at the top table. They too boast of their own well-oiled machine with its teacher research group and can be seen in the wings at conferences that operator teachers cannot afford to attend.

For Schein (2006), organizational learning is hampered by the conflicting nature of these three cultures.

> Organizations will not learn effectively until they recognize and confront the implications of the three occupational cultures. Until executives, engineers, and operators discover that they use different languages and make different assumptions about what is important, and until they learn to treat the other cultures as valid and normal, organizational learning efforts will continue to fail. (p. 210)

Organizations could learn much from Google's Aristotle project and the benefits that occur when different cultural groups gather and feel sage to share ideas.

The real problem of organizational learning is not a simple matter of pedagogy, teachers being persuaded to change their practice (engineering theory). There is an increasing misalignment between the three cultures, and this is caused by the executives (school CEOs) and engineers having reference points in a worldwide occupational community divorced from the tacit assumptions used by the operators who do the value work; they each face different challenges unique to their roles. There is in essence a communications and connectedness issue and one that the mixed-age organization is able to resolve!

CEOs and engineers are convinced that they know how the world works and what the world needs in terms of (say) future competencies. There is significant cultural buy-in whether right or wrong. Their frustration is persuading the operators to toe their party line and comply. They cannot understand any reluctance, let alone why people fall ill and walk away.

Each culture has its own way of seeing the world. Somewhere down the line, there has to be systemic change. For Schein, the learning problem rests with the *executives* and *engineers*. Wrapped in their own dialogue, they no longer know how to learn or that learning is needed and are unaware that they need help. Worse, they feel they don't have to learn. Schein's definition of culture shows what needs to be done. It identifies precisely where to seek the best system change lever, one in alignment with the school's tacit assumptions rather than one that ignores their value. At the heart of a school's tacit assumptions are empathetic learning relationships, knowledge, safety, and collaborative potential.

All schools believe in good learning relationships between staff, students, and parents. This is what makes the school and those in it tick! This is what schools say is important. The optimal approach to change is to lever these ideas in a direction that enhances their value rather than one that assumes them.

If there is any learning that needs to occur, it is understanding how the operational culture works and can be harnessed to bring about desirable change. For mixed-age groups, the problem is largely resolved when the CEO has the courage and foresight to return to frontline tutoring. This single act reconnects school culture and informs the CEO that trust is possible and that the conditions for improvement can be learned.

## EMERGENCE

One of the advantages of a complex system like VT is to promote systemic change despite the misalignment schools experience. When everyone is involved in the learning process and managers return to frontline tutoring, the school realigns itself and tacit assumptions become visible. When learning relationships extend to parents, community builds and it is this powerful force that is the most likely to lead any worthwhile systemic change. The weak point remains the group CEO increasingly divorced from the learning relationships he or she has cause to keep separate while somehow endorsing collaboration.

The theme of this book is that the biggest and most intransigent assumption within the school's compass to change is same-age organization. It is neither benign nor psychologically coherent and adds to cultural separation. It is also anathema to the idea of family and lodges like an irritant unseen among the school's tacit assumptions where it remains festering, unchallenged, and largely unopposed.

When exposed to the light of day, however, schools quickly realize how the same-age linear system leads to limitation and separation. Vertical tutoring works with the school's values by enhancing learning relationships and dares to speak of values, fun, and joy. The effect is to enable the school to realign artefacts, espoused values, and tacit assumptions in a holistic way, allowing the organization to be more self-managing, open, and emergent. It nourishes and further enhances the school's identity, how it sees itself, and improves the school's survival chances.

Cultural change happens through a process of *emergence*, the strangest concept in systems thinking. Change can emerge from within an organization that doesn't itself exhibit the properties of the change that happens. In other words, the interactions, the relationships between elements can complexify to produce something qualitatively different, more than the sum of the existing parts.

The system (our school) can change into a different kind of system, a move from a teacher-dependent system to one where everyone is a learner and a teacher. The trick is to flick the mixed-age change domino and to follow the pieces wherever they go: this means being guided only by values until all learning relationships are working as intended so enabling the conditions of emergence to occur.

As things stand, schools are not emergent nor can they be in their linear form; there has been no accelerated evolution of culture but a history of add-ons, fixes, and reinventions of the past. Neither is technology an answer when it detracts from human relationships; the ability of parents to access reports online can never be a substitute for the rich dialogics on which deeper learning depends.

Superficial change exhausts schools and runs counter to the school's tacit assumptions. It seems that schools have become tired by the physical and mental turbulence caused by *executives* and *engineers* unable to recognize system contradictions and unable or unwilling to learn and think in systems and across cultures. In their report to the World Innovation Summit on Education (WISE), Hallgarten et al. (2016) proposed that schools

> should create deliberate platforms for innovation that are future-focused, equity-centered, humanizing and crucially, teacher-powered.

While the RSA's call to arms is far from where schools are, this is not the time for schools to stand still frozen, moribund in time. We need our schools to be able to question organizational assumptions and reclaim their values.

To continue our search for new organizational thinking, we need to look at other organizations and how they approach the challenges of the future.

*Chapter 17*

# Learning from the Public Sector

In 2012, the King's Fund looked at how the National Health Service (NHS) in the UK might be improved and started a conversation intended to "shape policy, transform services and bring about behavior change." The Fund reminded everyone that the purpose of NHS leadership is to improve population health and patient care, and its recommendations signaled a shift in the way leadership is often conceptualized. The message from the King's Fund is clear; leadership has to change in ways that increase *engagement* both within the system and with patients.

The King's Fund is also very clear on its reasoning:

> Organizations with engaged staff deliver a better patient experience, fewer errors, lower infection and mortality rates, stronger financial management, higher staff morale and motivation and less absenteeism and stress.

In essence, engaged staff reduce failure demand—problems caused by a system unable to give patients the support and treatment they need when needed. There is much that schools can learn from other public service organizations seeking to escape the design spec of the past. So, why is it that traditional leadership and management ideas are so ineffective? Well, the King's Fund is clear on this, too:

> The dominant NHS approach [to leadership] is typified by laying down demanding targets, leading from the front, often being reluctant to delegate, and collaborating little—and is the consequence of the health service focusing on process targets, with reward depending on them.

It seems that communication and understanding between the operator, executive, and engineering cultures are exactly as Edgar Schein describes while the system in use is far from being VSM advocated by Stafford Beer. It is also far from being the well-oiled machine its engineering culture might wish it to be. It would seem that the sheer size of this organization makes change a daunting challenge; after all, the National Health Service as an organization:

- Provides comprehensive healthcare for over fifty-four million people;
- Sees over a million patients every thirty-six hours;
- Is funded by direct tax and provides 95% of all healthcare in England;
- Has twenty-two million service/user visits per year;
- Has 1.7 million employees, making it the fifth-largest employer on the planet and the largest in Europe.

## THE CURE IN CURATION

There is an increasing interest in *knowledge curation*, in effect applied systems thinking, and the past few decades have seen an increase in small teams of people doing their best to encourage new approaches to old problems. The Horizons Group is a small team within the NHS charged with bringing in fresh ideas to meet the challenge of rising customer demand.

This is a far cry from the delivery units and outcomes-based performance management orthodoxy advocated by NPM thinking. Instead of offering dogma and determinism, the Horizons team promotes fresh thinking through the dissemination of cutting-edge ideas from a variety of sources, based on those candidates best able to bring about systemic change over time.

The unit is unlike anything that exists in education. It is true that the UK's DFE (Department for Education) once had an innovation unit but it concerned itself with system add-ons and fixes and had no understanding of system change such as mixed-age organization. Like Edgar Schein's engineers, the concern of the unit was to make the same-age system work; any systemic change was paradoxically beyond its innovation remit. The Horizons Group has loftier intentions and is described in the following way:

> Its remit is about sharing the disruptive power of connecting—to influence change, leading edge knowledge, transformation and innovation. The aim is to support colleagues in health and care to think differently about the *"rules of change"* and make sense of it in their own context, leading to effective change practice and better outcomes for patients.

In 2014, team members Helen Bevan and Steve Fairman authored a white paper that advocated transformational change to the UK's much-treasured

NHS. It might have been reasonable to expect a call for greater efficiencies, another five-year plan, differential resource allocation, mergers, and new IT projects—NPM management paraphernalia all too familiar to schools.

The crux of the Bevan and Fairman approach is to move the change agency from the top of the organization to the edge and so build a more integrated and effective service based on patient need rather than service levels. This is the complete opposite of the kind of thought scaffolding that currently pertains in education and health. The idea is to replace top-down change programs with more dynamic, needs-based solutions better able to resolve the challenges posed by the complexity of demand on the service. The intention in systems thinking terms is to better absorb value demand and so reduce failure demand and remove waste.

There is widespread acceptance that the NHS is beginning to creak and cannot continue moving from crisis to crisis. Challenges facing the service are increasing in magnitude, and there are doubts whether the management thinking that has got NHS England this far can be successful in the future. The UK population is set to increase, people are living longer, drugs are becoming more expensive, and cases more complex. Demand is at an all-time high and set to rise year on year, and no one knows what Brexit might bring!

## ENGAGEMENT

The central theme of Bevan and Fairman's 2014 paper picks up on the notion of *engagement*. Staff expertise should accumulate at the point of delivery in the form of an enabled team capable of resolving complex problems first time round. Enablement through training and concurrent acceptance of responsibility allows staff to make effective interventions in line with organizational purpose. The result is improved care, happier patients, improved flow of information, and health workers intrinsically motivated by the work they do. The result is fewer people ending up in hospital, reduced management and bureaucracy, and people able to manage their lives more independently. When quality (care) increases, failure demand falls and costs go down.

To improve productivity, any system *waste* has to be tackled. According to Seddon (2008), there are five expensive types of waste in public services.

- The costs of people spending time writing specifications—drawing up standards, targets, guidance, reports *based on opinion and ideology* rather than knowledge. These not only fail to add value but also drive behavior in the wrong direction. We might add the hours spent on performance reviews!

- The costs of inspection. There is only one question inspectors should ask: *What measures are you using to understand and improve the work?*
- The costs of preparing for inspection. This also affects the way the work is done.
- The costs of the specifications being wrong. Regular rewrites, revised targets, and updates suggest an ongoing systemic problem.
- The cost of demoralization. The negative reaction of employees unable to do their job because of inappropriate systems management.

All are relevant to the context of schools. Removing waste releases the energy, time, and finances needed to resolve complex issues, allowing the organization to move from compliance to innovation. *Engagement* involves taking responsibility, being valued, and feeling part of a team, matters that resonate with teachers, students, and parents. At a profound level, it is part of the essence of what it is to be human, a higher state of consciousness buoyed by intrinsic motivation, matters that will feature in later chapters.

A system beset by waste is unable to adapt and just gets more and more complicated. It is bureaucratic, slow to resolve complex issues, unable to innovate its way free, and stifles systemic change. There is only one point to bear in mind. It is people who solve complex problems, but they can only do so if work complications are minimized. Such a close customer focus allows the organization to absorb complexity first time round and so reduce failure demand; organizational understanding of this concept is critical to organizational improvement. Leaders and managers need to think very differently about how the work is done, in a way that doesn't assume they know what it is or that they already do it!

The new model proposes a shift of training to the edge, one that enables people to handle complex challenges, take on responsibilities, and be an essential part of a multiskilled team. This is precisely what schools should be about. Niels Pflaeging (2014) expressed it like this.

> The main thing that organizations can do to stimulate performance is facilitate options for connection between individuals and throughout the organization, through purpose and meaningful work.

## ENABLERS OF CHANGE

To effect the kind of transition described above, Bevan and Fairman identify *five enablers* of the *emerging direction* of change—factors rarely, if ever, featured in books on school management and leadership. Too often, the ideas rarely considered are those that matter most and their curated list emanates from thought leaders, researchers, and experts across the globe. The five enablers are adapted here for schools and are outlined in greater detail later.

1. Activate disruptors, heretics, radicals, and mavericks. School leaders should identify and engage with these people to deal with challenges of organizational change; a very different version of the talent management approach has been discussed earlier!
2. Lead transformation from "the edge." Moving the change process to the organizational edge (to form tutors) leads to values-led change, radical thinking, faster interventions, and better outcomes, including improved equity. Schools remain doggedly top-down.
3. Change the narrative. Changing the story of school management requires the incorporation of a diversity of voices. When the narrative changes, so does the organization (a return to values). Mixed-age organization is such a narrative.
4. Curate rather than create knowledge. Schools should learn that the solutions they seek to better learning require them to evaluate, contextualize, and share knowledge from many sources within and beyond the school; being guided, not led, by research helps.
5. Build bridges to connect the disconnected. To effect successful organizational change, it is important to build bridges to those groups and individuals who feel most disconnected. This is what Laker and Hill's *architects* did (discussed previously)!

The underpinning psychology ensures a system that exhibits increased human commitment rather than increased compliance. In this section, the difference between same-age school systems and mixed-age organization becomes clearer and we are introduced to ideas that schools rarely have the chance to properly consider. So, let's join in the conversation and explore how these enablers of change might apply to schools and why mixed-age tutor groups are a sensible strategy to adopt. Readers can add their own input and infer other nuances but must be wary of claims that this is what schools already do.

## ACTIVATE DISRUPTORS, HERETICS, RADICALS, AND MAVERICKS

Bevan and Fairman call these "the people who rock the boat but somehow manage to stay in it." They are not destructive troublemakers but risk-takers who create improvement and do things in their own way despite the organizational obstacles that emanate from the systems in which they work. To survive and maintain identity, living systems have to reject hand-me-down ideas for ones able to move the organization from compliance to creativity, linearity to nonlinearity, and from complicated to complex using the careful and enabling design strategy of Laker and Hill's architects.

Many of these people operate at the edge of schools and most are part of Schein's operational culture. These are the teachers, tutors, and school managers who have a way of identifying system waste and getting to the heart of what matters. Every day in schools across the world these people come up with novel ideas, crazy whims, and schemes that don't follow accepted organizational dogma. Many ignore existing practice preferring collaboration. Occasionally, some even become head teachers and, when they do, values return to their schools.

Such creatives find clever ways to solve problems, take risks, and illuminate where a system is going wrong. They identify management failings, strategies, and policies that don't work and question the endless referral systems that delay effective intervention. Their operational breakthrough comes when they discover that the same-age system is the cause of the many obstacles to learning they seek to resolve.

Often, operational group members abandon set programs, ignore protocols, and decide to do their own thing, responding to a deeper values and a more relevant calling. Their gift is to inspire and tap the reservoir of intrinsic motivation inherent in schools. They do this by abandoning almost everything inherited under the label *school management*. NPM seeks to close this renegade activity down insisting on close alignment to the new *de facto* purpose, the measures derived from standardized outcome-based performance.

This disruptive group is unwelcome in schools and tends to be sidelined. Because they are not part of the perceived mainstream solution, they are viewed as noncompliant, resistant to change, and part of the problem. Disruptors, heretics, radicals, and mavericks present a challenge to linear thinking and stasis. They invariably reject reforms and find their own solutions, knowing that reforms have a short shelf-life and that normal service is always resumed after any initial enthusiasm wanes. This group is growing in membership and this is a healthy sign.

Few school leaders appreciate that engaging with these characters, if the school is lucky enough to have them, may be the school's salvation. They are the ones who suggest their school looks at vertical tutoring. They are not the kind of people likely to conform or stay silent, nor are they likely to take their APR seriously; APRs disrupt teaching and learning and do nothing to improve their school. Further, they are likely to ignore targets that serve to distort behavior rather than improve it, preferring their own *strategies for improvement*.

By engaging with this group to see more of what they see, school leaders might find that these characters are part of the solution after all. They hold the key to Kurt Lewin's unfreezing, cognitive restructuring, and refreezing. Their gift is empathy, to see the world through the eyes of others, and redefine the way service is provided.

## LEAD TRANSFORMATION FROM THE EDGE

To understand a system requires listening at the periphery at all the places where schools and customers meet because this is where any authentic talk of change occurs.

Richard Pascale (2010) reminds us that being overly task-focused leads to myopia and an inability to capture the gems of information carried in the white noise of the system. In a linear system, information is top-down and much is missing or fragmented across the piece. In an organization like a school, the relevant information comes from the edge, the periphery where parents, students, and tutors engage in the learning process and where information, opinions, and ideas are shared.

For every child, there has to be someone close who sees the child every day and knows them well (the tutor), a person able to intervene at the right time in the right way—a prerequisite for child development. This is why any school system has to be designed around the tutor. Surrounding the child with an enabling network of support ensures safer navigation through learning and this reduces system demand and supports both teaching and learning.

Similarly, for senior citizens needing medical support, it is more practical and economical to build an enabling support network in the community. Such a support strategy improves outcomes by removing from the patient the need to navigate a complicated referral and support system at a time when the patient is least able to do so. Intervention avoids delays, mistakes, and repeat treatment (complications and waste); a more bespoke team approach is able to absorb complexity.

At the edge of public systems there has to be *a nodal information hub*, the lynchpin of the system's *connectedness*. These are the places closest to students, staff, and parents where information is gathered that enables rapid intervention. In the health system, it is the community team leader and in school it is the form tutor who is the nodal information hub. Any failure at this juncture allows problems to fester and become worse downstream setting in motion the familiar results of higher costs, more bureaucracy, and lost human potential.

Bevan and Fairman (2014) are more succinct, proposing that "purposefully moving such processes to *the edge* can result in more radical thinking, faster change, and better outcomes." Their paper notes "a global trend for creative processes, including organizational development and change management, to move to the edges of organizations."

## CHANGE THE NARRATIVE (STORIES AND DIALOGICS)

To change the narrative, it is worth considering how people make sense of things. And this brings us to *dialogics*. In some ways, dialogics sits at the other end of the continuum to diagnostics yet can engage with diagnostics without being overly governed by data. Dialogics—conversations, stories, feedback, descriptive metaphors, and listening—comprise a range of learning strategies that bring about welcome organizational change but don't fit neatly into reformational approaches.

They involve the kind of social construction millennials might be the first to welcome, being an amalgam of social strategies that guide the way we think and act. This is what Google discovered as it burrowed deep to discover the human conditions that drive success and build generosity of spirit. It is also the essence of the socially collaborative school advocated here.

A data sheet of numbers and grades used to report on a child's performance is sent home, but behind each number and grade are a host of qualitative issues not recorded, vital and irrecoverable information lost by design, absent between the lines. Children are not data sheets; each is a living entity, referred to by Bertalanffy, an early systems thinker, as *active personality systems*. To make sense of data sheets requires dialogics, other summative information held by the parent and child coordinated through the child's tutor (the information hub). Without an opportunity for dialogics or a summative conversation between parties, strategies for improvement are both uncertain and unsupported at emotional and cognitive levels.

Dialogics enable assumptions to be challenged through a diversity of conversations and interactions that people play out in different spaces and settings, and especially through the agency of tutor time. Deep learning conversations between parent, child, and tutor at critical learning times are essential for promoting and supporting learning, and these need to be enacted, supported, and identified by the school. Dialogics help in system design by enriching data and identifying how information flows.

Out of this rich dialogic, change patterns emerge that have the capacity to redefine organizations. Bushe and Marshack (2009) describe the process as "complex responsive processes where people's thoughts and actions are in a continuous process of meaning making and emergence." This definition very much echoes Senge's defining characteristics of a learning organization. Change is not something that happens between periods of stability; rather, change is always happening at varying rates and times. In short, people are better at using their common sense when unfettered dialogue occurs.

For schools, these include learning conversations, information shared by staff, parents, and students used to inform and support learning and to make the learning and teaching system work better. By loosening these tightly controlled areas and designing such conversations into the way schools operate, the story of the school and its operational learning process starts to change. Using dialogics, the school can accommodate a wider view of the child so essential in complex matters like behavior management and assessment for learning.

## CURATE RATHER THAN CREATE KNOWLEDGE

We exist in a world where there is a massive amount of what Bevan and Fairman call "raw, unprocessed, context-free data." They postulate that

> improvement leaders will move from being "bench scientists" (creating and testing novel local improvement solutions to the challenges faced) to curators of knowledge (collecting, filtering, evaluating, contextualizing, and sharing knowledge from multiple sources). (p. 10)
>
> Curators gather significant change practices from diverse sources. They seek ideas that encourage new thinking, ones able to disrupt existing patterns of management behaviour. Curation reduces dependency on inward-looking solutions and improvement strategies while inviting schools to be more in line with organizations operating at the cutting edge where schools need to be. Curation is a learning invitation, a chance to question and reconsider, one able to challenge existing practice, expose assumptions and offer fresh thinking.

## BUILD BRIDGES TO THE DISCONNECTED

In a health system, older people, the lonely, and the disenfranchised are the hard to reach. But what about schools? The argument here is that same-age structures make all children hard to reach and that separating them out into same-age groups (and all the other separations) doesn't help. The linear system in play means that everyone knows a small piece of the child's learning jigsaw, but no one is able to collate the whole. This is left to the child and family to sort out. Simon Caulkin (2016) said this:

> At the extreme, organizations subject to the demands of today's management bureaucracy can become their psychopathic opposites, the reversed-out versions of themselves: banks that make people poorer, hospitals that kill patients, public services that destroy community rather than reinforce it. (p. 33)

To this, we can add school design that inadvertently causes bullying, limits potential, and increases mental health disorders among staff and young people and then has the temerity to accuse the victims of lacking character and resilience while offering a fix or add-on sticky-backed plaster to effect a cure. Schools assume same-age theory makes children happy, compliant, and easy to reach; the opposite is true. Using same-age organizational, social, and learning strategies, schools inadvertently introduce bullying on day one and setting on day two unaware of the damage caused.

This brings us to strong and weak-ties theory (Granovetter, 1973). Schools comprise a vast matrix of social networks, and the child on entry has to find a belonging group within a same-age network. Children like to have friends of their own age with common interests, but getting these friendship groups right is fraught with risk in a same-age school and there can be lifelong learning consequences if this goes wrong. Young people left to their own devices may find their needs met in anti-learning groups, anti-school groups, and gangs, and the immediate need to belong can override any long-term judgment to learn.

The point being labored is this: in an entirely peer-based system, a child's social network (in-group loyalty) tends to be tight and can also be a matter of fortune, one where any rejection or negative influence can have a debilitating effect. SEL or PSHE programs exist as antidotes to the way schools go about their induction processes and same-age organizational strategies. The problem with *strong ties* is their limitation and the considerable energy required to maintain any connectedness.

Granovetter's (1973) strong and weak-ties theory sheds light on school organizational assumptions. He starts with a simple idea: people often find jobs through *acquaintances* beyond their immediate circle of friends because they can span and access a much-extended network. In other words, immediate friends and associates can provide pathways to others who can be of help. If jobs are scarce, then a wide search strategy is essential for finding work. This leads to the counterintuitive strength of weak-ties theory. Someone always knows someone who knows a woman who knows a guy who. . . . It is an advantage to be part of an easily accessible extended network. Students in the private sector know this world well and the considerable advantage such networking offers. They were born into it.

Weak ties require no maintenance but nevertheless connect to other groups often very different from ourselves, expanding any contact network. Schools operate a strong-tie organizational strategy based on peer groups and intelligence. Because networks and loyalty groups tend to be confined to age, this restricts learning relationships but later, social mobility; it becomes a limiting factor. Not only is the linear school a closed system, but it perpetuates other closed systems throughout life.

Schools have the wherewithal to interrupt such a high-risk strategy by ensuring all children belong to a mixed-age loyalty group guaranteed to be pro-learning, pro-social, and pro-school—a face-to-face approach that expands both strong and loose-tie networks and crucially, the skill to develop and navigate through them. Importantly, joining such a network on induction satisfies many social and psychological motivational needs that enable better judgments later on when it comes to choosing a friendship group.

When a school operates tutor groups mixed by age for a short time each day, it expands the child's in-group loyalty in a pro-social, pro-learning way. In a sense, a mixed-age system expands the capability to *speak social*. It ensures that belonging and leadership needs are met first time round (a la Maslow, Bronfenbrenner, Bowlby discussed previously) besides increasing the child's weak-ties connections and networking skills beyond school. It develops social confidence, empathy, and a capacity to connect beyond immediate friends and is an essential part of security and well-being.

As far as community health is concerned, it is easy to appreciate how an understanding of weak and strong ties can support changes to community care. The patient and caregiver relationship forms the basis of a network of practice. The caregiver ensures the patient has an extended support network available with his or her direct interest at heart, just as the tutor does in a mixed-age setting. The real challenge is making the transition—the unlearning needed to escape current thinking.

The message of this section is simple. We are unlikely to find the solutions we need to the problems we face exploring old territory and leadership models. The curation community is inviting us to look again at the operational teams that deliver the goods every day, working at the edge of organizations and close to communities. They warn us to be beware of New Public managers baring gifts and to explore other models beyond our own and listen to those who have made a radical change and a meaningful difference.

## Chapter 18

# Learning Organizations and the Color Teal

The previous chapter offered new system possibilities by showing how and why large organizations must act like small organization with regard to service. Ken Wilber (2013) describes this as a move from large, inhibiting *dominator* hierarchies to small *actualization* hierarchies that arise as needed. Hierarchies don't disappear as such but are relocated as and where needed, the essence of the idea behind distributed leadership.

Before using the kind of changes outlined (chapter 17) as important arbiters of design, more background is required to match theory, practice, and context. Whatever the future, it is important that schools provide a humanizing experience able to produce people for all seasons. At the moment, there is a genuine fear that schools are being forged into something they should never be, soulless places unable to contribute to the goal of goodness, a situation summed up by Joe Hallgarten et al. (2016) in his online introduction to the RSA's submission to WISE (World Innovation Summit for Education):

> The current dominant paradigm of education reform tries to change behavior through top-down accountability measures, pay-related incentives and high-stakes testing and appraisal. These efforts appear to be having diminishing returns, and increase existing inequities. It risks creating a technocratic teacher identity, which reduces the teacher role to that of compliant technician, whose job is largely to implement protocols and carry out instructions.

This is not an argument against learning essential formulae, tables, and facts. Hallgarten is talking about systems and describes Schein's industrial design engineers with unnerving accuracy. It is a predicament echoed in the Taylor (2017) report on employment practices in the modern economy.

The choice facing organizations, we find, is whether to simplify reality to suit a preferred method of operation or to acknowledge the nature of the world, to challenge assumptions and to work in whatever ways are necessary to be able to make a difference.

Current thinking views teachers as somehow incongruent, the problem rather than the solution. There is a conflict between the *dominant paradigm* discussed earlier and Peter Senge's definition of learning organizations (below). As things stand, secondary schools are nowhere near to becoming the divergent learning organizations described by Senge:

Places where people continually expand their capacity to create the results they truly desire, where new and expansive patterns of thinking are nurtured, where collective aspiration is set free and where people are continually learning how to learn together. (p. 14)

This is not something the same-age system can achieve and is clearly not the NPM's current direction of travel. Senge's prophetic chapter "Education for the 21st Century" talks about "the ineffectiveness of the teacher-centric model." Children are "natural systems thinkers," though this is rarely what we ask of them. They are "hungry for leadership." Schools are "paralyzed" while "overstressed teachers and administrators try desperately to fend off pressures from business leaders and fearful parents" (p. 361). Senge reminds us that education for the nineteenth and the twentieth century is no longer appropriate.

While Senge gives an excellent picture of all that is wrong and a precise definition of a learning organization, the means of moving from a solely teacher-centric model that can get in the way of learning to one that is better balanced, where everyone learns and contributes, is less certain. Simply teaching students and staff to apply systems thinking by using a toolbox approach is insufficient and maintains sameness. While Senge is silent on mixed-age systems, he nevertheless points out how even the smallest change can lever a big effect.

## EVOLUTIONARY TEAL

To understand the bind, it is worth taking stock to gain a sense of where schools are and the direction schools might adopt to become more relevant. As Peter Drucker said and many others have intimated, in times of turbulence it is not the turbulence that should worry us but acting with yesterday's logic. For Drucker, *the best way to predict the future is to create it,* so it is important for schools to play their part and maximize all learning relationships by changing the way they manage themselves, a systemic shift to self-organization. Instead of preparing students for an unknown future, schools should see themselves as creating it.

This chapter highlights the contribution of Frederic Laloux and his seminal work, *Reinventing Organizations* (2014), a kind of *Fifth Discipline* reloaded. Laloux sets out his approach in the following terms. While the ability to collaborate more and more effectively has led to exponential advancement, there is still considerable disillusionment with organizational life reflected in posturing, bureaucracy, burnout, apathy, resentment, routines, and drudgery.

> At both the top and the bottom, organizations are more often than not playfields for unfulfilling pursuits of our egos, inhospitable to the deeper yearnings of our souls. (p. 4)

Laloux describes schools as "soulless machines where students and teachers simply go through the motions." Hospitals are described as cold, bureaucratic institutions that "dispossess doctors and nurses of their capacity to care from the heart."

To explain the present, Laloux looks at the past. He places organizations within a color-coded evolutionary framework as measured by their level of consciousness. When these levels are tracked over time, it shows that the evolution of organizational consciousness is accelerating, and we have reached a time when a number of paradigms are overlapping or operating alongside each other (figure 18.1). He argues that various organizational paradigms reflect stages of human consciousness and walk us through them.

Laloux assigns particular kinds of human organization to specific colors (epochs)—ones that best describe their organizational culture. Each juncture ushers in a new era of human history, including breakthroughs in our ability to collaborate. Laloux expresses the direction of organization as *Evolutionary*

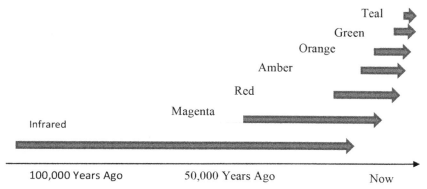

**Figure 18.1. The Accelerating Evolution of Consciousness: Direction of Change (from Laloux, 2014)**

*Teal—the next stage of human consciousness.* This phase sees a reduction in our concerns about ego and status and invites us into a world where decision-making shifts from externally imposed yardsticks to internally driven values, what is right and true to ourselves and to the ecology of mind that embeds us.

This is relevant to the situation in which schools universally find themselves and is in line with the RSA's report (discussed earlier). Organizations like schools are an expression of the worldview, a transitional stage en route to Teal. We can note where schools are in the world order (table 18.1). Teal is added later!

**Table 18.1.   Placing Schools in an Evolutionary Organizational Framework (from Laloux, 2014)**

| Corporate Descriptor | Current Examples | Key Breakthrough | Metaphor |
|---|---|---|---|
| RED: Exercise of power from chief to keep troops in line. Fear is the glue of the organization. | • Mafia<br>• Street gangs<br>• Tribal militias | • Division of labor<br>• Command authority | Wolf pack |
| AMBER: Highly formal roles within a hierarchical pyramid. Top-down command and control (what and how). Stability valued through rigorous processes. Future is repetition of the past. | • Catholic Church<br>• Military<br>• Most government agencies<br>• Public school* systems | • Formal roles (*stable and scalable hierarchies*)<br>• Processes (*long-term perspectives*) | Army |
| ORANGE: Goal is to beat competition; achieve profit and growth. Innovation is the key to staying ahead. Management by objectives (command and control on what: freedom on how). | • Multinational companies<br>• Charter schools<br>• Multiacademies<br>• Free schools | • Innovation<br>• Accountability<br>• Meritocracy | Machine |
| GREEN: Within the pyramid structure, focus on culture and empowerment to achieve motivation. | Culture-driven organizations. (*We might include Steiner schools, Jenaplan schools, VT schools*) | • Empowerment<br>• Values-driven culture<br>• Stakeholder model | Family |

*Public schools in this context are state schools, not independent and fee-paying ones. Multiacademy trusts have been added to Orange (machine metaphor) and VT schools to Green.

These paradigm shifts are becoming ever shorter, which infers that human consciousness is evolving at an accelerating rate albeit differentially. But while there is hoped-for progress, the route is far from linear; there are oscillations, overlaps, and setbacks. The first column (corporate descriptors) sets out overlapping or coexisting organizational paradigms. Examples in column 2 have school exemplars added; otherwise, the table is as it appears in Laloux (p. 36). Organizations aren't bound to any one paradigm and can sometimes shift between paradigms given the circumstances they face; but each paradigm *includes and transcends the previous* one, an evolution of consciousness.

Note where public or state school systems feature and the descriptors Laloux applies to depict their particular paradigm. It appears that schools have spent much of their time stuck at the Red traffic light. Now, they hesitate between Orange and Amber. Given the length of time in these domains, it would seem that schools are long overdue for change, to *flip the system*.

Not included in this first table is the color *Teal*. The Teal paradigm is the equivalent of what Maslow (1943) called self-actualization. This occurs when decision-making moves from external to internal yardsticks to create more values-led organizations, ones able to design well-being in rather than as an afterthought, add-on, or fix. Laloux invites us to consider how Teal organizations (explained below) change the metaphor in use from machines to those inspired by *life and nature*.

Preceding the framework (illustrated in table 18.1) were small kinship groups that Laloux calls *the Infrared Paradigm* (fifty to one hundred thousand years ago). This is followed by the tribal organization of *Magic Magenta* (around fifteen thousand years ago) and then the *Impulsive Red* epoch of around ten thousand years ago, which saw the first proto-empires and chiefdoms. These proposed epochs are each marked by states of consciousness and sense of self. We never escape our tribal success and must be forever aware of this very human need to belong and the price sometimes paid for membership!

Schools may like to ponder the attributes and descriptors akin to their particular organization (table above). What they will find are elements of every color in operation at any single moment in both practice and perception. How those in charge see the world (perhaps a globally competitive marketplace where winners take all, where fear is the organizational driver) determines the particular paradigm and color code. For those working to make sense of it all, there will always be a limited palette from which to choose.

This, however, is to let regimes and the engineering culture that run school systems off the hook. The reaction to a changing world by many governments remains the polar opposite of what might be hoped for as they toy with the past, guided by the ways of Red and Orange to make progress. This indicates a blockage in our organizational consciousness, one that requires the kind of shift in thinking needed to execute systemic change.

We know that we live in a time when knowledge is expanding beyond our capacity to grasp even a fraction and where the rate of change is accelerating along an exponential curve—so much so that our current epoch goes by several names: the Post-Industrial Age, the Knowledge Society, the Digital Age, Post-Modernism, and so on. Organizations have to adapt faster than has ever been the case in such uncertain times, and that means change and the ability to absorb complexity; but there is only so much mileage in Red and Amber. Some schools (charters, free schools, multiacademy trusts, and voucher schools) now find themselves purposefully placed in Orange, perhaps with the intention of providing competition to those schools stuck in Amber and glued to repetition of the past.

In fact, Laloux places most schools in Amber and Orange guided respectively by the metaphors *Army* and *Machine*. Some teachers might feel less generous and view themselves more in the *Wolf Pack* of the *Red zone*. Head teachers and managers may choose to believe they operate almost entirely in deeply caring Green schools where everyone is valued through a family ambience and where parent partnership is *de rigueur*. Unfortunately, trying to reflect using a seemingly immovable industrial mind-set can often be difficult, delusional, and self-deceiving.

For Laloux, organizations like schools that often exhibit a palette of behaviors are organizationally stuck at a particular level of consciousness, none of them as high as they might be. This might explain why schools with aspirations to be bona fide *learning organizations* have yet to materialize and why so few of us can claim to work in such places.

For organizational theory, the classroom ceases to be the overriding problem we are led to believe, and if we seek a learning solution there we are likely to be disappointed. Of primary importance is the way schools go about realizing issues of connectedness to enable learning relationships to form, which explains why Teal, a higher level of consciousness, is about wholeness and integration.

Schools may aspire to Green and even argue vociferously that this is their patch, their dictum. They may even point to evidence in their school to back their case, but their actual home remains largely in the command structure of Amber where the future is repetition of the past, or Orange where purpose is still heavily controlled, leaving schools limited elbow room to decide the *what* and *how*. Green organizations are driven by values—something linear schools are unable to design-in, having been obliged to abandon them under prevailing NPM conditions.

## GREEN AND TEAL SCHOOLS

In the model, VT (mixed-age) schools designed using principles of systems thinking feature in Green. These schools reignite their values because they have figured out a way to embrace complex learning relationships; they are *connected schools*, and this reflects their higher level of consciousness, their ecology of mind—one that safeguards well-being. Their guiding metaphors are "family" (Green) and "living system" (Teal)—ones reliant on values related to family, teams, and collaboration, attributes of what Laloux terms "higher levels of consciousness."

*The Teal organization* transcends previous models and presents challenges both to schools and to the idea of *schooling* that on first sight may seem insurmountable. It is worth pausing and returning to Peter Senge (1990) and his idea of the learning organization:

> Organizations where people continually expand their capacity to create the results they truly desire, where new and expansive patterns of thinking are nurtured, where collective aspiration is set free, and where people are continually learning to see the whole together.

This is the philosophical and psychological essence of all that truly high-performing Teal schools might be. Teal represents a higher level of evolutionary consciousness that transcends previous paradigms. In the postmodernity of the West, millennials (system survivors) desperate to avoid becoming homo economicus strive for the higher values of Green, an epoch typified by equity, acceptance of diversity, cooperation, fairness, inclusion, action on climate change (ecological embeddedness), and tolerance.

It seems that having experienced the trauma of Orange with its uncontrolled greed, biases, and damage to the commons, many (millennials) now aspire to something better. The Teal organization seeks wisdom and promotes the kind of spiritual and emotional intelligence (SQ and EQ) that enables people to connect and be more of who they were meant to be. Unsurprisingly, the metaphor that Laloux assigns to Teal is *a living system* and represents a way in which ego can be set aside and replaced by a more joyful, fulfilling, and creative experience. It is the epoch of Beta organizations, ones unwilling to leave the future to the deliverologists of the past. It is also where this book started its journey.

In Teal organizations, management and leadership take on a very different form. In fact, the idea of the manager virtually disappears from the organization as a permanent feature, echoing Beer's VSM (viable systems model). In a mixed-age tutor group, leadership, learning, and mentoring are integrated and collaborative approaches that work to ensure any learning support is on tap. Hierarchies form and reform wherever needed between students

**Table 18.2.  The Teal Organization (from Laloux, 2014 with VT and Lumiar added)**

| Organizational Descriptors | School Examples | Breakthrough | Metaphor |
|---|---|---|---|
| Teal: Self-management replaces the hierarchical pyramid. Organizations are seen as living entities, oriented toward realizing their potential. | ESBZ School, Germany (used by Laloux as an exemplar). Also Jenaplan, Holland. Steiner, Montessori, Lumiar. Mature VT schools | • Self-management<br>• Wholeness<br>• Evolutionary purpose | Living system |

as mentors and sometime staff. Mentoring and leadership are everywhere appearing as needed to service and reduce demand. (In the chapter that follows, these design imperatives are set out.)

A significant feature of Teal is a trend for self-employment. One of the purposes of schools has always been to prepare students for employment. Teal suggests that schools should expand this to prepare young people for a future whereby they need and want to create their own jobs. It is an area in which the UK has enjoyed success. In Teal, groups of professional people become self-managing and self-organizing and (servant and systems) leadership is more about the enablement of others. In table 18.2, types of schools that aspire to Teal have been added.

Many schools experience fleeting moments when they stand on tiptoe and shine as organizations. But look closely and pay is tightly linked to status (Amber), and leadership leans toward Amber and Orange while aspiring to Green. *De facto* purpose and targets remain rooted in Orange blocking the intrinsic motivation on which Teal organizations depend.

The breakthroughs attributed to Teal organizations are self-management, wholeness, and evolutionary purpose. Donella Meadows (2009) doesn't shy away from their value.

> The most stunning thing living systems and some social systems can do is to change themselves utterly by creating whole new structures and behaviours. In biological systems that power is called evolution . . . The ability to self-organise is the strongest form of system resilience. A system that can evolve can survive almost any change, by changing itself. (p. 159)

For Laloux:

> Our schools today are probably further away from self-management than most other types of organizations. We have turned schools, almost everywhere, into soulless factories that process children in batches of 25 per class, one year at

a time. Children are essentially viewed as interchangeable units channeled through a pre-defined curriculum. (p. 93).

For Teal, responsibility is distributed across the organization enabling decisions and strategies to be used creatively and quickly just as it is in mixed-age schools. It is an interconnected system based on trust that not only allows more complex information to flow and be absorbed but reduces feedback lags and speeds up interventions. The purpose is to create organizational interconnectivity determined and managed through collaboration and teamwork. When information is accessible and able to flow freely, the organization starts to learn, adapt, and improve quality without recourse to arbitrary targets and incentive bonuses.

Wholeness for Teal is the shift from an environment where only the narrow professional self with its many external and internal impositions is permitted, to one that is more ego-free, enabling people to realize much more of their true selves. This brings additional benefits to the organization like renewed energy, loyalty, enthusiasm, and creativity. Resultant teamwork can enable a school to perform well above its fighting weight.

If a key purpose of a school is to increase the stock of goodness in the world, release creativity, and develop individual potential, then growing young people into who they were meant to be is preferable to the serendipity of current practices with constant repetition of the past (Amber*)*.

Evolutionary purpose defies the ambivalence of paradox. For Laloux, Teal organizations "base their strategies on what they sense the world is asking from them." When they do, they respond with *agile practices* that no longer require the expense and delays of long-term plans, targets, and incentives. The upshot is they perform better and achieve more because human organizational energy and intrinsic motivation are replenished rather than depleted. In turn, this demands a more sophisticated and ecological mind-set regarding judgments about performance and therein is the challenge. The danger is always atrophy.

While this may sound metaphysical, schools despite their circumstances are more than familiar with such ideas, and this makes them well placed to aspire to Teal styles of self-organization. Besides, it is the karma of schools to prepare for the future without the bits of the future they need, and this means being reliant on values, organizational resilience, and connectivity framed within an ecological mind-set.

Table 18.3 compares Teal structure with Orange, the dominant frame of reference for today's management thinking. It needs to be said that this comparison from Laloux runs to several pages covering many areas. A small selection is adapted here for schools to give a flavor. All of these ideas stem directly from organizational practices of existing and named companies, including at least one school.

**Table 18.3.** The Next Stage of Organizational Evolution (adapted for schools from Laloux, 2014)

| Structure | Orange Practices | Teal Practices |
|---|---|---|
| Coordination | Fixed meetings at every level leading to overload | No executive team meetings: coordination mostly ad hoc as need arises. This frees time for real work |
| Staff functions | Plethora of central staff for HR, IT, curriculum, risk management, counselling, support services, finances | Most functions performed within teams. In a VT school, the tutors are the design hub. They connect all other groups fostering learning relationships. They can pull down resources as needed. |
| Recruitment | Interviews by trained senior staff, focus on fit with the job description | Interviews by future colleagues based on fit with school ethos, teams, and ecological purpose |
| Training | Based on response to external diktat (exam changes) and inspection needs/protocols | Personal and group responsibility for training. Critical importance of common training for all and especially training based on studies of value demand and pedagogy |
| Performance management | Focus on individual teacher as the problem that needs addressing Appraisal from superior highlighting past performance and new targets often determining pay/reward | Focus on the team; peer-based evaluation used to explore *calling* and organizational purpose. Feedback is regularly given as needed and designed in, not annual. |
| Office spaces | Standardized, soulless, and abundant status markers | Self-decorated, warm, open to children, animals, and plants. Shared and flexible. No status markers |
| Information flow | Need to know, restricted and minimized, the default is secrecy to outside world | All info available in real time, including school finances/protocols. Transparency invites suggestions for improvement. |
| Purpose | To achieve test pass rates; related to self-preservation; this drives decision-making and teacher method | The school has its own evolutionary purpose/values. Competition and comparisons are largely irrelevant. |

## TEAL IDEAS

The idea of training against value demand has been featured throughout, and Teal seals the deal. In Teal, power is not empowered nor is it delegated or distributed solely as a set of permissions. Such ideas hide command structures, a matter discussed earlier and concerning distributed leadership.

It is the willing acceptance of responsibility that enables teams at the edge to manage demand and do the work in the most efficient and humane way possible. The traditional idea of training people to progress along chosen career pathways ceases to be valid because the structures cease to be dominator-pyramidal, far better to resource training against demand than spend valuable time and resources dealing with organizational failure demand. Besides, all important decisions are taken by those working at the base and edge of organizations, on shop floors, and in tutor groups and classes.

At a skills level, Teal colleagues lead much of the training. Why? Because they know the work that needs to be done and have access to the ideas and suggestions of other teams. External consultants enable such a process. For schools changing to a mixed-age system, there is a commonality of training around values-led culture that continually develops the learning relationships between school, students, and parents so essential in absorbing complexity. To support transformation, any external trainer will need to lean toward being a Teal systems practitioner, heretical, noncompliant to orthodoxy, and versed in curation and systems thinking.

The removal of the traditional management scaffolding to one that is self-managing (self-organizing) may seem high-risk with the potential for chaos, but people are too smart for that. Laloux describes the replacement structures used by major companies as "complex, participatory, interconnected, interdependent, and continually evolving systems, like ecosystems in nature."

## SCHOOLS

Laloux focuses on the ESBZ, a parent start-up secondary school that opened in 2007 in the center of Berlin with sixteen students. From his description, the following design principles emerge.

1. Students toggle between being learners and being teachers. A child's first port of call is another student. Older students are trained to help younger ones. Empathy and leadership are built-in.
2. Every child has a one-to-one meeting with their tutor each Friday. The tutor acts as an academic and pastoral guide. This ensures every child is known and feels cared for.

3. Every class has two teacher tutors. Teaching shouldn't be an isolated and lonely activity.
4. Twice a year, there are deep learning conversations where students arrive at goals via strategies for improvement.
5. The school is divided into mini-schools, the kind of nested system advocated by Bronfenbrenner and others.
6. Parents contribute to costs by giving a regular time commitment to the school.

There is much about the values of this inclusive oversubscribed school to admire and the innovative way it goes about its work (there are no grades until a student is fifteen). These are precisely the organizational principles that the mixed-age system employs, describing vertical tutoring with unswerving accuracy.

In the chapter that follows, we leave Germany and switch to Holland for inspiration. All the design principles needed to build a connected Teal school are then listed. None cost a school a penny to implement. All require management change.

*Chapter 19*

# The Buurtzorg School

Before anyone Googles this, there is no such thing as a Buurtzorg School. All will become clear, but first another diversion. In this chapter, design principles learned from other organizations and Teal practices are put into practice to create a self-organizing school, something every secondary school can do given care and a little systems knowledge.

To get us there, we travel to Holland. The Dutch have not only managed to build an education system that performs well but, according to UNICEF, have the happiest and most well-balanced kids in the world. Among the factors noted by Rina Mae Acosta and Michele Hutchinson (2017) are the importance of family life, simplicity, and a practical view of equity and equality.

Their parents too, according to surveys, are happy. Dutch children can play freely outside and ride their bikes to school, while Dutch babies, it is claimed, sleep longer and are more contented than those in the USA. There is also less pressure to excel, although there is a kind of 11+ called the CITO that helps parents determine the type of secondary school most appropriate for their children.

The authors describe Dutch culture as one that is able to downplay anxiety by adopting an adult perspective on life. Acosta and Hutchinson note that in New York and London, "parenting has evolved into a highly competitive, exhausting business, and schooling into a war zone." The Dutch are good at taking in the big picture, and schools and parents seem to be better systems thinkers and more adept child psychologists. Schooling in both structure (choice architecture) and expectation seems in many ways to be an extension of family life.

Alma Harris and Michelle Jones (2017) describe *The Dutch Way* as "a best kept secret." There are three key lessons to be learned and one, judiciously, that seems to be missing!

1.  Like Finland, the Dutch have avoided the angst of the UK and the USA by not relying on competition, preferring strong collaboration between teachers, schools, and municipalities.
2.  The Dutch approach is inclusive and students leave school better able to participate in the world of work. Schooling provides flexible pathways, and any decisions about which pathway is the more appropriate involve family and school collaboration, not just examination passes.
3.  The system always seeks to combine equity and equality.

Like Finland, there is a sense that there must be a careful balance between school inspection, intervention, and constructive support. There are other factors; primary school children and teachers are free from the anxiety of homework, while school inspectors play a less intrusive role than they do in (say) the UK. Fee-paying schools are relatively few, and much of the learning groundwork is done prior to the children starting school.

The Dutch also have the advantage of not having a middle school system. This is missing from the list and the heresy is that this is the sensible way to go. Even the UK managed to give up on the idea of middle schools and, among the numerous advantageous reasons, one stands out. Given that the formation of long-term learning and support relationships is critical to learning and child development (connectedness, belonging, attachment, etc.), there can be no justifiable reason to increase anxiety by adding an unnecessary middle stage to schooling that disrupts the sense of safety children need if they are to be at their best. In terms of systems, middle schools and junior highs cause an unnecessary obstacle to learning by interfering in long-term learning relationships.

## WELCOME TO BUURTZORG

The point of that little detour is simply to show that the Dutch are good at solving systems problems and seeing past the fear-mongering nonsense that NPM brings to the table; it is wise to remember that fear is an inhibitor and the organizational opposite of trust and responsibility. The Dutch also have a strong sense of community and the kind of organizational know-how required to inspire happiness and well-being. They tend to get their priorities and values right.

Over the past decade, a Dutch nursing company called *Buurtzorg* (it means *neighborhood care*) has won international recognition as an exemplar of how service organizations work at their best. Buurtzorg has become self-organizing (the ability to create a different structure, to learn, complexify, and be adaptive) and because of this capability it is able to provide services internationally recognized as being among the very best. It has achieved a reputation as an organization where team workers are genuinely happy, a disposition evidenced by high measures of intrinsic motivation.

Buurtzorg is one of the exemplars identified by Laloux as a Teal organization. Its mission statement reads as follows (as ever, we need to think *school* as we look at how this service sector model operates):

> To change and improve the delivery and quality of home health care through the leadership and collaboration of the community nurse, allowing the individual to receive the kind of care they most need, where they most want it, and thus avoid more costly institutional care for as long as possible.

It is a model that parts of National Health Service (NHS) England are beginning to explore and practice. Such a systems approach saves time and money, something that NPM advocates might note. The mission statement acts to limit failure demand, the cost of not doing things right the first time, by predicting where intervention is needed (studying demand) and having the power to act (trust, training, and responsibility). It does this by building an enabling support structure around patients when and where they need it based on the support team's judgment and that of the patient as service receiver. Further, the community team can *pull* down from the system the resources needed to do the work.

For community nurse, think form-room or homeroom tutor! The purpose of Buurtzorg is quite straightforward and, like most ideas stemming from systems thinking, boils down to common sense. It understands that service providers working directly with those needing help are best placed to identify and absorb the complexity of demand on the system. The Buurtzorg system is individualized, one where the system adapts and responds to client need rather than the client having to adapt to a one-size-fits-all system. It is classic pull theory using Beta thinking; the client, working with the community nurse, can more easily access (pull down) the resources needed to enable the best possible outcome.

Buurtzorg builds self-managing teams that work with minimal bureaucratic support. The counterintuitive approach of Buurtzorg is to strengthen the team by reducing regulation, rules, and targets from above (sources of waste). There are no bosses or middle managers, and the removal of obstructive hierarchy alters everything.

> The teams of nurses aren't simply empowered by their hierarchy; they are truly powerful because there is no hierarchy. (Laloux, 2014, p. 69)

Customer need (value demand) determines the service provided.

* The right care and coordination are provided at the point of contact where decisions are also made.
* Decisions are not delayed or lost in myriad referral procedures.
* Responsibility and training also move to the edge of the system where increased trust and responsibility stoke intrinsic motivation needed to do the work in a quality way.

Research relating to Buurtzorg shows that such a system not only prolongs and increases the quality of life, but also saves money through the avoidance of institutional care and bureaucracy. It is the model that the UK's NHS is anxious to adopt should it ever be able to untangle the messiness, waste, and mistrust within the current approach.

## THE UK APPROACH

The bureaucracy that emanates from regimes, especially in the UK, is massive and leads to a sea of paperwork, complications, and bureaucracy that slows everything down and leads to low morale. Work problems are resolved through add-ons, fixes, and increased investment rather than distributed leadership, training, and trust. It was Ricardo Semler (of Maverick fame) who noted that bureaucracies are built by people to prove they are necessary, a process achieved through the forlorn hope of trying to add value from the top.

The Alpha model in use (UK) is a command model whereby the person needing care has to cope and comply with the complications and bureaucracy involved in provision. One-size-fits-all remains the NPM case, a system that leads to gaming, inequity, and post-code lotteries. The service is prespecified, dependent on economies of scale, and budget-driven, and results in vulnerable people having to navigate a host of obstacles and complications to access the care they need. There is a world of difference between services contracted out to private companies and the approach adopted by Buurtzorg that has no visible management bureaucracy.

In effect, older people and the sick cannot easily *pull* down from a bureaucratic and difficult-to-access institution the help they need to live their lives with the independence they want. Buurtzorg ensures this is not the case. Buurtzorg has done away with complications and built a system where complex teams resolve the complex issues faced by complex people. The system is flexible, fast, and able to handle the variety of demand it is there to absorb.

Community care as it exists in the UK suffers from a litany of assumptions and a style of management inherited from Taylorism through Thatcher,

Major, and the Blair years to the present time. The command model directs a community helper to a host of patients at set hours to perform preprogrammed tasks in the shortest possible time at the lowest cost. This allows performance (the wrong performance) to be superficially measured and efficiencies gauged.

It returns us to the old model where purpose is replaced by simplistic measures that constrain method and prevent innovation. Dominant thinking *pushes* and assumes such an approach to be an efficient use of precious resources when all it really does is provide unnecessary layers of management and increased costs. It is all too easy and highly expensive to create a failure demand system, one that builds with complications.

The nurse or helper follows direction from on high, has targets to achieve, and a workload to cover in a given time. If she or he discovers a problem, this is written up, referred to another group who might eventually make an assessment and refer it on yet again: it is a failure demand process that is unable to predict, causes dangerous delays, and increases costs while the client's condition deteriorates, further complicating the process. The community nurse or equivalent is often under workload stress, suffers low morale, and has to be paid a minimal amount to cover the costs of bureaucracy.

In such a system, no one knows the patient well and, like the student in school, he or she is known only through data sheets and snatched conversations. The patient then ends up in hospital in a bad condition requiring massive care from a host of other service interventions. Once in hospital, it seems the patient cannot be released because of other service complications. Nobody benefits, no relationships form, and no savings are made for system investment.

The visiting nurse and most others are robbed of intrinsic motivation just as Laloux suggested. Care is designed to suit the system in use, not the individual, just as it is in schools where school counsellors, deans, and heads of year become a dumping ground for a system ironically driven by care but organizationally unable to express it.

There is a choice: *Alpha* or *Beta*. We can either unlearn and replace existing linear thinking with systems thinking (Teal) or perpetuate as the NPM engineering culture suggests.

## BACK TO BUURTZORG AND THE DUTCH WAY

So how does Buurtzorg do it? Buurtzorg, care in the community, thrives on self-management, an extension of self-organization. In a self-organizing system, teams decide how the work is done and who should do it. Buurtzorg is self-managing. It hands over complete responsibility and autonomy to small teams of nurses (maximum twelve) who handle between forty and fifty vulnerable clients, each of whom may present a different challenge. The team decides not only how the work should be done and who should do it but what the work priorities are. This includes managing their own training and budgets.

The team has to support the chronically ill, the severely disabled, and those struggling with dementia. Each area team has its own budget, decides on the best intervention and support strategies, builds informal community networks, collaborates with specialists, and spends time with each patient on a needs basis decided by the circumstances.

Buurtzorg team member undergoes training in "Solution-Driven Methods of Interaction," to ensure that listening and communication skills lead to better team decisions, underpinning the research conducted by Google. Training is not designed for career progression but for personal satisfaction and increased work expertise—to get better at doing rewarding work. The Buurtzorg system inspires learning. Nurses, like teachers, want to be trained in more advanced techniques so that they can be of the greatest benefit to others, such is their self-motivation. Their reward is intrinsic motivation.

You may think that team leadership is the key and search above the teams for managers and controllers, but there are none. Even leadership is designed in and shared. The seven thousand workforce is administered by thirty people, none of whom set targets or demand extra paperwork. There are no regional managers, but there are regional team coaches and these too have no targets, no incentive bonuses, no responsibility for outcomes, and no managerial career structure.

In effect, hierarchies (some nurses will always have more expertise than others in given situations) are relocated to where they are needed according to the group's need and patient context. Because of this, individuals experience high job satisfaction, feel trusted, and are highly intrinsically motivated. Training is decided by the team and is based on demand (what is needed to improve the way the system works for patients). The team can also review individual performance, recruit, and *set free* those unable to meet the team's standards.

The team decides all pertinent issues. These include how many patients they can serve, holiday scheduling, whether they need to rent an office, which doctors and pharmacies should be involved, how to work with hospitals, how to determine tasks, who to employ, and how to monitor their own performance. They ensure that patients are known, listened to, and trust established. They might arrange for a hairdresser to visit or relatives to call. Laloux describes Buurtzorg care as follows:

> Over the course of days and weeks, deep trust can take root in the relationship.
> Care is no longer reduced to a shot or a bandage—patients can be seen and

honored in their wholeness, with attention paid not only to their physical needs but also their emotional, relational and spiritual ones. (p. 65)

Patients are not only known, but able to contribute far more to their own wellness because of the relationship with the nurse and support network. They practice optimal self-management. The result is a happier client who thrives more and who requires less specialist and expensive care in hospital. As caregivers, nurses are valued, respected, and listened to, and survey after survey reports extremely high job satisfaction. Management of the team is absent in this self-organizing structure, and bureaucracy kept to a minimum to allow the team to develop any good practice that other teams share.

There is much more, but the message is clear. So how might a school start to build a self-organizing system, a kind of viable systems model that has high work satisfaction and better outcomes? It has to be worth a try.

## DESIGNING A BUURTZORG SCHOOL

Because schools like mission statements, the one used by Buurtzorg can be adapted:

To change and improve the delivery and quality of education in our school through the leadership and collaboration of the community, tutors, staff, and parents, allowing the individual to receive the kind of care and support they most need, where they most need it, and thus avoid the community cost of failure demand.

This adapted statement is a Teal-style blueprint and contains the word *change*, a call for action. The three Teal descriptors are *self-management, wholeness, and evolutionary purpose,* so we need to bear these in mind. The Buurtzorg School needs to enable self-managing style groups to form, and this means unlearning most of the management tenets that dominate current (Orange) organizations.

In particular, Orange preaches a neoliberalist view of meritocracy that all can achieve and prosper; a view, to quote Charlotte Pell (2016), that people are "perfectible . . . if only they tried hard enough" (p. 7). Such a situation fails to deconstruct the formality of Amber with its bureaucratic command scaffolding, one where the route to meritocracy is based on examination success. The school has to mitigate the existing management processes until it can collude with communities to remove such obstructions and design something more relevant and more likely to lead to systemic change.

Given the restrictions of conformist Amber, the promise of achievement Orange, and the ideals of pluralistic Green, designing a school based on Teal thinking and the Buurtzorg approach seems fraught with difficulty, but all is not lost. It is still possible to set out the design parameters schools need. The means is mixed-age organization with its redesigned learning relationships. Remember, for Teal organizations the aim is for self-actualization, the final destination in Maslow's (1943) hierarchy of needs.

Set out below are the basic design parameters, and why vertical tutoring with its mixed-age tutor groups fits the bill.


## THE DESIGN PARAMETERS OF A BUURTZORG SCHOOL

- Children need to feel looked after, known, listened to, and valued for all they bring to school. These are not specious claims made by schools but psychological imperatives that must be organizationally enabled—a need to belong and feel safe based on a better understanding of the dynamics of family dynamics and mixed-age in-group loyalty.
- There must be at least two adults (tutors) in the school who know the child well and who offer a sense of permanence and ongoing support. This is the lead tutor and co-tutor who see their tutor group for around twenty minutes each day. They do not teach programs as such. There are sufficient staff and adults to achieve two tutors per tutor group, at least one of which is a teacher. Every adult/employee is a tutor.
- No adult joins the school in any capacity without realizing he or she will be expected to be a tutor. All adults are form tutors, including ancillary staff, the head teacher, CEO, and leadership team. It is not a promotion to abandon working with students for the perceived higher task of administration. It is essential for school leaders to remain in the value work if they are to study demand and understand a pull system and the training and trust needed to absorb the variety of demand on the system.
- All information about the child from within school and from the community (parents) flows through form tutors who are enabled to intervene as needed. The tutor is the learning hub through whom information flows. They can access and pull down any organizational resources and any information needed to support learning and teaching. Schools have long identified this role but have disabled tutors from making their job profile a reality.
- Any information sent home must be more than numbers and grades and include strategies for improvement (enhanced summative assessment for learning). Quality conversations require quality information and time for discussion in a safe environment at critical times.
- Parents and students have to be active partners in learning and support. The school has to reach out and extend its (strong and loose-tie) network. This

means designing-in parent partnership via deep learning tutorials lasting about forty-five minutes each year at all critical learning times.

- Schools must identify these critical learning times (occasions when school, child, and parent need to share information to guide decisions) and coordinate these with report evenings (assessment for learning) and reporting processes to guide agreed strategies for improvement. These are the first items to be placed on the school's academic calendar. Subject (full) reports containing learning strategies should never come at the end of the school year.
- The child needs to belong to a mixed-age home base of around eighteen students. This greatly reduces bullying, optimizes well-being, and expands the student's pro-social, pro-school support network.
- Every child has to be enabled to fulfil a leadership and mentoring role as he or she grows. Every child is a learner, a mentor, and a leader. This occurs easily in mixed-age groups. Empathy is designed in (not added on) through mentoring and leadership training for all students.
- Citizenship, wellness, and pro-social programs will not be required as add-ons and fixes! These can be absorbed into the way the school operates as a nested system; each tutor group is democratically involved in how the school as an organization operates. In this way, care is not added on but it too is redefined and designed in. Once the system is running, PSHE and pro-social programs can be made complementary as needed. The tutors will decide what is needed with students.
- The curriculum will contain not only what we do know but will also allow time for personal development and for exploring what we don't know. There has to be balance. STEM remains vital but not at the cost of other learning areas as Projects Aristotle and Oxygen showed.
- The school will measure itself not only on outcomes easily measured but also by its capacity to nurture empathetic behavior, enthusiasm, goodness, helpfulness, wellness, and leadership for all—the school's capacity to grow young people into the capable citizens they were meant to be. We might call this the school's *genius loci*, the spirit of the place.
- There will be no student council or student voice add-ons. Each tutor group is a student council, and every student's voice will and can be heard, attributes incorporated within the nested house structure to which tutor groups belong.
- Reports will be redesigned within a revised assessment for learning process to illuminate learning progression. The tutors take the overall or summative view of learning in conjunction with the students and parents. These are important as the baseline of learning discussions and reflection and general strategies for improvement.

- Managers will no longer manage people as such but will facilitate change to the mixed-age system and self-organization. They manage the change to an enabling system (the viable system model) until the school can self-manage.

And so the list builds, and so the management dominoes fall, driven by values and sound common-sense principles. This is precisely the model that mixed-age design builds. Each guideline is underpinned by psychology (Bronfenbrenner's six principles, Maslow's hierarchy of needs, Dweck's growth mind-set, Duckworth's ideas on grit and perseverance, Rutter's studies of resilience, Bowlby's attachment theory, etc.). None are treated as add-ons but as matters that combine to provide a more holistic and humane approach to learning and to organization, one able to embrace complexity and one with empathy and collaboration incorporated within the design as imperatives, not add-ons.

The design process starts with the needs of those trying to make the system work, the teachers, staff, students, and parents. These players form an intricate and interweaving matrix of essential learning relationships focused on learning. The school has to get the underpinning psychology right and not assume attachment, care, and support. These socioprofessional networks have intricate feedback loops and to work optimally, they need to flow and contain usable information, not just data.

Learning relationships cannot be a consequence of separation and limitation, a matter of fortune, but must be a minute one, day one, and week one, designed-in requirement. Students cannot wait until a teacher actually speaks to them and a further year until a relationship forms only to dissipate when a teacher leaves and a new one starts.

There can be no long feedback delays in forming in-group loyalty. Critical to successful growth and better learning outcomes is what happens in the first hour of the first day in the new school; who the child meets and how. The school has to apply Buurtzorg principles and design in as much self-organization as possible. If this is the general essence of the Buurtzorg organization, the Buurtzorg school, it is possible to look at particulars too.


## THE IN-GROUP


A child aged eleven (say) is about to join secondary school. Instead of that child having to fit into the school organization, learn its ways, and find friends, why not approach induction from the child's point of view as Buurtzorg would? We can bear in mind value demand, psychology, and the need to develop supportive learning relationships with immediacy. The student is one of a group of four children (same-age) joining their tutor group in the school.

On the first day, they will meet their two tutors, both of whom have prepared themselves by studying the students' transfer files.

Twenty minutes later, these young children will meet four older students from the same tutor group who have been trained to mentor and look after them and guide them through the first few difficult weeks. They are experts in Google and Aristotle and Oxygen. These students will show the younger ones around the school, sort out timetables, and explain systems. They will be there every day for them.

The next day, the students meet the whole tutor group, another empathetic and belonging group that has been together a long time and understands what it is like to be new to the school. No getting-to-know-you games are played; these come later when the newcomers feel safe and are used to being heard.

These *belonging* and support groups form around the new students aided by other students who willingly take on leadership and mentoring roles; young people long to be leaders, trusted, respected, enabled, and to be seen to be cool, an ultimate accolade! The work is done by the group. The group changes the group. The school organizes the first stage by ensuring all children are members of a self-supporting and self-managing in-group loyalty team with a wide strong and loose-ties framework. This provides a firm base, a home group, one that is safe and one from which young people can venture out with, knowing the group has their back.

New-intake students are not abandoned to the risk of finding new friends in the chaos of the peer group, circle time, and getting-to-know-you games; these come later when the child feels secure and settled! It is what a Dutch family would do—explanation, preparation, alleviate anxiety, trust.

At the end of the very first day of school, the tutors contact home and begin a professional dialogue with parents that will last for the entirety of the student's school career. Tutors build the pull system. They pull the parents in. They reach out and engage. The complete tutor group size will be around eighteen and meet once a day during the twenty minutes before break time in the morning, the optimal time for tutoring. There is no pro-social program to follow as such, but a civic life to be practiced in safety with all its authenticity just as Mary Parker Follett advised over a century ago.

The tutor group is not a friendship group as such, even though this group will be and act as the best friends ever! But it is the starting place for each child to build and manage her own networks, a lifelong skill she will need beyond the school gates. On no account should a child begin school life with circle time, team-building exercises, and settling-in or getting-to-know-you games something often *de rigeur* for same-age institutions. Such strategies are *Lord of the Flies* variations more likely to have an opposite effect, including long-lasting detrimental consequences. If this kind of activity is

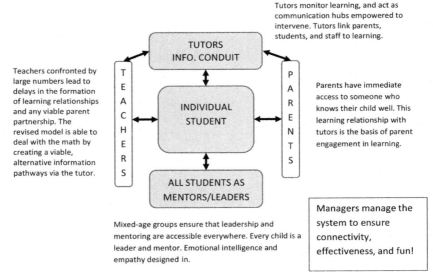

Tutors monitor learning, and act as communication hubs empowered to intervene. Tutors link parents, students, and staff to learning.

TUTORS INFO. CONDUIT

Teachers confronted by large numbers lead to delays in the formation of learning relationships and any viable parent partnership. The revised model is able to deal with the math by creating a viable, alternative information pathways via the tutor.

T E A C H E R S

INDIVIDUAL STUDENT

P A R E N T S

Parents have immediate access to someone who knows their child well. This learning relationship with tutors is the basis of parent engagement in learning.

ALL STUDENTS AS MENTORS/LEADERS

Mixed-age groups ensure that leadership and mentoring are accessible everywhere. Every child is a leader and mentor. Emotional intelligence and empathy designed in.

Managers manage the system to ensure connectivity, effectiveness, and fun!

**Figure 19.1. The Basic Self-Organizing School**

introduced before a child feels secure, it can be a sure way to design bullying in rather than out.

The Buurtzorg approach is to create self-managing autonomous groups capable of building community and drawing down from the system all that is needed to make progress. For the child, the tutor group is ideal—a cost-effective way to absorb value demand before it becomes failure demand. The mixed-age tutor group is self-organizing, so it creates its own agenda based on need and context, an ideal place for learning support in all its guises.

A mixed-age group built on empathy and support grows resilience and encourages a can-do mind-set. It ensures well-being through complex learning relationships coordinated by tutors and students whereby the tutors are the nodal link between child, home, and school. For schools, this means establishing long-term support and mentoring relationships around each child. Mentors include everybody in the school, including every other child. This makes every child a leader, mentor, and role model.

In other words, the school creates self-managing tutor groups. Every child is surrounded by advisers and mentors who have their back in trying times. Parents have direct access to someone in the school who knows their child well (a front office system). Slowly, a nested system builds as all players connect to each other in a network of socio-learning relationships. The effect is to build multiple complex groups all exchanging information; a new front-office information system replaces the existing back-office menagerie that parents were required to battle through.

The next stage is to ensure that tutor group belongs to a school within a school, sometimes called a house or college. In turn, each house has its own head teacher, the equivalent of the Buurtzorg coach. When combined, the houses form a school, and the nested system that started with the tutor meeting a child for the first time builds. All that remains is to meet the design specifications outlined above.

When the mixed-age lever is activated, management responsibilities migrate to the edge of the school to where the value work takes place. The feedback loops are reestablished, the information flow improved, and intrinsic motivation restored. The basic mixed-age model is set out conceptually in figure 19.1, a template derived from schools that have made a successful transition to a mixed-age structure. In this model, the child is surrounded by a support network (team child) coordinated by the child's tutor. And here is the only difficult bit. Can managers change in ways that support and promote the nonlinear, viable systems model—the socially collaborative school?

# Chapter 20

# Moving from Complicated to Complex—The Strange Case of the Effect List

Reform solutions, fixes, and add-ons take a mechanistic and reductionist view of what is really a living system; the idea behind such thinking (the engineer's approach) is that by applying the right tools to complex structures like schools, they can be repaired or somehow made to work better with either a new addition or replacement part. When this approach fails, they act on the operatives with any crude management tools they can find.

The problem with schools organized on a same-age basis is that they work precisely as intended (POSIWID). When the engineer tries to correct what has clearly become a basic design fault with a scatter-gun approach oblivious to cause, the machinery becomes ever more complicated to run and injurious to participants. The school is unable to absorb the variety of demand on its system, and this is especially so in jurisdictions low in both equity and social mobility.

An indicator of how complicated and off-course schools in the UK have become is provided by the Office for National Statistics (2016). In general terms, 48% of school employees are teachers, 28% are teaching assistants, and 25% are nonclassroom-based support staff. The engineering and executive cultures created a teacher workload problem that they then made the mistake of trying to fix. When they simplified (sought to reduce complexity), failure demand increased creating even more work. To solve the subsidiary problem, schools employed more support staff until the system became support staff dependent. This created more bureaucracy and new managers; all the while costs rose and quality plateaued.

How can it be that there are less teachers than support staff combined, and what improvements might there be if we employed a lot more teachers? Ken Robinson put it this way:

We have to rethink how we do school. These are systems we've created for efficiency, not to get people to learn things. We organize our kids' learning by their date of birth. We don't do that anywhere else, except school.

Unfortunately, the system once designed for separational and limitational efficiency has now become incredibly inefficient. It seems we've got efficiency all wrong and achieved complicated by mistake, but the engineers persist.

Readers who have got this far may have already picked up the difference between *complicated* and *complex* organizations. A clock is complicated. Treat a school like a clock, and it remains stuck in time and persists in doing the same things over and over. A living system is complex and treating it as complicated is a big mistake. Eileen Johnson (2008) notes the pathway followed by schools and the processes that direct them.

> The call for accountability within education has led to the increased examination of the academic achievement of students across the nation. Too often, however, schools and school districts are scrutinized by means of overly simplistic linear models that fail to consider the complexity of interactions that result in student achievement.

Johnson rightly describes education systems like schools as complex and dynamic with *multidirectional linkages and processes that interconnect different layers*. However, it is clear from previous chapters that the linkages and processes intended to connect different layers are by no means joined up. When faced with complexity, it cannot absorb (the variety of demand on the school); the school reacts by separating out people, parts, and issues. It treats complexity as a set of separate matters, component parts, a reductionist approach to solving problems that explains the employment ratios above.

The effect is to make things very complicated and rule-bound. This is reflected in the way the school organizes itself and the work it does. Johnson (2008) describes the situation as follows:

> Currently, many methods of investigating the educational outcomes of individual schools . . . are based on linear algorithms that simplify and break down systems into isolated, component parts. The premise of such linear models is that inputs into the system will result in predictable outcomes. While appropriately predictive of some static, closed systems, these models fail to adequately predict the behavior of or capture the essence and emergent properties of complex systems involving three or more interacting components. (pp. 5–6)

In effect, things have got so complicated that there is no natural entry point into the system for reformers. Schools are inherently complex, and this requires an organizational strategy that doesn't treat such inherent complexity as complications to be minimized and controlled. The school itself has to be complex if it is to absorb the complexity it faces. We have seen what happens when schools try and exert control of complexity using the same-age system in use. This takes us to John Hattie.

## EFFECT LISTS

This is what the statistician Pierre-Jérôme Bergeron (2017) says of John Hattie's work.

> To believe Hattie is to have a blind spot in one's critical thinking when assessing scientific rigor. To promote his work is to unfortunately fall into the promotion of pseudoscience. Finally, to persist in defending Hattie after becoming aware of the serious critique of his methodology constitutes willful blindness.

OK. But this time round, we'll be a little kinder. Hattie (2015a) believes that the variability in the effectiveness of teachers is the reason for underperformance in learning—variance between schools and individuals. The answer he suggests is to improve teacher expertise, not fix the teacher, or clumsily call them to account (complex vs. complicated). For Hattie, three matters have to coalesce: expert and passionate teachers operating collaboratively, school leaders able to maximize teacher effectiveness, and a system able to offer more support, training, and time. We are in danger of losing the first while training leaders in ways that assume the system is OK.

So it comes down to the system and any changes that are still within the limited remit of schools. In the unlikely event of wholesale systemic change, the aim must be to disturb the complicated thinking behind the same-age legacy and nudge schools in the direction of a more complex mixed-age system. Hattie will never attain what he seeks (in effect, the socially collaborative school) in the same-age system we have. Schools must be complex as systems, not complicated as nonsystems are. The idea of collaborative professionalism is not realizable in the same-age model (complicated), and this is the blocker. What is needed is the socially collaborative school (complex)—a mixed-age design whereby the school is dependent on collaboration as the means by which the work is done, not forcing it—this brings into play better assessment, improved knowledge flow, and the organizational learning Hattie seeks.

The *effect list* is intended to help such a process but is ultimately counterproductive. It does afford insights into important aspects of teaching and learning, and while this is helpful, it has no system impact as such and so is compensatory. It is the reception of such a list by the receiving system that is problematic. Jurisdictions take an organization like a school, apply the reductionist analysis of the engineer (the repair and fix list), and then blame the operators (teachers) for failing to follow *what works*, and the CEOs for lack of leadership rigor in implementation. Teachers need no reminding of visible learning; they simply crave a system that recognizes their agency, one more teal than orange.

Despite the criticisms regarding effect lists including the alleged errant use of statistical data and meta-analyses, the headlines that emanate from such lists rule the day. The effect list has in many ironic ways become part of the *politics of distraction* (Hattie, 2015b) from which Hattie urged escape. It is why this book concentrates on system change; the system has to change first if learning and teaching are to develop, and the real means of escape is the designed-in connectedness of the mixed-age model, the only one able to make sense of Hattie's guidance and able to connect all the dots.

Here's the systems rub. Everything in John Hattie's effect list is connected to everything else (complex) and has to be so given the variety of demand schools face. The list is not a list but a matrix; it is complex, not complicated. The system itself has to learn and be self-organizing, a state unobtainable in the industrial model in use, with all players garnered to the learning cause.

The heresy is simple; the effect list is interesting and not unhelpful but it delays the kind of systemic change schools and civic society needs. This is because the problem that needs to be dissolved is far more wicked than messy. For all students, smaller tutor groups are top of the effect list, not near the bottom, because the school is a living system. The teacher and student in the classroom depend on the rest of the school being effective at learning.

Hattie's concerns and statements of intent are correct; it is important to maximize impact and yes, teaching is important and can be improved, and yes, teachers working together are more effective, and yes, it is important to have credibility and high expectations. Schools know this. No meta-research analysis is needed for what teachers already know and want to do! The fact is everything on the effect list is connected to everything else on the list. Class size does matter! Having breakfast at school does help. None can be isolated from the other. An effect list is a guide, not a creed; everything works somewhere just as Dylan Wiliams said. This is why teaching is an art as well as a vocation and why agency is all.

And this is what the system should ensure. The effect list is interesting but to be useful it needs to be seen through a complex lens, not the engineer's microscope. Besides, the meta-research all stems from a same-age system, not one designed on mixed-age. And there it stops. In the absence of systems thinking, we look at parts rather than the whole and much research is necessarily of this kind. Research is there to ensure we engage with System 2 thinking when making decisions, to guide us rather than shore-up any biases.

Glouberman and Zimmerman (2002) set out a table (table 20.1) to illustrate the difference between tasks labelled simple, complicated, and complex.

Glouberman and Zimmerman argue that we are "trapped into a narrow way of defining and responding to current issues as if they were merely complicated." See how tempting it is to place an effect list (what works) in the first two columns when its home and its intention should be in column 3.

If schools follow effect lists, then teachers and schools belong in the Simple column under menus. Unfortunately, children are in the Complex column and this provides a better reality of the challenges schools face. Learning is complex, multifaceted, and requires an approach that is holistic, involving all players. How our players work, their connectedness, is what is important and this is highly complex, a systems issue.

John Hattie is right to call our attention to teaching and learning variables, but in the absence of systems thinking there are inherent dangers in the use of effect lists. These are described by Ivan Snook et al. (2009) as follows:

- Despite his own frequent warnings, politicians may use his (Hattie's) work to justify policies that he does not endorse and his research does not sanction.

**Table 20.1. Simple, Complicated, and Complex (from Glouberman and Zimmerman)**

| Simple | Complicated | Complex |
|---|---|---|
| Follow a Recipe | Send a Rocket to the Moon | Raise a Child |
| The recipe is essential | Formulae are critical and necessary | Formulae have a limited application |
| Recipes are tested to assure easy replication | Sending one rocket increases assurance that the next will be OK | Raising one child provides experience but no assurance of success with the next |
| No particular expertise is required. But cooking expertise increases success rate | High levels of expertise in a variety of fields are necessary for success | Expertise can contribute but is neither necessary nor sufficient to assure success |
| Recipes produce standardized products | Rockets are similar in critical ways | Every child is unique and must be understood as an individual |
| The best recipes give good results every time | There is a high degree of certainty of outcome | Uncertainty of outcome remains |
| Optimistic approach to problem possible | Optimistic approach to problem possible | Optimistic approach to problem possible |

- Teachers and teacher educators might try to use the findings in a simplistic way and not, as Hattie wants, as a source for "hypotheses for intelligent problem solving."
- The quantitative research on "school effects" might be presented in isolation from their historical, cultural, and social contexts, and their interaction with home and community backgrounds.
- In concentrating on measureable school effects, there may be insufficient discussion about the aims of education and the purposes of schooling without which the studies have little point.

Snook is being very fair but unfortunately, the horse may have bolted! We have been diverted from the organizational issues that influence learning and, at the risk of mixing metaphors, placed all our eggs in the teacher basket rather than that of the school as a joint social enterprise or social collaboration.

All we need do is make a subtle change. Forget the classroom for a moment. We need a school to believe that students can achieve more than they may think, and we need all players to have a collective response, not just teachers. Instead of seeing an effect list as a menu of separate parts, we need to see it through complex eyes all at the same time, as a guide to a connected learning system. In this way, the effect list adds to the design specification schools seek rather than being separate to it—a reminder of priorities.

We need the school to be complex, not simple and certainly not complicated. To handle complex problems requires complex people enabled to work in creative, collaborative, and flexible ways. When this happens, there is a higher likelihood of innovation and fresh approaches. We need our schools not just to believe they can make a difference but also to know they can with the right connectedness and enabling management approach.

The self-organizing Buurtzorg teams are constantly learning because they feel trusted and are self-enabled; they constantly innovate and discuss fresh approaches, ideas, and solutions. We need schools to behave similarly as organizations, able to learn and self-manage; but this can happen only when managers understand their enabling role and that there is no formula to follow other than the complexity that derives from the connectedness of a community of kindred spirits. Without systems thinking, this is very difficult to achieve.

## MANAGEMENT

It is all too easy to get hung up on the question, "What should a school management structure look like?" Most schools cover the regulations, what they perceive inspectors expect to see, what the new CEOs and commissioners demand, plus a few fringe benefits they interpret from research.

A more interesting question is this: "How do we enable our players (staff, students and parents) to collaborate, communicate and show care in order to support and promote learning and maintain aspiration?" Such a question is as spiritual and moral as it is practical in so far as the underpinning requirement is to connect people, build learning relationships, and ensure that all information feedback loops are current and working. Living systems like schools organized on a mixed-age basis exist to ensure that all the relationships needed to promote learning are all in place; that's what makes them complex. Controlling, separating, and minimizing them make things complicated, induce failure demand, inculcate fear, and increase costs!

As Larry Cuban (2010) observed, sending a rocket to the moon is a complicated task and so is brain surgery, while raising a child or getting children to succeed in school is complex. A complicated linear system, like the same-age schools we have, assumes expert and rational leaders, top-down planning, smooth implementation of policies, and clockwork organization—the well-oiled machine. It is simply not enough in a complex society low in equity.

It is a push production-line approach of plans, policies, and experts whereby students must adapt to the system rather than the enabling system to the learner. Cuban describes the way a school sets about organizing its affairs as becoming reliant on reductive assumptions where any attempt to change procedures and practices is a major event—such is the school's deep-seated need to stay true to its identifying features.

## COMPLICATED AND COMPLEX SCHOOL STRUCTURE

Most *successful* systems in terms of their interconnectedness and service coherence are complex. The more connections there are, the more stable the system, the more resilient it becomes, and the more it learns. The complex strategy is ultimately stronger, more flexible, and reduces failure demand. An example is Ontario. Fullan (2003) notes:

> The Ontario strategy is based on three overriding sustaining elements: respect for staff and for professional knowledge, comprehensiveness, and coherence and alignment through partnership between the government and the field (schools and districts). (p. 108)

Ontario minimized mandated approaches preferring to build on ideas from schools themselves—reform designed in and built from the base up. Schools that build feedback loops, collaboration, and interconnectivity tend to be more innovative, achieve more, and are happier!

Table 20.2 sets out the characteristics that exemplify the two approaches, *linear* and *nonlinear* or, more broadly, *complicated* and *complex*. On the left, the linear system is dominated by structures, permission levels, hierarchy, delays, bureaucracy, expert managers, one-way information, long-term plans, and assumed communication linkages. Any change in this column can become not only a major event, but also a crisis. The school is unable to adapt, evolve, and self-organize; it has no emergent capability. H. L. Mencken once noted, "For every complex problem, there is an answer that is clear, simple and wrong."

On the right is the vertically tutored school. This list is a descriptive template derived from those schools that have made a successful transition from

**Table 20.2.  Complicated and Complex; Applied to Schools**

| *Complicated (Structures)* | *Complex (Relationships and Structure)* |
|---|---|
| Same-age organizational base (linear) | Mixed-age organizational base (nonlinear) |
| Low student leadership opportunities | Every child a leader |
| Low mentoring opportunities | Every child a mentor and mentee |
| Learning relationship slow to develop | Learning relationships formed immediately |
| Disobedient of child psychology | In line with child psychology |
| Values assumed (logistics driven) | Values-driven |
| Tutors and tutoring as low status | Tutors and tutoring critically important |
| Peer group pressure sometimes negative | Groups balanced by mixed-age, supportive |
| Information-out system | Interconnected communications throughout |
| Tutor isolated | Tutor as the communications hub |
| Data sheet reporting | Reports rich in strategies for improvement |
| Variable emotional/spiritual intelligence | High EQ and SQ: empathy designed in |
| Low coconstruction and personalization | Coconstruction and personalization designed in |
| High on rules, referrals, procedures, meetings | High on problem-solving at source (trust) |
| Nonecological, nonemergent, non-self-organizing | High innovation, self-organizing, emergent |
| Leading from the top | Leading from the edge; servant/leadership |
| Weak parent partnership; added on | Strong parent partnership designed in |
| Emphasis—formative assessment for learning | Formative and extended summative assessment |
| High potential for bullying/poor behavior | Low potential for negative behavior |
| School causal in mental health issues | Child psychology designed in and supported |
| High need for add-ons and fixes and programs | PSHE designed in via networked relationships |
| High in management inefficiency and cost | Self-organizing and efficient. Lower costs |
| Command-and-control approach | Systems thinking |

the same-age system to the mixed-age system. It reflects what schools have learned from their field trials over time.

In the right-hand column, students belong to tutor groups carefully balanced by age, gender, learning dispositions, and capability. Every tutor group belongs to a house (or school within a school), creating a supportive network and nested system. There are two tutors in every tutor group, and tutors are chosen from everybody in the school regardless of their status. Everyone is a leader, mentor, teacher, and learner. Parent partnership is designed in, not added on. Such a nonlinear system is socially collaborative and intervention fast because work at the edge is enabled. It is a high-trust organization.

The nonlinear school reconnects all feedback loops and rewires them through the auspices of the tutor as the *learning and communications hub* of the school. The support network established ensures that resilience, perseverance, empathy, and a can-do mind-set are designed in, not added on using programs. Many other positive dispositions to learning are nurtured (personal organization, collaboration, networking, etc.) while avoiding many of the mental health issues plaguing the same-age model.

## SELF-ORGANIZING TEAMS AND NETWORKS

The working paper of Sean Snyder (2013) provides a useful overview of where schools are. He describes complexity and schooling in different jurisdictions but unsurprisingly makes no specific mention of the same-age assumption and how an individual school can execute change from within. Snyder makes the following important systems point:

> Key to all of this—and problematic for policy makers trying to steer from the center—is the fact that there is often no guiding central hand in the evolution of the system. What the center can do is create a fertile environment that embraces the emergent nature of complex systems and work to create processes that maximize the flow of feedback between and across levels in a safe and manageable space. This will allow for self-organization in which structures will emerge born from the collaboration of all stakeholders. (p. 12)

Unfortunately, policy makers do not create this fertile environment because essentially they belong to the engineering culture, one unable to learn (Schein). Schools, however, can! It seems that VT provides many of the answers Sean Snyder seeks. While his worthy statement of intent focuses on system-wide approaches, schools themselves have a small window of opportunity and sufficient autonomy to deal with their issues now, despite the position in which they find themselves.

Jurisdictions hooked on reform, and business strategies have run out of ideas, and it will be a while before they come to their senses and opt out of NPM complicatedness in preference for PVM (Public Value Management) complexity. For those schools already embracing a mixed-age organizational base by shifting from the linearity of grade or year systems to more complex and interconnected house and family-type structures are capable of designing the more effective learning relationships Snyder describes. By connecting to more of themselves, such schools start an approach likely to lead to emergence and systemic change; forward to a better future rather than backward to the sameness of the past.

There is always a paradox. Complexity has a chaotic quality and like ecology readily resolves itself if understood. Berlow (2010) put it neatly, "Complexity leads to simplicity." He might have added, "Complicated leads to even more complicated and precedes atrophy!"

Raewyn Connell (2013) offers us the complex view of education that we are in danger of losing, one where care is being crudely redefined and learning relationships go unsupported. Real learning is complex, nonlinear, and complex, a combination that requires the school to be operationally connected on all fronts. Care has to be redefined not as an isolated empathetic interaction when things go wrong but as the way the school is designed to prevent things going wrong. As Connel says:

> Education involves encounter between persons, and that encounter involves care. Learning from a computer is not care. Learning from a computer is not education: the machine does not care. Learning from a person behaving like a machine is not education; that person's capacity for care is being suppressed. It is care that is the basis of the creativity in teaching, at all levels from Kindergarten to PhD supervision, as the teacher's practice evolves in response to the learner's development and needs. Encounter between persons implies people capable of encounter; that is, people with significant autonomy (p. 104).

Complex schools based on mixed-age groups require complex leaders, wicked problem solvers, and heretics able to thrive in conditions that often feel messy at best. To these we can add facilitators, brokers, advocates, and stewards, the entrepreneurial spirit recommended by the RSA and discussed earlier. Such people are more likely to be driven by values and an enabling belief in the development of others.

They will know how to release their school from the complications of the architecture of control and its accompanying industrial mind-set, to one more complex and based on participation and collaboration, one where every child, teacher, and parent is known and supported to be the best they can be. Theirs will be a constant battle to abandon the industrial mind-set and the assumptions and failed methodologies of the same-age past, and to relish self-organization and the diverse and emergent nature of a more ecological mind-set.

# Chapter 21

# Concluding Remarks—
# Two Management Models and
# Systems Thinking

There are two models, and each requires a very different approach to leadership and management; each has its own unique features and both are living systems. One model is spawned from a same-age leverage point and depends upon static hierarchical command structures that separate, limit, and frustrate. It responds to the world using methods that are characteristic of itself, ones that serve only to maintain its rigid identifying features.

An inability to flex and evolve means it requires constant add-ons and fixes, and this makes it more and more complicated and difficult to work. Over time, it becomes fragile and moribund and is only tenuously connected as a living system. When put under pressure, the model fails and its operators and clients suffer untold stress. This is made worse because the cause of its ills, the same-age structure it has used seemingly forever, is regarded as benign and unaddressed.

It is a model that is taking us to a very dark place guided by engineers with a reductionist mind-set who work to control the communications and connectedness on which learning depends—precisely the way their schools taught them to think about the world and how it is organized. A cultural feature of this model is cognitive dissonance; the huge discomfort and loss of well-being caused when actions and beliefs are in conflict, and little in the way of resolution is in sight; self-deceit is the opt-out clause.

The second model is alive, bright, and complex. It is driven by a mixed-age change lever, one that is constantly inviting the school to connect to more of itself. It defies the rational analysis favored by engineers in preference for the welcome complexity that comes with greater connectivity, social collaboration, and self-organization. The mixed-age design is ecologically minded, constantly learning, and collaboration dependent. Complexity is resolved by distributing leadership to wherever decisions need to be made and by connecting all learning relationships in ways that allow information to flow where needed.

As a living system the mixed-age model does no harm and is entirely built on principles of social psychology and child development. This model is complex and adaptive and relies on collaboration to function—designed in, not added on!

Each model demands a very different form of leadership. One seeks followers of an insecure vision, willing to suffer cognitive dissonance and travel a perilous route to a bad place; this leader, like all other players, must fit the system and be judged only against standardized tests. The other, the servant leader, seeks the reality of service, building leadership and trust in others and following the goal of goodness. This leader judges herself against higher values, including tests! While the first leader manages people from an office, this leader manages from a tutor room and shapes the system to enable people to be her.

In the USA, teachers are called instructors and learning is called instruction. When teachers are called by the wrong name, something profoundly and managerially odd has occurred. Both are terms derived from industrial thinking. Both deny the deeper calling of the teacher as learner and spirit guide. In the UK, teachers are still called teachers but they are increasingly coerced into being instructors. Niels Pflaeging (2014) has an excellent take on complexity and instruction:

> Problem-solving in a life-less system is about instruction. Problem-solving in a living system is about communication . . . complexity can be neither managed, nor reduced. We can only confront it with human mastery. (p. 9)

What we see in schools is never all there is. We operate heuristically with our biases never far away and our intuition on full alert, trying to keep us safe, and running the show. But we ask the wrong questions of ourselves, thinking they are the right questions. We are, in Daniel Kahneman's terms, System 2 indolent, and this makes us vulnerable and compliant to false authority and accepting of ideas with little substance. We too willingly absorb the *fake news* of what Jonathan Haidt called *enthusiastic scholarship*.

It was Thomas Kuhn who did so much to reveal the nature of paradigm shifts. He pointed out how orthodoxy and old bureaucracies amass significant intellectual capital, a lifelong investment they are unwilling to jettison even when confronted with the common sense of systems thinking. The world of schools is now a mess of paradoxes, social fixes, and add-ons; a piecemeal world of reductionism at a time when holism is needed. The system is just about held together by wonderful teachers still clinging to their deeper values, not realizing that the same-age system they try so valiantly to make work undermines them.

# PLATO'S ALLEGORY

Plato's *Allegory of the Cave* tells the story of three people, lifelong prisoners since birth. They are tied, so all they see is the wall of stone in front of them. Behind them is a walkway where people pass each and every day carrying animals, wood, food, and plants; beyond the walkway is a fire that casts terrifying shadows of these figures in front of the prisoners. Their total experience of the world is of these strange and frightening silhouettes on the wall.

Eventually one of them escapes and slowly realizes that there is a new reality, one that embraces beauty and meaning. The realization emerges that his former existence was merely a sham. He returns to the cave to rescue the others, but to his surprise they threaten to kill him if he tries to set them free. They refuse to be persuaded, preferring the security of their prison, what they think they know.

Those who control our education systems are prisoners of the past, smug in their own reality and beset by bias. What they see (Schein's engineers) is far from all there is and what they know is determined by an inherited industrial mind-set. It is they, not teachers, who are unable to change and who refuse to be rescued. They believe that with enough add-ons and fixes, all will be well and the machine will run better. Many dream of a day when teachers are replaced by technology.

All that is needed, they claim, is an upgrade, some means of turning teachers into better instructors and deliverers of data. They ignore the system's increasing sameness, its convergent direction, and its inability to be complex and adaptive. They ignore the dangerous world such a system has created. To the mix, they add the management ways of business, a last and possibly fatal throw of the neoliberal dice.

It was Machiavelli, an early systems thinker, who understood the consequences of change. He observed that any heretic who innovates and becomes a leader of change threatens the existing order and makes powerful enemies and lukewarm supporters. He noted how most profit from retaining the status quo.

> It must be considered that there is nothing more difficult to carry out, nor more doubtful of success, nor more dangerous to handle, than to initiate a new order of things. (*The Prince*)

It seems that any call for change like universal mixed-age schools, even for twenty minutes a day, will meet with resistance, incredulity, and outright opposition.

Ed Schein's idea of the three levels of organizational culture offers a means of escape. Understanding cultural assumptions involves traveling through the contested spaces of the school as an organization with its multiplicity of relationships and feedback loops. It involves following the experience of our players, reinterpreting the shadows on the wall, and exposing assumptions to the light of day. Only when the same-age linear model is understood can it be unlearned and any underpinning assumptions exposed for what they are.

For schools, emergence involves creating a new work culture from the old. While it may not yet be possible to take the school out of the factory, it is possible to take the factory out of the school. But to do this involves going deep into the psyche of the school as a living system, where the teachers, students, and parents interact and where their collective knowledge and community know-how makes the difference.

All we need do is follow our players' interactions as they loop around the system, and then redesign these loops in ways that enable information to flow and emotional intelligence to flourish. Initiating the mixed-age lever brings about a subtle change in the way the school operates. The learning relationships, complex at first, start to settle and redesign themselves in the way chaos tends to do. Here is the first domino of systemic change; all that schools need do is follow it wherever it goes using their values and applied common sense as a guide.

As for cognition, we are only just beginning to understand how we see and know things. Our System 1 and 2, as Kahneman says, are a clever team but left to their own devices can outwit the best of us when it comes to decisions and judgments. As for networks, these are a source of information and cross-border energy just as Frank Betts (1992) suggested, but we need to understand how to rewire them to ensure access to all areas.

Duffy (2016) holds firmly to the heresy that governments cannot innovate. They are crippled by administrative incompetence, driven by ideology, and unable to distinguish good advice from bad. Their modus operandi at best is to keep things the same by clinging to the past:

> Genuine and valuable social innovations involve real people and complex changes in behavior and organizational structures. They require changes in human understanding and attitude and not just formal rule changes.

The linear school is an information-out system, not a two-way communication system. Reopening the channels between players and extending loose-ties opportunities will be an enriching experience for those schools wishing to be better connected. When students join and participate in mixed-age groups, their own horizons expand and for a time they are safe, protected from any negative peer pressure until they are ready to explore. By creating this place of security and attachment, resilience grows and this allows them to venture out with confidence rather than trepidation. It is what the Google research discovered and is what psychology teaches.

In such conditions, every child learns to lead and leads to learn. Well-being is assured, resilience grows, and grit is nurtured and supported. Some call this character building; if it is, it needs no social program to build it, just an enabling system to grow it and let it flourish. Practice does not make perfect; perfect practice makes perfect just as Mary Parker Follett intimated.

## SYSTEMS THINKING

This book began with systems thinking, and it is only right to end in the same way. Donella Meadows (1999) suggested the highest leverage point of all, the power to transcend paradigms. Set out in this book is a mixed-age paradigm as a better way of working. It should help schools in this blink in time but that's all. Meadows said this:

> Magical leverage points are not easily accessible, even if we know where they are and which direction to push on them. There are no cheap tickets to mastery. You have to work at it, whether that means rigorously analyzing a system or rigorously casting off your own paradigms and throwing yourself into the humility of Not Knowing. In the end, it seems that power has less to do with pushing leverage points than it does with strategically, profoundly, madly letting go. (p. 19)

This book concludes with the *Twelve Rules of Systems Thinking for Complex Global Issues* written by Louise Diamond (2017) via the Plexus Institute. They are interpreted here for schools (italics).

1. Connect the disconnected.
   In complex systems, all the elements or agents are interconnected, as in a giant web. They are also interdependent—what happens to one affects all others. Therefore, connect the disconnected. *Learning is best achieved when the learner feels they are at the center of a support web, so does the teacher. It is important to attach the teacher, tutor, parent, and child to each other not separate them. Every voice needs to be heard and every child needs to feel safe. In a mixed-age system, the tutor is the hub of a matrix composed of students, teachers, and parents.*
2. Ground yourself in unpredictability.
   Complexity is the nature and condition of living systems and the world we live in. What we know about complex systems is that there are multiple agents or elements, combining and interacting in unpredictable and nonlinear ways. This means decisions often lead to unintended consequences. Therefore, ground yourself in unpredictability.

*Learning and teaching is full of surprises; there is no easy science to the art. Schools can only create the conditions that maximize flexibility, intervention, connectedness, and social collaboration between groups. Expect mistakes and learn from them. A mind-set embracing of complexity is key. See the school as a social collaboration and leadership distribution as essential. The more connections the better.*

3. Create Conditions for quality engagements.

   In that giant web of interconnectedness, the points or nodes where the agents meet are the relationships, or opportunities for interaction. These interactions determine what will happen to the system. The nature and quality of these relationships, therefore, are critically important. Therefore, create conditions for quality engagements.

   *The key here is that first meeting when older students show care, empathy, and support to younger children. From this point, the system builds relationship on relationships until the complex web is built. The tutor is the enabling nodal point that unites teachers, students, and parents. Make the interactions high-quality learning relationships. Remember quality reduces demand and costs.*

4. Rebalance the flows across boundaries.

   We know that all living systems exchange energy, matter, and information across their boundaries. When we can identify imbalances in these flows—stuck places, over or underaccumulation—we can shift things to be more equitable and more sustainable. Therefore, rebalance the flows across boundaries.

   *Let's not assume parent partnership but live it. Wherever our players meet, make it a quality experience and an energizing source that recognizes every player's contribution. Everyone is a learner and a leader, and this combination enables organizational learning and is the source of system energy. Don't create boundaries but embrace complexity. Living systems need to be complex.*

5. Repattern for sustainability and well-being of the whole.

   All living systems develop patterns. Often, these patterns are self-reinforcing and become deeply embedded and difficult to change. Many of these patterns in human systems are common and recognizable. Patterns also show up in similar forms at different scales or levels of the system. Therefore. repattern for sustainability and well-being of the whole.

   *This book is all about changing a deeply embedded pattern of behavior, one we all recognize—same-age construction. Changing to a mixed-age base (vertical tutoring) ensures the sustainability and well-being currently under threat. Instead of adding mindfulness on, create a mindful school where empathy is designed in and everybody is a mentor. Break the pattern while you can and build a better one! Above all, recognize the forces that create a negative self-enforcing feedback loop.*

6. Attend to ever smaller parts and ever larger wholes. We know from living systems that everything is a whole in itself and at the same time part of a larger whole. Therefore, attend to ever smaller parts and ever larger wholes.

*See the individual child as a whole and always set the child within the whole school and within the levels and groups between—teachers too. This will help embrace the complexity of variation. By attending to child psychology design a better and more ecologically minded system. See the school through the eyes of players. Move from one-size-fits-all system to one with the complexity able to absorb the variety of demand.*

7. Pay attention to emerging networks.

Living systems organize themselves through the interactions of their agents or parts. The basic format of that organization is networks—that is, groups of parts joined together in a decentralized way for some period of time. Therefore, pay attention to emerging networks.

*At any one time, one network will hold sway in the learning process. The school ensures that the network matrixes formed by fellow students, tutors, and parents are thriving and viable. As power shifts to the organizational edge, leadership and hierarchy form and reform as needed (the VSM and Buurtzorg Model). Ensure agency in loose and tight networks. Let these networks build and sustain them.*

8. Seek coherence within chaos.

Systems move between various degrees of stability and instability, order and disorder. When the disorder, or chaos, becomes too great, things fall apart. When the order is too rigid, things cannot grow or develop. Yet a certain degree of instability, or the edge of chaos, can also be a powerful moment of creative change. Therefore, seek coherence within chaos.

*Be courageous. Innovation and systemic change die in rigid, machine-like systems that only breed complications and loss of well-being. Allowing power to move to the edge invites the school to a new order and disorder all at the same time. This is where most organizational learning occurs. Embrace complexity with human ingenuity. Recognize that wherever the value work is being done, there will always be a degree of self-organizing chaos.*

9. Look to the intangible as well as the concrete to see the potential.

All living systems exist within a single field of potential, where the observer is a player, our thoughts have consequences, and creative solutions emerge. Therefore, look to the intangible as well as the concrete to see the potential.

*It is easy to know the schools we have and how they are run, and yet most feel there is far more in them trying to escape. Every school must emerge from its chrysalis. We need them to be butterflies; remember, a school is not a caterpillar with wings strapped on its back. Dreams are important, and children have many. As Ken Robinson famously said, let's not tread on their dreams! Tests and tests results are important, but they are far from everything.*

10. Articulate, communicate, and validate the stories you tell yourself.

    Living systems exist within their own unique context. For human systems, that context is the narrative that gives meaning to our choices and actions. Therefore, articulate, communicate, and validate the stories you tell yourself.

    *Keep telling stories of the good teacher, the great school, the great moment, but don't use self-deceit and self-delusion; recognize cognitive dissonance, validate, and prepare to be challenged until the school becomes a system that is true to its values and the goal of goodness.*

11. Define and revisit goals and purpose.

    The parts of living (human) systems cohere around a common shared purpose. Therefore, define and revisit goals and purpose.

    *Any failure to do this creates a vacuum, and we end up with a de facto purpose (passing tests). Systems must have a shared purpose. Living systems need to be values driven, values that reflect goodness, an ecological mind-set, and both EQ and SQ.*

12. Learn and change from inner and outer messages.

    Living systems are learning systems. That is, they adapt from the feedback they receive from their internal and external environments. Therefore, learn and change from inner and outer messages.

    *Effect lists and research provide insights and guidance for system users. They are some of the many sources of information. Staff members are another, and so are students, parents, and community. All contribute messages that guide the whole process for individual and organizational learning to occur. The school needs to consider and absorb them all to ensure it learns and adapts. Build a socially collaborative school.*

## SHORT CHANGED

In 1957, Charlton Ogburn wrote a short article for *Harper's Magazine* about his experiences in the Burma Campaign. In 1959, it became a book and was later made into the film *Merrill's Marauders*.

We trained hard, but it seemed that every time we were beginning to form up into teams we would be reorganized. Presumably, the plans for our employment were being changed. I was to learn later in life that, perhaps because we are so good at organizing, we tend as a nation to meet any new situation by reorganizing; and a wonderful method it can be for creating the illusion of progress while producing confusion, inefficiency, and demoralization. During our reorganizations, several commanding officers were tried out on us, which added to the discontinuity.

Real change is tough, especially so when so much of what we believe is based on long-held and unchallenged assumptions and shadows on a wall. But when the lightbulb moment occurs, the shadows disappear, and it is possible to do and see so much more. The school connects to more of itself, a sense of community is restored, and leadership moves to the edge where it's most needed; well-being improves as the system starts to recover its purpose and sense of belonging. All that schools need, as Donella Meadows said, is to strategically, profoundly, and madly let go.

When this happens, the living system that is the school will again *nurture a strong skeptical mind, a kind heart, and an abiding interest in advancing the common good*, just as Deborah Kenny said. And when this happens, the world will be a better more tolerant and safer place, and our children will achieve so much more because they went to a great school, one where their teachers were enabled to live out their working lives according to their deeper and more soulful values.

# Chapter Summaries

## SECTION 1

### Chapter 1

This first chapter introduces the major themes. We think we are smart enough to control systems, but it turns out this is not the case. If we were any good at system design, the education systems we have wouldn't keep going wrong in such spectacular ways. So, a major challenge is to improve our systems understanding. In this chapter, we introduce the concept of leverage points, places in a system that determine how the (living) system thinks and behaves. For schools, that pivotal point in the system's design is the determination to organize schools into peer groups for tutor time. This seemingly benign aspect of design now 150 years old sets in motion all of the errant behavior we see and explains our complete inability to respond using reform methods and even research. Unfortunately, this only becomes clear for schools that have adopted mixed-age groups in tutor time; that is, such schools have taken a new design lever, one that connects rather than separates. A key message of systems thinking is system connectedness and its importance socially and psychologically to learning.

Terms used in this chapter included *cognitive dissonance, theory-in-use and espoused theory, failure demand and value demand*, and *single- and double-loop learning*.

### Chapter 2

Here we start to note some of the collateral damage that our current approach to school organization has started to cause. It seems that when the current model is asked to upgrade its output (note the machine metaphor), nasty things happen to people. They get ill, lose heart, and people start to cheat (game) the system. The problem occurs because we think we have a teacher problem. This is not true. We have a systems problem, and this requires a very different approach. The real question mark is the systems inability to adapt. The effect of same-age organization is to disrupt system connectivity, especially information flow. When this happens, the school deviates from child development, learning, and psychology in general. When we look at mixed-age schools, this connectedness returns and is built from the base up and outside to in, a very different management and leadership approach.

## Chapter 3

In chapter 3, the theme of connectedness continues by looking at collaboration. Terms like *collaborative professionalism* and *collective teacher efficacy* (CTE) (high on Hattie's effect list) are introduced, and the thinking behind them traced. This book endorses social capital (another term) and promotes the idea of the *socially collaborative school*. In effect, CTE and collaborative professionalism veer off-course from social capital and the reason for this is explained by the same-age driver. To be effective, the whole school (parents, students, and staff) have to be socially collaborative to support learning, not just teachers. One route continues to separate and see teachers as the solution to all learning endeavors while the other (the socially collaborative school) adopts learning and teaching as a joint community enterprise able to adapt to whatever is required. This chapter looks at models and suggests a design where the organization is collaboration dependent, not one where collaboration is tacked on. The reason it is missing is because the same-age model blocks its being.

## Chapter 4

Here, attention is turned to push-and-pull management styles and how we are diverted by the economics of the student as a unit of production, a financial measure of worth. Push management is prescriptive and increases dependency on the center for direction by narrowly defining purpose and means. The teacher exists to deliver programs that meet the output measures. This leads to a comparison between command-and-control versus systems thinking and to a direct correlation between the same-age system and the mixed-age system. It seems relevant to establish very early on how the two system drivers leverage opposing thinking and management. In particular, the same-age structure relies on endless add-ons and fixes (pro-social programs) to make it (appear) to work. It has to repair the damage that the system itself causes. Mixed-age tutoring designs in what is needed regarding empathy and well-being, so need fewer add-ons and fixes.

## Chapter 5

Changing the metaphor from machine to the school as a living system changes the way we see and understand schools. A biological system is concerned with identity and survival, so it should be approached with care. It doesn't respond well to disturbances like reforms. When we understand the school in this way, we also learn how to help the school transform by changing tactics. I can't make a school change. The school decides this in its best interests, often when self-preservation concerns increase. One of the strange concepts that arises is simplification and how any attempt at simplifying a same-age system leads to complication and failure demand. When the school complexifies (mixed-age) chaotic conditions temporarily increase, but these tend to simplify matters by reducing demand. Examples of failed reform strategies are offered and explained in part by showing how reforms such as add-ons and fixes take a mechanical view of the school. Part of the collateral damage occurs when children are seen as deficit in character, grit, resilience, and a can-do mind-set. This is not true but has led to the development of a social repair industry that schools errantly endorse.

## Chapter 6

This chapter explores some of the ways that schools tackle bullying. Most are fixes and add-ons that occur after the event. One of the most challenging (heretical) statements states that same-age organization is the single primary cause of school bullying, which schools then spend five years and considerable resources trying to fix. I introduce some of my research regarding influences on learning. School staff place peers high regarding influence. At the same time, research into bullying indicates how peer groups provide near perfect conditions for bullying to occur, yet this is the system schools use as the basis for learning and social relationships. This chapter shows how mixing the age groups reduces bullying by increasing (designing-in) student empathy and leadership. Bullying is designed out! The latter uses psychology, the former assumes it.

## Chapter 7

Chapter 7 starts with a general overview of different jurisdictions and how we judge performance and try to increase system output. There is a link between mental health and our seemingly futile attempts to get more from the system. The heresy here is that efforts to increase the performance of a bad system (same-age) have given rise to a dramatic increase in mental health issues and a loss of well-being, all detrimental to learning. This is not a resilience issue but a systems issue, one directly connected to same-age assumptions. While it may not be possible to take the school out of the factory, it is possible to take the factory out of the school.

## Chapter 8

Out search for a better model leads us to the connection between systems, psychology, and purpose and, in particular, the work of Stafford Beer and the viable systems model (VSM). He made a very important point POSIWID—the purpose of a system is what it does! We can make all kinds of claims for our schools, including engaging in self-deceit and delusion (as living systems do), but in the end, if the system makes people ill, anxious, and fearful, that is its purpose. The VSM is a model in which power is distributed to where decisions need to be taken and its connective nature is described. Only then can we consider concepts like collaboration and distributed leadership. A comparison is made between the same-age system and the VSM.

## Chapter 9

Using the VSM, it is possible to show how parent partnership (PP) fails as a concept. While recognized as highly productive in learning terms, the pressure on schools is such that PP has been simplifying and minimized to the point where it is barely connected regarding learning engagement and support. School claims the opposite (self-deceit and assumption). This lead to a discussion on wicked problems and messes. In this chapter, the same-age structure is the culprit that throws up a numbers problem that the school cannot resolve. Like all wicked problems, it is only really understood once a solution is discovered. This is related to the research literature, the VSM model, and the mixed-age answer.

## Chapter 10

Part 1 ends by bringing together two major (hot) topics (collective teacher efficacy [CTE] and distributed leadership) with psychology. We start by looking at leadership, its context, its followers, and how different styles have different outcomes when faced with the challenge of school improvement. The heresy is simple: distributed leadership cannot exist in a same-age model because of the hierarchies that such a model necessitates. It is a contradiction in terms reflected in the confusion of research and definition. This brings us to the work of Mary Parker Follett and the psychology of Bronfenbrenner, Bowlby, and Maslow. Next comes CTE, and it too fails the systems test. It is the right idea, but the same-age system acts as an obstacle to implementation. This section ends by updating table 10.1 where we started out.

## SECTION 2

### Chapter 11

The scientific principles of Taylorism are our start and finishing point in this chapter. We move on through Fayol and Weber to the 1960s and McGregor's Theory X and Theory Y, where X sees people as lazy and Y as self-motivated and capable. This sets in motion two management models Alpha and Beta. Alpha is used when a Theory X dominates management thinking and Beta when Theory Y is the case. We look at the work of Kurt Lewin in this context touching on intrinsic motivation but end with the realization that very little has changed regarding institutionalized management thinking. This brings us up to the past three decades.

### Chapter 12

The period of the past three decades is dominated by neoliberalism and the birth of NPM (New Public Management). We look at NPM as an example of push theory and a view of people that leans toward Alpha but claims to be Beta. A comparison is made between health service as a system and schools. A picture emerges of constant change and systems moving from crisis to crisis as investment deteriorates. In particular, we examine the problem of system purpose, one where values have been sidelined, and pass rates/measures have taken over as the new *de facto* purpose: the effect is to change method (how teachers teach). This is discussed and explained. Public Value Management (PVM) is promoted as a better service model.

### Chapter 13

In this chapter, we look at NPM close up and in particular the concept of deliverology. We start by returning to the school as a living system and how it copes with change. Deliverology is Taylorism updated but still Taylorism with a heavy mix of Weber. In an organization where time and costs are at a premium, deliverology is a cumbersome and bureaucratic approach as far from modern management as it's possible to get. Nobody wins. From here, the annual performance review (APR) or appraisal process is critically examined. It seems that just as many major companies are abandoning the APR, schools are required to use it to set targets and decide pay issues. This comes under in the guise of personal development. In all the tables present, the reader is forced to return to column 1 where school management is stuck.

## Chapter 14

The lessons to be learned from this chapter are about teams and teamwork. Because talent management has always been a topic in NPM thinking, it needs to be challenged/questioned as a concept for organizational improvement. This provides an opportunity to look at the work of Laker and Hill and head teachers engaged in school improvement. Again a conflict arises between NPM push style of management and the design-oriented head teacher *architects* who are slow but best at getting the job done. This chapter ends with the wise words of W. Edwards Deming.

## Chapter 15

The aim here is to move from dominant thinking, the way we see organizational structure and work, to emerging thinking where power is distributed and purposes based on shared values. In a way, this completes our management journey. Of importance here is the research conducted by Google into teams and how they work best. For a high STEM employer, Google's findings in Project Oxygen and Project Aristotle appear counterintuitive, and the implications for school design are very important. Above all else, emotional safety—in terms of freedom to speak and make mistakes in a supportive environment—was the top priority. This returns us to the mixed-age system that designs in the precise characteristics discovered by Google's research teams.

## Chapter 16

We return to school culture and the work of Donald Schein. In many ways, Schein verifies the living system model. Schein's three cultures are of particular interest. He calls the first culture the *operators* (school staff, students, and parents in our case); then *engineers*—those who determine curriculum and what counts as measures of success, people who operate at the highest levels; and finally *CEOs*—this is the executive culture that manages schools. These groups have different agenda, language, and different assumptions that act detrimentally on schools. Finally, we come to emergence, the strangest systems concept of all.

## Chapter 17

We now start to look at alternatives and return to health and to the Horizon's Group for inspiration. As there is no education equivalent, their work is applied to the school situation and seems a good fit. The *five enablers of the emerging direction* are outlined and applied to schools. The first requirement is to activate disruptors, heretics, radicals, and mavericks. Schools will find some interesting new concepts here that inform the design process; these include weak-tie theory and dialogics.

## Chapter 18

In chapter 18, we arrive at evolutionary Teal, and a discussion based on the work of Frederic Laloux tracks the journey of organizations against levels of consciousness. It is a journey toward self-organization and one reflected in this book. Laloux provides exciting insights into the plight of schools, where they are taking us and, by inference, the effect on participants. Tables 18.1 and 18.2 indicate the new parameters for the self-organizing school. This concludes with a look at a high-conscious school model (ESBZ) nominated by Laloux, which has adopted mixed-age principles and practices.

## Chapter 19

Here we find the community nursing company Buurtzorg. This group is one of the best examples of Teal and self-organization. It is a team approach that has no management or leadership structure and minimal bureaucracy. The team decides everything, including who leads at any one time and is high in intrinsic motivation and the need to build quality relationships (connecting the disconnected). This chapter draws out the similarities of the design principles of the Buurtzorg approach and mixed-age organization or vertical tutoring. A model (figure 19.1) shows how such a school works.

## Chapter 20

Having talked about complicated and complex systems throughout, the differences are now explained. It is possible to treat Hattie's effect list in the three ways listed. If the list becomes a recipe, we end up with "what works" and training becomes one dimensional and so does the school as a system. If the list falls in the complicated column, the system becomes formulaic but will still work differently in different places; the variation to be absorbed is far too high. Neither approach changes any system fundamentals. Far better to accept the list as a guide as a means of connecting players within a better system, one that recognizes teacher agency and the complexity of the teaching and learning task. Table 20.2 sets out the differences between complicates structures (same-age) and complex (mixed-age) and builds on table 1.1. The key understanding comes from Snyder (2013) "the emergent nature of complex systems" and Connel (2013) regarding how schools define what it is to care.

## Chapter 21

This chapter has three narratives: Plato's Allegory, the systems thinking concepts set out by Louise Diamond, and Meryl's Marauders! All offer sage advice.

# A Handful of Heresies Relating to Same-Age Organization

NB. These heresies stem from twenty years of intensive work with hundreds of schools transitioning from one system (same-age) to another (mixed-age) and the feedback these schools have generously shared. Most have field-trialed VT, adapted the model, and retrialed, gradually building collaborative organizational practices dependent on distributed leadership and parent partnership. I call these socially collaborative or VT schools. These heresies (below) are system realizations that come from the experience of change by these pioneering VSMs (viable systems models). From the mixed-age system, it is possible to see more clearly the obstacles to learning that same-age schools have to deal with every day.

1. The concept of distributed learning within a same-age system is a contradiction in terms, a confusion recognized in the research literature. It does not and cannot lead to organizational change and may even have an opposite effect. A living system does not respond to such add-ons. A mixed-age system is dependent on distributed leadership; that is, distributed leadership has to be designed-in, not added-on: it cannot be simply mandated.
2. Collaborative professionalism is of this type. It is an add-on that is welcome but difficult to implement in a system that abhors innovation. Far better to adopt a systems approach and consider a viable systems model or socially collaborative school involving all players—one that is collaboration dependent.
3. School organization by age is a root cause of bullying and underachievement. Schools that have same-age tutor groups introduce the conditions for bullying to occur on day one and then spend five years, with mixed fortunes, trying to fix what they broke. Had school anti-bullying strategies and agencies been effective, bullying behavior should be in steep

decline; in fact, it simply reappears elsewhere because the cause is never addressed and the pro-social repair programs and strategies put in place are not as effective as claimed. As many consultants, training agencies, think tanks, and smart people know, there is good money to be made from prolonging organizational problems by treating symptoms (complications) and ignoring causes (complexity).

4.  There is no parent partnership or engagement worthy of the name in schools where tutor groups are defined by same-age, nor can there be. Not one of the hundreds of (same-age) school teams with whom I have worked has been able to show me a coherent partnership model. The same-age approach used by schools to handle large numbers simply doesn't allow it. Claims made by schools organized on a same-age basis, which laud their parent partnership initiatives, are baseless by design and largely delusional. Consultants who organize courses and certificate schools for reaching some kind of parent partnership level are mistaken.

5.  The increase in mental health problems among young people and teachers is almost entirely attributable to the system of same-age organization and the fragmentation of relationships such organization causes. Vital learning relationships between players (teachers, students, and parents) stemming from same-age school organization are a matter of serendipity, not design, and place children at risk. Most work only partially. Safeguarding policies have completely ignored systemic issues and simply add to the list of inherent complications.

6.  Deprofessionalization of teachers and teacher agency and even problems of teacher retention and recruitment flow directly from complications arising from school organization by same age and the linear management mind-set and organizational complications it perpetuates. It leads directly to what Michael Fullan (2011) calls *the juggernaut of wrong drivers*. These include merit pay, teacher appraisal, excessive testing, and treating alleged world-class standards as a panacea. These may not seem connected, but I've tried and show that they definitely are! Mixed-age organization directly addresses and complements Abraham's Maslow's hierarchy of needs, Bronfenbrenner's ecological systems theory, Bowlby's attachment theory, and the sense of belonging to something greater than ourselves, as proposed by Jonathan Haidt in *The Happiness Hypothesis*. Research indicates mixed-age organization leads to happier schools and people.

7.  Same-age organization acts to maintain inequity and increase separation, and ultimately undermines learning. It limits and it separates, which is what it was designed to do a 150 years ago. In fact, nearly all separation, including separation by ability (setting and streaming),

causes limitation and sets in motion the kind of thinking that results in unintended relationship damage.

8.  Acting directly on teachers to effect better student outcomes will fail and simply adds to the harm. It also leads to a loss of value purposes. Teachers are not the single cause of underperformance, nor are they the route to school improvement. This is not to say that they don't deserve better training, more time, and support to do their work. Better performance starts and ends with the design of an enabling and supportive system and this requires a complex (not complicated!) mixed-age base.

9.  Acting on students to increase their resilience, grit, character, and a can-do growth mind-set using pro-social programs (add-ons and fixes) without system change cannot work by itself, and it too is high-risk. Neither is such an approach in line with the root research. These so-called dispositional deficits are not what they seem. They are the result of a system unable to cope with the stresses imposed and are exacerbated by the same-age way schools as systems operate. Children do not have a character problem and do not need repair. They need a system that supports their learning capability. To grow and develop better dispositions to learning requires systemic change, not programmed add-ons (above) and fixes. There is a symbiotic relationship between the school's organizational structure and the behavior of those trying to make the learning and teaching work, work. When we understand the same-age design assumptions in use, it is possible to shift the system to better practice so that it builds learning behavior. After that, and only after that, should we complement the system with social and emotional education.

10. The world focus on teacher improvement is insufficient and turns a blind eye to other equally important learning relationships involving staff, students, and parents. Such a focus should be replaced by a systems approach that first understands the vital role of the form tutor, the person who sees the students every day. The adoption and understanding of a systems thinking approach enables the school to mend itself, to self-reform and self-organize. It becomes more connected and values-led! Understanding why this is and how the change is achieved is the key to school improvement and building civic society.

11. An obscure phrase so often quoted by *smart* people and those who claim to know goes as follows: *The quality of an education system cannot exceed the quality of its teachers.* If there is such a thing as a misleading, inaccurate, and unhelpful tautology, one that sets jurisdictions scurrying in wrong directions, then this is it! Teachers are only part of the variation in a system. As far as systems thinking is concerned, quality is not a simple measure of a teacher's ability to ensure students

pass tests but is one that concerns the (emotional) learning relationship between players (Langford and Cleary, 1995, p. xi).

11. Given that schools might be described as a wicked problem and living systems, we are not going to impact on them using reforms alone. A wicked problem is understood and dissolved only when a solution is discovered. Those schools that have changed to a mixed-age system are the ones able to understand the problem of the same-age system.

# The Ten Tenets of Collaborative Professionalism

Analysis of the case studies points to ten tenets of collaborative professionalism that distinguish it from earlier versions of professional collaboration.

1. Collective Autonomy

    In collective autonomy, educators have more independence from top-down bureaucratic authority, but less independence from each other. Teachers are given or take authority.

2. Collective Efficacy

    Collective efficacy is about the belief that, together, we can make a difference to the students we teach, no matter what.

3. Collaborative Inquiry

    In collaborative inquiry, teachers routinely explore problems, issues, or differences of practice together in order to improve or transform what they are doing. At its best, collaborative inquiry is embedded in the very nature of teaching itself. Teachers inquire into problems before rushing into solving them.

4. Collective Responsibility

    Collective responsibility is about people's mutual obligation to help each other and to serve the students one has in common. Collective responsibility is about our students, rather than just my students. It is about our schools in our community, not just my school on my own piece of land.

5. Collective Initiative

    In collaborative professionalism, there are fewer initiatives, but there is more initiative. Teachers step forward, and the system encourages it. Collaborative professionalism is about communities of strong individuals who are committed to helping and learning from each other.

6. Mutual Dialogue

  Both collaborative professionalism and professional collaboration involve teachers talking. What distinguishes collaborative professionalism is that talk is also about doing the work. Difficult conversations can be had and are actively instigated. Feedback is honest. There is genuine dialogue about valued differences of opinion about ideas, curriculum materials, or a student's challenging behavior. This dialogue is often facilitated, and its participants are protected by protocols that insist on clarification and listening before any disagreement is brought forth.

7. Joint Work

  To collaborate is to labor or work together. Joint work exists in team teaching, collaborative planning, collaborative action research, providing structured feedback, undertaking peer reviews, discussing examples of student work, and so forth. Joint work involves actions and sometimes products or artefacts, like a lesson, curriculum, or feedback report, and is often facilitated by structures, tools, and protocols.

8. Common Meaning and Purpose

  Collaborative professionalism aspires to, articulates, and advances common purpose that is greater than test scores or even academic achievement on its own. Collaborative professionalism addresses and engages with the goals of education that enable and encourage young people to grow and flourish as whole human beings who can live lives and find work that has meaning and purpose for themselves and for society.

9. Collaborating with Students

  In the deepest forms of collaborative professionalism, students are actively engaged with their teachers in constructing change together. In this respect, student voice is the ultimate end point of student engagement.

10. Big Picture Thinking for All

  In collaborative professionalism, everyone gets the big picture. They see it, live it, and create it together.

# Bibliography

Ackoff, R. 1979. "The Future of Operational Research Is Past." *Journal of the Operational Research Society*, 30(2): 93–104.

———. 2004. "Transforming the Systems Movement. The Systems Thinker." Presented at the 3rd International Conference on Systems Thinking in Management, May 19, 2004. Available online at https://thesystemsthinker.com.

Acosta, R. M., and Hutchinson, M. 2017. *The Happiest Kids in the World: Bringing up Children the Dutch Way*. New York: Doubleday.

Ames, C. 1992. "Classrooms: Goals, Structures, and Student Motivation." *Journal of Educational Psychology*, 84(3): 261–271.

———. 1990. *Overcoming Organizational Defenses: Facilitating organizational learning*. USA: Pearson.

———. 1995. "Action science and organizational learning." *Journal of managerial psychology*, 10(6): 20–26.

Astle, J. 2017. *The Ideal School Exhibition*. RSA: RSA Reports.

Atkinson, J. 2016. "Working with Systems—Heart of the Art." Available at www.heartoftheart.org/?p=4617 and also, Atkinson, J. 2015 in Atkinson, J., Loftus, E., and Jarvis, J. *The Art of Change Making*. London: The Leadership Centre. Accessed July 11 2018.

Banathy, B. H. 1991. *Systems Design of Education*. Englewood Cliffs, NJ: Educational Technology.

———. 1996. *Designing Social Systems in a Changing World*. New York. Plenum.

Barber, M., Moffit, A. and Kihn, P. 2011. *Deliverology: A Field Guide for Educational Leaders*. London: Sage.

Barnard, P. A. 2000. *Chaos, Culture and Third Millennium Schools*. Guildford: Apocalypse Press.

———. 2010. *Vertical Tutoring: Notes on School Management Learning Relationships and School Improvement*. Guildford: Grosvenor House Publishing.

———. 2013. *The Systems Thinking School: Redesigning Schools from the Inside-Out*. New York and London: Rowman and Littlefield.

————. 2015. *From School Delusion to Design: Mixed-Age Groups and Values-Led Transformation.* New York and London: Rowman and Littlefield.

————. February 2018. "A Systems Thinking Explanation into the Rise in Mental Health and Well-Being Issues in UK Secondary Schools with Particular Reference to Same-Age and Mixed-Age Systems." *Mental Health in Schools.* February 2018. Leeds Beckett University.

————. 2016b. "The Management of 'Emotional Labour' in the Corporate Reimaging of Primary Education in England." *Journal of International Studies in the Sociology of Education,* 26 (1): 66–81.

Bateson, G. 2000. *Steps to an Ecology of Mind: Collected Essays in Anthropology, Evolution, and Epistemology.* Chicago, IL: University of Chicago Press.

Bennett, N., Wise, C., Woods, P., and Harvey, J. 2003. *Distributed Leadership.* Nottingham: National College of School Leadership.

Bergeron, Pierre-Jérôme. 2017. "How to Engage in Pseudoscience with Real Data: A Criticism of John Hattie's Arguments in Visible Learning from the Perspective of a Statistician." *McGill Journal of Education,* 51 (1)McGill: [S.1].

Berlow, E. 2010. "How Complexity Leads to Simplicity," TED Talk, accessed August 10, 2013. www.ted.com/talks/eric_berlow_how_complexity_leads_to_simplicity.html.

Betts, F. 1992. "How Systems Thinking Applies to Education." *Educational Leadership,* 50 (3): 38–41.

Bevan, H., and Fairman, S. 2014. "The New Era of Thinking and Practice in Change and Transformation: A Call to Action for Leaders of Health and Care." NHS Improving Quality NHS. http://www.nhsiq.nhs.uk/resource-search/publications/white-paper.aspx. Accessed July 11, 2018.

Block, P. 2007. "Civic Engagement and the Restoration of Community: Changing the Nature of the Conversation." http://www.asmallgroup.net/pages/images/pages/CES_jan2007.pdf. Accessed July 11, 2018.

Blond, P. 2010. *Red Tory: How Left and Right Have Broken Britain and How We Can Fix It.* London: Faber & Faber.

Boden, R., and Epstein, D. 2006. "Managing the Research Imagination? Globalisation and Research in Higher Education." *Globalisation, Societies and Education,* 4: 223–236.

Bowlby, J. 1969. *Attachment and Loss.* Vol. 1, Attachment. New York: Basic Books.

————. 1988. *A Secure Base: Parent-Child Attachment and Healthy Human Development.* New York: Basic Books.

Brennan, M. 1996. "Multiple Professionalism for Australian Teachers in the Information Age?" Paper presented at the AERA Annual Meeting, New York, April 1996.

Bronfenbrenner, U. 1970. *Two Worlds of Childhood: U.S. and U.S.S.R.* New York: Pocket Books.

————. 1977. "Towards an Experimental Ecology of Human Development." *American Psychologist,* 32(7): 513–531.

Brooks. D. 2011. *The Social Animal: The Hidden Source of Love, Character, and Achievement.* London: Random House.

Burbidge, I. 2017. "Altered States." *RSA Journal,* 1: 10.

Bushe, G. R., and Marshack, R. J. 2009. "Revisioning Organization Development: Diagnostic and Dialogic Premises and Patterns of Practice." *Journal of Applied Behavioural Science*, 45: 348. doi: 10.1177/0021886309335070.

Caine, R. N., and Caine, G. 1991. *Making Connections: Teaching and the Human Brain*. Alexandria, VA: Association for Supervision and Curriculum Development.

Cambell, D. T. 1979. "Assessing the Impact of Planned Social Change." *Evaluation and Program Planning* 2 (1): 67–90

Carter, A. 2017. "Mobilising the Middle—The Key to Cultivating Collective Teacher Efficacy." Minnis Journals; *Education Today*, 17 (4), Term 4.

Caulkin, S. 2016. "Everything you know about management is wrong." In Pell, C., Wilson, R., & Lowe, T. (Eds.) *Kittens are Evil: Little heresies in public policy*. 2016. Triarchy Press.

Cohen, S. 2001. *States of Denial: Knowing about Atrocities and Suffering*. Cambridge, UK: Polity Press.

Coleman, J. 1990. "Social Capital in the Creation of Human Capital." *American Journal of Sociology*, 94: 95–120.

Connell, R. W. 2013. "The Neoliberal Cascade in Education: An Essay on the Market Agenda and Its Consequences." *Critical Studies in Education*, 54 (2): 213–229.

Cornish, L. 2015. "Are Mixed-Grade Classes Any Better or Any Worse for Learning. The Conversation." Available online at https://theconversation.com/are-mixed-grade-classes-any-better-or-worse-for-learning-38856. Accessed July 11, 2018.

Crawford, D. 2012. "Solo and Distributed Leadership: Definitions and Dilemmas." *Educational Management, Administration and Leadership*, 40 (5): 610–620.

Crehan, L. 2016. *Clever Lands: The Secrets behind the Success of the World's Education Superpowers*. London: Random House.

Cuban, L. 1989. "The At-Risk Label and the Problem of Urban School Reform." *Phi Delta Kappan*, 70 (10): 780–784.

———. 2010. "The Difference between Complicated and Complex Matters." Larry Cuban on School Reform and Classroom Matters. Blog at https://larrycuban.wordpress.com.

Cuban, L., and Tyack, D. 2004. *Tinkering to Utopia: a century of public school reform*. USA: Harvard College.

Davidson, C. N. 2017. "The Surprising Thing Google Learned about Its Employees—and What It Means for Today's Students." Article by Valerie Strauss in the *Washington Post*, December 20, 2017.

Davies, B., and Davies, B. J. 2011. *Talent Management in Education*. London: Sage.

Deming, W. Edwards. 1986. *Out of the Crisis*. Cambridge: MIT Center for Advanced Engineering Educational Services.

Desforges, C., and Abouchaar, A. 2003. *The Impact of Parental Involvement, Parental Support and Family Education on Pupil Achievement and Adjustment: A Literature Review*. Research Report No. 433, Department of Education and Skills.

DfES. 2007a. *Social and Emotional Aspects of Learning (SEAL): Guidance Booklet*. Nottingham: DfES

Díaz-Gibson, J., Zaragoza, M. C., Daly, A. J., Mayayo, J. L., and Romaní, J. R. 2017. "Networked leadership in educational collaborative networks. *"Educational Management Administration & Leadership*, 45(6): 1040–1059.

Donohoo, J. 2017. *Collective Efficacy: How Educators' Beliefs Impact Student Learning*. Thousand Oaks, CA: Corwin.

Duffy, S. F. 2016. In *Kittens Are Evil*, edited by C. Pell, R. Wilson, and T. Lowe. UK: Triarchy Press. Chapter 5, p. 54, *Government Cannot Innovate*.

Dunleavy, P., Margetts, H. Bastow, S., and Tinkler, J. 2006. "New Public Management Is Dead—Long Live Digital-Era Governance." *Journal of Public Administration Research and Theory*, 16(3): 467–494.

Durlak, A., Weissberg, R. P., Dymnicki, A. B., Taylor, R. D., and Schellinger, K. B. 2011. "The Impact of Enhancing Students' Social and Emotional Learning: A Meta-Analysis of School-Based Universal Interventions." *Child Development*, special issue: *Raising Healthy Children*, 82(1): 405–432. Online library: Wiley. com.

Dweck, C. 2006. *Mindset: The New Psychology of Success*. New York. Ballantine Books.

Education Support Partnership Health Survey. 2017. The mental health and wellbeing of education professionals in the UK. A report from YouGov (online).

Ericsson, K. A., Prietula, M. J. and Cokely, E. T. 2007. *The Making of an Expert*. Managing People. *Harvard Business Review*, July–August 2007.

Espejo, R., and Gill, A. 2015. "The Viable Systems Model as a Framework for Understanding Organizations." Available online at http://www.moderntimesworkplace. com/good_reading/GRRespSelf/TheViableSystemModel.pdf. Accessed July 11, 2018.

Evers, J., and Kneyber, R., eds. 2016. *Flip the System: Changing Education from the Ground Up*. Abingdon, Oxon: Routledge.

Fayol, H. 1916. Administration Industrielle et Générale. Le texte fondateur du management. First published in *le Bulletin de la Société de l'Industrie minérale*, then by Dunod, 1918; re-edited in 1979 and 1999.

Fisher, A. 2012. "Are Annual Performance Reviews Necessary?" Blog: Fortune. com [Online]. http://fortune.com/2012/06/27/are-annual-performance-reviews-necessary/.

Flook, L., Goldberg, S. B., Pinger, L., and Davidson, R. J. 2015. "Promoting Prosocial Behavior and Self-Regulatory Skills in Preschool Children through a Mindfulness-Based Kindness Curriculum." *Developmental Psychology*, 51(1): 44–51.

Forrester, J. W. 1961. *Industrial Dynamics*. Cambridge: MIT Press.

Follett, M. P. 1918. *The New State: Group Organization the Solution of Popular Government*. California, USA: The Pennsylvania State University Press.

———. 1924. *Creative Experience*. New York: Longman Green and Co. (reprinted by Peter Owen in 1951).

Fox, C. 2016. *I Find That Offensive!* London: Biteback.

Fuchs, L. S., Fuchs, D., Karns, K., Hamlett, C. L., Dupka, S., and Katzaroff, M. 1996. "The Relation between Student Ability and the Quality and Effectiveness of Explanations." *American Education Research Journal*, 33(3), 631–664.

Fullan, M. 2003. *The Moral Imperative of School Leadership*. Corwin Press.

———. 2011. "Choosing the Wrong Drivers for Whole System Reform." Centre for Strategic Education Seminar Series: Paper No. 204, May 2011. Available online at www.michaelfullan.ca?media/13436787590.html.

———. 2014. *The Principal: Three Keys to Maximizing Impact*. New York: Jossey-Bass.

Fullan, M., Quinn, J., and McEachen, J. 2017. *Deep Learning: Engage the World to Change the World*. CA, USA: Corwin.

Gallo, P. 2016. "Why Positive Relationships at Work Matter More Than You Think." Paper for World Economic Forum, 2016. Available online at www.weforum.org/agenda/2016/03/why-positive-relationships-are-key-to-real-success-at-work.

Gladwell, M. 2002. "The Talent Myth: Are Smart People Overrated?" *New Yorker*, July 22, 2002, 28–33.

Glatter, R. 2017. "Because We Can: Pluralism and Structural Reform in Education." *London Review of Education*, 15(1): 115–125.

Glouberman, S., and Zimmerman, B. 2002. Complicated and Complex Systems: What would successful reform of medicare look like? Discussion Paper No. 8. Commission on the Future of Health Care in Canada. Online at CP32-79-8-2002E. pdf (PDF, 1192 KB).

———. 1995. *Emotional Intelligence: why it can matter more than IQ*. Bantam.

———. 1998. *Vital lies, simple truths: The psychology of self deception*. Simon and Schuster.

———. 2005. *Emotional Intelligence: Why It Can Matter More Than IQ*. New York: Bantam Books.

Goodall, J., and Montgomery, C. 2014. "Parental Involvement to Parental Engagement: A Continuum." *Education Review*, 66: 399–410. http://dx.doi.org/10.1080/00131911.2013.781576

Goodall, J., and Vorhaus, J. 2010. *Review of Best Practice in Parental Engagement*. London: DfE.

Graeber, D. 2013. "On the Phenomenon of Bullshit Jobs." *Strike! Magazine* (Online). http://strikemag.org/bullshit-jobs.

Granovetter, M. S. 1973. "The Strength of Weak Ties." *The American Journal of Sociology*, 78(6): 1360–1380.

Greenleaf, R. K. 1970. *The Servant as Leader*. Westfield, IN: Greenleaf Center for Servant Leadership.

Grint, K. 2010. "Wicked Problems and Leadership". Paper submitted for the Windsor Leadership Programme's, Strategic Leaders event, 27–30.

Gruening, G. 2001. "Origin and Theoretical Basis of New Public Management." *International Public Management Journal*, 4(2001): 1–25.

Guilfoyle, S. 2016. "The Performance Manager Emperor Has No Clothes." In *Kittens Are Evil: Little Heresies in Public Policy*, edited by C. Pell, R. Wilson, and T. Lowe. Devon: Triarchy Press.

Hallgarten, J., Hannon, V., and Beresford, T. 2016. *Creative Public Leadership: How School System Leaders Can Create the Conditions for System-Wide Innovation*. Innovation Unit; Royal Society of Arts; Dubai: WISE.

Hanushek, E. A. 1986. "The Economics of Schooling: Production and Efficiency in Public schools." *Journal of Economic Literature*, 24(3): 1141–1177.

———. 2014. "Boosting Teacher Effectiveness." In *What Lies Ahead for America's children?*, edited by Chester E. Finn Jr. and R. Sousa, 23–25. Stanford, CA: Hoover Institution Press.

Hanushek, E. A., Kain, J. F., and Rivkin, G. S. 1998. "Teachers, Schools and Academic Achievement." Working Paper 6691 Cambridge, MA: National Bureau of Economic Research. www.nber.org/papers/w6691.

Hanushek, E. A., Piopiunik, M., and Wiederhold, S. 2014. "The value of smarter teachers: International evidence on teacher cognitive skills and student performance (No. w20727)." *National Bureau of Economic Research*.

Hanushek, E. A. 2016. "What matters for student achievement." *Education Next*, 16(2): 18–26.

Hardin, G. 1976. *Exploring New Ethics for Survival: The Voyage of the Spaceship Beagle*. New York: Penguin.

Hargreaves, A., and Fullan, M. 2012. *Professional Capital: Transforming Teaching in Every School*. New York: Teachers College Press.

Hargreaves, A., and O'Connor, M. T. 2017. *From professional Collaboration to Collaborative Professionalism*. WISE Research #12. Available at http://www.wise-qatar.org/2017-wise-research-collaborative-professionalism.

Hargreaves, D. 2006. *A New Shape for Schooling?* UK: Specialist Schools and Academies Trust.

Harris, A. 2003. "Distributed Leadership in Schools: Leading or Misleading? Management in Education." *British Educational Leadership, Management & Administration*, 16(5): 10–13.

Harris, A., and Jones, M. S. 2017. *The Dutch Way in Education: Teach, Learn & Lead the Dutch Way*. Netherlands: Onderwijs Maak Je Samen & De Brink Foundation.

Harris, A., and Spillane, J. 2008. "Distributed Leadership through the Looking Glass. Management in Education." *British Educational Leadership, Management & Administration Society*, 22(1): 31–34.

Hattie, J. 2015a. *What Works Best in Education: The Politics of Collaborative Expertise*. Pearson (online).

———. 2015b. *What Doesn't Work in Education: The politics of Distraction*. Pearson (online).

Hattie, J. 2017. The Australian Society for Evidence Based Teaching. Online at www.evidencebasedteaching.or.au

Henderson, A. T., and Mapp, K. L. 2002. *A New Wave of Evidence: The Impact of School, Family, and Community Connections on Student Achievement*. Austin, TX: Southwest Educational Development Laboratory.

Henderson, A., Mapp, K., Johnson, V., and Davies, D. 2007. *Beyond the Bake Sale: The Essential Guide to Family School Partnerships*. New York: New York Press.

Higton, J., Noble, J., Pope, S., Boal, N., Ginnis, S., Donaldson, R., and Greevy, H. 2012. *Fit for Purpose? The view of the higher education sector, teachers and employers on the suitability of A levels*. Ipsos Mori: Social Research Institute.

Hill, A., and Laker, B. 2016. "We Are Rewarding the Wrong School Leaders." *Schools Week*. Available online at https://schoolsweek.co.uk/we-are-rewarding-the-wrong-school-leaders/.

Hill, A., Mellon, L., Laker, B., and Goddard, J. 2016/2017. "The One Type of Leader Who Can Turn around a Failing School." *Harvard Business Review*, October 20, 2016/Updated March 3, 2017. Available online at https://hbr.org/2016/10/the-one-type-of-leader-who-can-turn-around-a-failing-school.

Hoy, A. W. 2000. "Changes in Teacher Efficacy during the Early Years of Teaching." Paper presented at the Annual Meeting of the American Educational Research Association, New Orleans.

Huizinga, J. 1938. *Homo Ludens: A Study of the Play Element in Culture.* Boston, MA: Beacon Press.

Humphrey, N., Lendrum, A., and Wiglesworth, M. 2010. "Social and Emotional Aspects of Learning (SEAL) Programme in Secondary Schools: National Evaluation." Research Report DFE-RR049. UK: DFE.

Humphrey, N., Wigelsworth, M., and Lendrum, A. 2012. "A national evaluation of the impact of the secondary social and emotional aspects of learning (SEAL) programme." *Educational Psychology*, 32(2): 213–238.

Hunter, D. J. 2006. "The National Health Service 1980–2005" (Editorial). *Public Money and Management*, 25(4): 209–212.

Huttenlocher, P. 1990. "Morphometric Study of Human Cerebral Cortex Development." *Neuropsychology*, 28(6), 517–527.

Jenkins, L. 2013. *Permission to Forget*. 10th ed. Milwaukee; WI: American Society for Quality Press.

Jerald, C. D. 2007. *Believing and achieving*. Washington, DC: Center for Comprehensive School Reform and Improvement.

Johnson, D. W., and Johnson, R. T. 1991. *Learning Together and Alone: Cooperative, Competitive, and Individualistic Learning*. Englewood Cliffs, NJ: Prentice Hall.

Johnson, D. W., Johnson, R. T., Johnson-Holubee, E., and Roy, P. 1984. *Circles of Learning: Cooperation in the Classroom*. Alexandria, VA: Association for Supervision and Curriculum Development.

Johnson, E. S. 2008. "Ecological Systems and Complexity Theory: Toward an Alternative Model of Accountability in Education." *Complicity: An International Journal of Complexity and Education*, 5(1). Available online at: https://ejournals.library.ualberta.ca/index.php/complicity/article/viewArticle/8777.

Kandel, D. B. 1978. "Similarity in real-life adolescent friendship pairs." *Journal of personality and social psychology*, 36(3): 306.

Kandel, E., R., and Hawkins, R. D. 1992. "The Biological Basis of Learning and Individuality." *Scientific American*, 267(3), 79–86.

Kenny, D. 2014. "Our Philosophy." Harlem Village Academies Webpage. http://harlemvillageacademies.org/our-philosophy/.

Kerstein, E. L. 2005. *The Art of Demotivation: A Visionary Guide for Transforming Your Company's Least Valuable Asset, Your Employees*. Austin, TX: Despair.

King, K., and Frick, T. 1999. "Systems Thinking: The Key to Educational Redesign." Paper presented to the American Educational Research Association; Montreal, Canada.

The King's Fund. 2012. *Leadership and Engagement for Improvement in the NHS.* London: The King's Fund.

Kohn, A. 1993. *Punished by Rewards: the trouble with gold stars, incentive plans, A's, praise, and other bribes.* USA: Houghton Mifflin Co.

Komatsu, H., and Rappleye, J. 2017. "A New Global Policy Regime Founded on Invalid Statistics? Hanushek, Woessmann, PISA, and Economic Growth." *Comparative Education*, 53(20): 166–191.

Laloux, F. 2014. *Reinventing Organizations: A Guide to Creating Organizations Inspired by the Next Stage of Human Consciousness.* Brussels, Belgium: Nelson Parker.

Langford, D. P., and Cleary, B. A. 1995. *Orchestrating Learning with Quality.* Milwaukee, WI: ASQC Quality Press.

Leana, C. 2011. "The Missing Link in School Reform." *Stanford Social Innovation Review*, 9(4): 30–35.

Lebow, R., and Spitzer, R. 2002. *Accountability: Freedom and Responsibility without Control.* San Francisco, CA: Berrett-Koehler.

Leicester, G., Stewart, D., and Bloomer, K. 2013. *Transformative Innovation in Education: A Playbook for Pragmatic Visionaries.* Devon, UK: Triarchy Press.

Leonard, A. 1999. "A Viable Systems Model: Consideration of Knowledge Management." *Journal of Knowledge Management Practice.*

List, J. A., Livingston, J. A., and Neckermann, S. 2016. "Do Students Show What They Know in Standardized Tests?" From *The Selected Works of Jeffery A Livingston.* Bentley University. Available online.

Lougee, M., and Graziano, W. 1985. *Children's Relationships with Non-Agemate Peers.* Unpublished manuscript.

Lucas, B. 2013. "Engaging Parents: Why and How." *Redesigning Schooling-6.* SSAT; London.

Maccia, E., and Maccia, G. 1966. *Development of Educational Theory Derived from Three Models.* Project No. 5–0368. Washington, DC: US Office of Education.

Marler, P. 1976. "On Animal Aggression: The Roles of Strangeness and Familiarity." *American Psychology*, 31, 239–246.

Marsden, D. 2010. "The Paradox of Performance-Related Pay Systems: Why Do We Keep Adopting Them in the Face of Evidence That They Fail to Motivate?" In *Paradoxes of Modernization: Unintended Consequences of Public Policy Reforms,* edited by Hood, C. and Margetts, H. and 6, Perri, 185–202. Oxford: Oxford University Press. See also, Marsden, D. and Belfield, R. 2010. "Institutions and the Management of Human Resources: Incentive Pay Systems in France and Great Britain." *British Journal of Industrial Relations*, 48 (2): 235–283.

Marsh, H. 2015. *Relationship for Learning: An Overview. The Relational Teacher. Relational Schools: Self-published by Relational Schools:* http://relationalschools. org

Maslow, A. 1943. "A Theory of Human Motivation." *Psychological Review*, 50(4): 370–396.

Maturana, H. R., and Varela, F. J. 1980. *Autopoiesis and Cognition: The Realization of the Living.* Oston Studies in the Philosophy of Science. Vol. 42. D. Reidel Publishing Co., London, Dordrecht in Holland and Boston, USA. See also, Mechanism and biological (1972) explanation, in *Philosophy of Science* 39(3) available at http://cepa.info/540.

McAdams, Dan P. 2001. "The Psychology of Life Stories." *Review of General Psychology*, 5(2): 100–122.

McClellan, D. E. 1994. "Multiage Grouping: Implications for Education." In *Full Circle: A New Look at Multiage Education*, edited by Panelle Chase and Jane Doan, 147–166. Portsmouth, NH: Heinemann.

McClellan, D. E., and Kinsey, S. J. 1999. "Children's Social Behavior in Relation to Participation in Mixed-Age or Same-Age Classrooms." *ECRP*, 17(1).

McDonald, D. 2014. *The Firm: The Story of McKinsey and Its Secret Influence on American Business*. New York: Simon & Schuster.

McGregor, D. M. 1960. *The Human Side of Enterprise*. New York: McGraw-Hill.

Meadows, D. H. 1999. *Leverage Points: Places to Intervene in a System*. The Sustainability Institute (online).

———. 2009. *Thinking in Systems: A Primer*. Edited by Diana Wright. London: Earthscan.

Meadows, D. H., Meadows, D. I., Randers, J., and Behrens, W. W. 1971. *The Limits to Growth: The 30-Year Update*. White River Junction, VT: Chelsea Green.

Mental Health Foundation. 2016. Fundamental Facts About Mental Health. Online at www.mentalhealth.org.uk

Michaels, E., Handfield-Jones, B., and Axelrod, B. 2001. *The War for Talent*. Boston, MA: Harvard Business School Press.

Mifsud, D. 2017. "Distribution Dilemmas: Exploring the Presence of a Tension between Democracy and Autocracy within a Distributed Leadership Scenario." *Education Management Administration and Leadership*, 45(6): 978–1001.

Miller, W. 1995. "Are Multi-Age Grouping Practices a Missing Link in the Educational Reform Debate?" *NASSP Bulletin,* 79(568), 27–32.

Mockler, N. 2013. "Teacher Professional Learning in a Neoliberal Age: Audit, Professionalism and Identity." *Australian Journal of Teacher Education*, 38(10).

Nevis, C. E., Lancourt, J., and Vassallo, P. C. 1996. *Intentional Revolutions: A Seven-Point Strategy for Transforming Organizations*. San Francisco, CA: Jossey-Bass.

NFER. 2018. *Spotlight on multi-academy trusts: A glimpse into performance*. Online at www.nfer.ac.uk

Nickols, F. 2010. *Performance Appraisals: A final criticism*. Online at www.nickols.us/afinalcriticism.pdf

O'Connell, P., Pepler, D., and Craig, W. 1999. "Peer Involvement in Bullying: Insights and Challenges for Intervention." *Journal of Adolescence*, 22: 437–452.

O'Flynn, J. 2007. "From New Public Management to Public Value: Paradigmatic Change and Managerial Implications." *Australian Journal of Public Administration*, 66: 353–366. doi:10.1111/j.1467–8500.2007.00545.x

Office for National Statistics. 2016. Online at https://www.ons.gov.uk/

Ogburn, C. 1957. "Merrill's Marauders." *Harper's Magazine*.

Pascale, C. M. 2010. "Epistemology and the politics of knowledge." *The Sociological Review*, 58(2_suppl): 154–165.

Peck, J., and Theodore, N. 2015. *Fast Policy: Experimental Statecraft at the Thresholds of Neoliberalism*. Minneapolis: University of Minnesota Press.

Pfeffer, J. 2001. "Fighting the War for Talent Is Hazardous to Your Organization's Health." Working paper no. 1687. *Organizational Behavior Dynamics*, 29:
248–259.

Pflaeging, N. 2014. *Organize for Complexity: How to Get Life Back into Work to
Build the High-Performance Organization*. New York: BetaCodex.

Pink. D. 2009. *Drive: The Surprising Truth about What Motivates Us*. New York:
Riverhead Books.

Plato (427–347). *The Allegory of the Cave. Book V11: The Republic*. Available online
at https://web.stanford.edu/class/ihum40/cave.pdf and elsewhere.

Pollitt, C. 2007. "New Labour's Re-Disorganization: Hyper-Modernism and the Costs
of Reform—A Cautionary Tale." *Public Management Review*, 9(4): 529–543.

Reay, D. 2017. *Miseducation: Inequality Education and the Working Classes*. Bristol:
Policy Press.

Rittel, H. W. J., and Webber, M. M. 1973. "Dilemmas in a General Theory of Planning." *Policy Sciences*, 4(2): 155–169.

Rogoff, B. M. 1990. *Apprenticeship in Thinking: Cognitive Development in Social
Context*. New York: Oxford University Press.

Runciman, D. 2016. "Deliverology." *London Review of Books*, 38(7): 29–30.

Sahlberg, P. 2015. *Finnish Lessons: What can the world learn from educational
change in Finland?* 2nd. Edition. Teachers College Press

Salmivalli, C. 2009. "Bullying and the Peer Group: A Review." *Aggression and Vio-
lent Behaviour*, 15: 112–120.

Salmivalli, C., A. Huttunen, and K. Lagerspetz. 1997. "Peer Networks and Bullying
in schools." *Scandinavian Journal of Psychology*, 38: 305–312.

Schein, E. H. (1992). *Organizational culture and leadership (2nd ed.)*. San Francisco,
Calif: Jossey-Bass.

———. 1996a. "Three Cultures of Management: The Key to Organizational Learning." *Management Review*, Fall 1996. Available online at www.sloanreview.mit.
edu.

———. 1996b. "Culture: The Missing Concept in Organization Studies." *Administrative Science Quarterly*, 41(2): 229.

———. 2006. "Kurt Lewin's Change Theory in the Field and in the Classroom:
Notes towards a Model of Engaged Learning." *Reflections*, 1(1): 59–74.

———. 2009. "Sense and Nonsense about Culture and Climate." Available online at
http://lab4.psico.unimib.it/nettuno/forum3/free_download/sense_and_nonsense_
about_culture_and_climate_112.pdf. Accessed July 12, 2017.

———. 2016. *Organizational Culture and Leadership*. 5th ed. San Francisco, CA:
The Jossey-Bass Business and Management Series.

Seddon, J. 2000. "From 'Push' to 'Pull'—Changing the Paradigm for Customer Relationship management." *Journal of Interactive Marketing*, 2(1): 19–28. Palgrave
Macmillan UK. Seddon, J. J Direct Data Digit Mark Pract (2000) 2: 19. https://doi.
org/10.1057/palgrave.im.4340064.

———. 2008. *Systems Thinking in the Public Sector: The Failure of the Reform
Regime and a Manifesto for a Better Way*. Devon: Triarchy Press.

———. 2016. "New Public Management: Dystopian Interventions in Public Services." In *Kittens Are Evil: Little Heresies in Public Policy*, edited by C. Pell., R.
Wilson, and T. Lowe, 11–17. Devon: Triarchy Press.

Senge, P. M. 1990. *The Fifth Discipline: the art and practice of the learning organization*. London: Nicholas Brearley Publishing.

Senge, P. 2006. *The Fifth Discipline: The Art and Practice of the Learning Organisation*. London: Random House.

Se-Woong Koo. 2014. "An Assault upon our Children: South Korea's Education System Hurts Students." *New York Times Sunday Review*, August 1.

Shaughnessy, M. F. 2004. "An Interview with Anita Woolfolk: The Educational Psychology of Teacher Efficacy." *Educational Psychology Review*, 16(2), 153–175.

Sherman, P. 1980. "The Limits of Nepotism." In *Sociobiology: Beyond Nature-Nurture*, edited by George W. Barlow and James Silverberg, 505–544. Boulder, CO: Westview Press.

Smyth, J., and Simmonds, P. 2017. "Where Is class in the Analysis of Working Class Education?" In *Education and Working Class Youth*, edited by J. Smyth and P. Simmons, 1–28. London: Palgrave Macmillan.

Snook, I., O'Neill, J., Clark, J., O'Neill, A-M. and Openshaw, R. 2009. "Invisible Learnings? A Commentary on John Hattie's Book—'Visible Learning: A Synthesis of Over 800 Meta-analyses Relating to Achievement'" [online]. *New Zealand Journal of Educational Studies*, 44(1): 93–106.

Snyder, S. 2013. "The Simple, the Complicated, and the Complex: Educational Reform through the Lens of Complexity Theory." OECD Education Working Papers, No. 96, OECD Publishing. http://dx.doi.org/10.1787/5k3txnpt1lnr-en

Song, R., Spradlin. T. E., and Plucker, A. 2009. "The Advantages and Disadvantages of Multi-Age Classrooms in the Era of NCLB Accountability." *Education Policy Brief*. Center for Evaluation and Education Policy, 7 (1).

Spratling, D. 2017. "This beautiful profession has been transformed into a beast that is damaging mental health. Who will break the spell?" *Times Educational Supplement:* November, 2017.

Squire, L. R. 1992. "Memory and the Hippocampus: A Synthesis from Findings with Rats, Monkeys, and Humans." *Psychological Review*, 99(2), 195–231.

Straw, E. 2016. Blog Post online: www.edstraw.com.

Sutton, J., and Smith, P. K. 1999. "Bullying as a Group Process: An Adaptation of the Participant Role Approach." *Aggressive Behaviour*, 25: 97–111.

Taubman, P. 2009. *Teaching by Numbers: Deconstructing the Discourse of Standards and Accountability in Education*. New York: Routledge.

Taylor, M. 2017. *Taylor Review of Modern Working Practices: An Independent Review of Modern Working Practices*. Royal Society of Arts.

Tizard, B. 1986. "Social Relationships between Adults and Young Children, and Their Impact on Intellectual Functioning." In *Social Relationships and Cognitive Development*, edited by Robert A. Hinde, Anne-Nelly Perret-Clermont, and Joan Stevenson-Hinde, 116–130. Oxford: Clarendon Press.

Van Damme, K. 2015. "OER and the Innovation of Learning." Presentation to OE Global, available at www.slideshare.net/oeconsortium/key-note-open-education-global-conference-banff-23-april-2015-final. Accessed 12 January, 2018.

Vygotsky, Lev S. 1978. *Mind in Society*. Cambridge, MA: Harvard University Press.

Wheatley, M., and M. Kellner-Rogers. 1996. "The Irresistible Future of Organizing" [online]. Margaret J. Wheatley; available at http://www.margaretwheatley.com/articles/irrisistiblefuture.html. Accessed 16 February, 2018.

Wheatley, M. J., and Kellner-Rogers, M. 1998. "Bringing life to organizational change." *Journal of Strategic Performance Measurement*, 2(2): 5–13.

Wheatley, M. J. 1999. *Bringing Schools Back to Life: Schools as Living Systems. Creating Successful School Systems: Voices from the University, the field, and Community*. Norwood, MA: Christopher-Gordon publishers.

Wilber. K. 2013. Foreword to Laloux, F. 2013. *Reinventing Organizations: A Guide to Creating Organizations Inspired by the Next Stage of Human Consciousness*. Brussels, Belgium: Nelson Parker.

———. 2016. "The Secret of Effective Feedback." *Educational Leadership*, 73(7): 10–15.

Williamson, B. 2017. "Fast Psych-Policy & the Datafication of Social-Emotional Learning." Paper prepared for the Annual Ethnography Symposium, University of Manchester, August 30–September 1, 2017. Available online at https://codeactsineducation.wordpress.com/2017/08/29/fast-psycho-policy.

# Index

Note: Page numbers in *italics* indicate figures and tables.

# About the Author

By nature, **Peter A. Barnard** is foremost a lateral thinker, and this makes him a contrarian. After leaving school, he tried his hand at a number of jobs, including work on building sites, postal delivery, painting and decorating, catering, and as an operative assembling TVs on the conveyor belts of a large factory, experiences that were to prove invaluable. He claims he drifted into teaching by accident and worked his way through the ranks to become a very successful school principal in three different places.

It was during this time that Peter discovered systems thinking and the ideas of Ludwig von Bertalanffy, Jay Forrester, W. Edwards Deming, Peter Senge, Russell Ackoff, Donella Meadows, Margaret J. Wheatcroft, and many others. The realization dawned that most of the challenges faced by schools are caused by the inability of schools to operate as complex, connected systems, ones that value people and recognize their essential contribution to the activity of learning and teaching. He set about the process of school redesign, not realizing that he was using the viable systems modeling (VSM) approach of Stafford Beer. The purpose of leadership is to manage the system in an enabling way, not manage people to cope with a system that undermines them and does them no favors.

The breakthrough came when his schools adopted mixed-age tutor groups—a systems change now called vertical tutoring. By redesigning the school around this construct, it was possible to reconnect the school in complex ways to more of itself, essential to a systems approach. The fragmented learning relationships between staff, students, and parents, previously marked by separation and limitation, became integral to the school's success. As Peter so often says, only when the change from one system to another is complete do the severe limitations and dangers of the same-age model in universal use become apparent.

For Peter, same-age organization as a design application is 150 years old and intended for very different purposes. As such, it is ignorant of social psychology and child development besides being the primary cause of bullying and loss of well-being. Because of its unquestioned familiarity, it has also flown under the radar of research. For Peter, there is nothing wrong with the quality of our teachers or the character of our kids, but much wrong with the NPM route that schools are compelled to travel.

In 2010, Professor Frank Duffy invited Peter to contribute to his prestigious online papers on schools and systemic change. Peter then wrote two books for Rowman and Littlefield as part of the Leading Systematic School Improvement series: *The Systems Thinking School* and *From School Delusion to Design*. This book is the last in his series.

Peter facilitates schools wishing to adopt mixed-age approaches, work that has taken him to Japan, China, Qatar, and Australia, and includes links with South Africa, New Zealand, and Ukraine. He is now involved in research work and spends time growing fruit and veg on his allotment. He also claims to be the oldest and most annoying groupie of his son's new band, Gold Keys!

Printed in Great Britain
by Amazon